My Lovely Wife

My Lovely Wife

A MEMOIR OF
MADNESS AND HOPE

Mark Lukach

bluebird
books for life

First published 2017 by HarperWave

First published in the UK 2017 by Bluebird
an imprint of Pan Macmillan
20 New Wharf Road, London N1 9RR
Associated companies throughout the world
www.panmacmillan.com

ISBN 978-1-5098-0595-2 HB
ISBN 978-1-5098-0594-5 TPB

1 3 5 7 9 8 6 4 2

A CIP catalogue record for this book is available from the British Library.

Designed by Leah Carlson-Stanisic
Printed and bound by CPI Group (UK) Ltd, Croydon, CRO 4YY

Visit *www.panmacmillan.com* to read more about all our books
and to buy them. You will also find features, author interviews and
news of any author events, and you can sign up for e-newsletters
so that you're always first to hear about our new releases.

For Giulia and Jonas, true believers all the way.

I can see a lot of life in you

I can see a lot of bright in you

And I think the dress looks nice on you

I can see a lot of life in you

—SUFJAN STEVENS, "THE DRESS LOOKS NICE ON YOU"

Contents

My Lovely Wife

one

August 2000

The first time I saw my wife, she was walking around the Georgetown campus and I shouted out, *"Buongiorno, Principessa!"* like a buffoon. She was Italian, radiant, way out of my league, but I was fearless and almost immediately in love. She had a smile *bello come il sole*—I learned some Italian to impress her—and when I saw her at a party, we spent the whole night immersed in flirtatious conversation. I walked her to her room, and I snuck in a quick good-night kiss, and she kissed me back. We both already knew what was happening. She lived on the floor below me in the same freshman dorm. I knocked at her door the next morning to take her out to breakfast. She answered with a tone that was almost like "Where have you been, it's about time you got here."

Within a month we were a couple. She'd stop by my room to wake me up if I was oversleeping class; I taped roses to her door. Giulia had a perfect GPA; I had a Mohawk and a Sector 9 longboard. We were both blown away by how amazing it feels to love someone and be loved back.

The night before winter break freshman year, the first time we'd be apart since we met, we sat up together late into the morning, perched at my dorm window, watching snow blanket the quad below. We cried our guts out at the prospect of being separated for two weeks. It felt as though we were anticipating a death. I hoped that the snow would postpone or cancel her flight and we'd steal a few more hours together, but the snow backed off, she flew off to her family in Italy, I to my family in Delaware. Our fragile hearts somehow survived. By the time we got back to school, we were already talking about the Future, as if it were a certainty. Our love was inevitable, like graduation or gravity, a foregone conclusion that neither of us wanted to escape. It didn't matter that we were only eighteen years old.

The more we got to know each other, the more we delighted in our commonalities. We were both left-handed, and our moms shared a birthday. My family moved abroad from the U.S. to Japan in 1989; Giulia's family moved abroad from Italy to the U.S. in the same year. We told ourselves that these mere coincidences were something much more, and they became part of our mythology that we were destined to be together.

The most important thing we shared was an emphasis on family. I had three siblings and Giulia only one, but for each of us, family was at the core of our identities.

Our two families first met on Christmas Eve, a few blocks from the Spanish Steps in Rome, the winter break of our sophomore year. My family was there on vacation; Giulia was visiting her extended family, all of whom were still in Italy. Another coincidence to be spending the holidays in the same country.

Giulia's mom, Mariarita, gave me her cell phone number in a time when few people had cell phones, so I could call to arrange for us all to meet. Giulia arrived a few days before we did. On my family's first night in Rome, we ate dinner and then walked through the cobblestone streets back to our hotel. My mom, Mary, led the way—she had studied in Rome in college and was giddy to be showing the city to me and my three siblings. Every few blocks I ducked into a bar or a restaurant to try to call Mariarita from a pay phone, but she never picked up.

I had just about given up, and then we turned a corner and I saw Giulia coming our way, the collar of her winter coat drawn tight against the lightly falling snow, arm in arm with her mom, her dad and brother laughing about some joke. They stopped short when they saw us walking their way. Mariarita's cell phone was in hand, waiting for the call. The phone lines didn't find each other, but we did anyway.

No one knew what to say, we were so shocked. This was one coincidence too many.

My dad, C.J., was the first to snap out of it, and he eagerly introduced himself to Giulia's dad, Romeo. The moms met, and all the siblings exchanged hugs, and then we parted ways, with a plan for a proper meeting scheduled the next day.

No one said it, but I think everyone left knowing that these two families would gather again someday down the road, in a church, for a wedding, a formal blessing of the union, and maybe that was what we had just done anyway.

Back at our lives in college, our plans expanded, from what we were doing that weekend—like crashing a wedding reception, which we did one Saturday night—to what we were going to do beyond college. Ever since high school I had been planning to go to law school, but now in my critical college years, I wasn't doing a very good job of convincing myself of that. I haphazardly signed up for whatever humanities courses sounded interesting to me and cobbled together a history major with an English minor. During summer break, I escaped to a small beach town in Delaware and wandered from surf session to beach volleyball and then worked for tips in restaurants.

Giulia could not have been more opposite and certain of her path. She wanted to be a marketing director and have three kids by the time she was thirty-five, and she was ready for whatever work was necessary to get there. Which meant internships, and meeting with professors during office hours, and even spending Friday evenings at the library. She used to dress herself up for Friday night by four p.m. in order to go to the library for a few hours before meeting me—straight from the books to her boyfriend. She always covered her tracks, pretending that she was doing something with friends rather than studying, afraid that I might think she was too nerdy.

Summer for Giulia meant an internship in New York City—the first summer it was with a fashion house, then a boutique ad agency the following summer, and then a major ad agency the summer after that. In the summer after our junior year, that major ad agency celebrated the end of the season by taking the interns out to a concert. I came up to New York for the weekend to be Giulia's plus-one.

"Now remember, my boss is going to be there, so make sure you say hi to him, and, you know, be good," Giulia said to me. We were cramped in the bathroom of her rented apartment. Giulia was in a skirt and a bra, applying eyeliner. I was ready to go and didn't need to still be in the bathroom, but I liked to be there as she got herself ready. I got to see Giulia before she presented herself to the world and felt like I was getting to become a part of her secrets. I closed my eyes and imagined us getting ready for concerts and parties together like this for the rest of our lives.

"I'll be good," I insisted, hands up, innocent of the implied charges.

"I mean don't say anything about the band," she said.

"Oh, you mean Evanescence? You don't want me to say anything about the fact that we're actually at an Evanescence concert?" I had been mocking Evanescence to her over the phone since she'd first told me about the concert.

"Yes," she said. "That's exactly what I don't want you to say."

She was impatient with me, but I leaned in and kissed her on her bare shoulder. I couldn't help it. Makeup, no makeup, in the act of putting on makeup, it didn't matter. She was stunning in all contexts.

"What's the name of that song of theirs that you love so much again?" I asked, teasing, knowing she didn't know.

"You know, that one song," she said, now applying lipstick.

"Oh yeah, right, that song," I said back, smirking.

"Don't be a jerk," she said.

"I'm not, it's just . . . Evanescence."

"Mark . . ." She turned, trying to be mad. This was a big night for her, and she was taking it seriously, which she should, but I knew that even she couldn't take Evanescence seriously. Finally, she couldn't contain it. The laughter spilled out of her, a bellowing laugh that outshone even her smile with joy. Giulia laughed longer and harder than anyone I'd ever met. It took control of her whole body. She often had to hold herself up when she started laughing, to keep herself from falling down. No matter what mood you were in when she started, you were always laughing along with her before she finished. I loved to make her laugh, because it was like creating a little private memory that was ours and ours only, to add to the growing pile of trivialities that no one else could possibly care about but were becoming the foundation of our intimacy. Little things like this— knowing that we would wordlessly laugh about the band all night long together, through smiles and glances—pulled me deeper into my infatuation. As she laughed in her bra and half-applied makeup, I knew that I would never be able to be away from her.

At the concert it was the boss who tried to be good around me, rather than vice versa. He wobbled on drunken legs and leaned into my ear to shout over the loud music about just how great Giulia had done this summer, the best intern they had ever had, so hardworking and team oriented, the ideal combination of creative thinking and attention to detail, and they were going to miss her and hoped she'd apply for a full-time job when she graduated.

I beamed. I had my understanding of Giulia—her passion, her fire, her smile, her ambition—but I knew the professional Giulia only through hearsay. She studied business, and I was in the humanities, so we were never in the same classes, and I certainly never saw her at work in an office. But any time I met a boss, or a professor, or even another student who was in a group project with her, it was always the same refrain: Giulia was exceptional, the kind of worker who made everyone around her want to do better.

Of course, not everything was 100 percent perfect, even though it felt that way at the time.

One Saturday night Giulia stayed in to work on a paper for a religion class, and she called me in a panic. Her computer had frozen, and a cryptic window had popped up that asked whether to proceed: yes or no. I left the friends I was with and marched across campus with a purpose. I found her in her room, in tears, frantic, her pillow clutched to her chest.

"I don't know what to do, Mark," she said through her sobs. Her eyes were fixed on the ominous computer screen. "If I click the wrong option, I'll lose the whole paper."

"Okay, let's settle down, we'll figure this out," I said, taking a place next to her on the bed, my arms immediately on her shoulders for gentle massaging. "We'll figure out what to do."

"But what if we don't figure this out?" She shook me away, agitated by my touch.

"Then it's okay, it's not a big deal, it's just an essay."

She exploded. "How can you say that?" she shrieked. "Do you know what will happen to my GPA if I don't do well on this paper?" She squeezed the pillow tighter, her body hunched and shaking as the tears fell harder and her sobs grew louder.

It took almost an hour to calm her down before we clicked together and salvaged the essay. But by then, to me, whether or not we saved the essay was beside the point.

After we graduated, I moved to Baltimore to teach high school, and Giulia moved to Manhattan to work in fashion.

We tried every possible angle to end up in the same city and all along had a certainty that we would. But that didn't happen.

Giulia moved with a college girlfriend into an apartment on the Upper East Side, laundry and gym in the basement, frozen yogurt spot just around the corner. She loved it: living in the big city, walking briskly down Lexington Avenue in her stylish sunglasses and designer jackets to her office in the morning, coffee in hand, each step in the direction of that director job and those three kids.

My life in Baltimore was bleak in comparison. I knew no one and rented a depressing one-bedroom apartment in a run-down condo unit named Cherrybrook Meadows, an insulting homage to the disappeared scenery that the condos replaced. My bedroom windows looked out over a parking lot. I barely decorated. The room held a bed, a table with a few chairs, and stacks of books towering along the floor. I was a first-year history teacher at an all-boys school, and also coached soccer and swimming. I enrolled in a grad school program at Johns Hopkins that offered night classes so I could pursue another degree in history. Giulia was my future, and she was in New York, so I flooded my life with as much work as possible to fill the emptiness. I often stayed up lesson planning and grading papers until two a.m., with the alarm set the next morning for five a.m. If I was falling asleep, I did a bunch of push-ups to wake me back up. Fifty push-ups could usually get me another fifteen minutes of concentrated focus, no matter what time it was.

One day at school, another history teacher named Cas came up to me and put his hand on my shoulder. Cas was short, stocky, and the only person I ever met with a louder voice than I have. A direct, warmhearted, but sometimes cranky Australian, Cas looked me in the face, saw my loneliness, and said, "I can see that you need to spend time with a family. Come have dinner with my family tonight."

With that, I made my only close friend in Baltimore, a man twenty years my senior. For dinner, he cooked up an assortment of Indian and Chinese vegan dishes, and he and his wife, Leslie, along with their two young boys, Bronimir and Blaize, marveled in awe at how much food I ate. After dinner, they cranked David Bowie followed by Bruce Cockburn, and we all danced together wildly in their living room, their dog, Brutus, barking at me as I spun and swung the boys.

Giulia and I committed to seeing each other every other weekend and alternating who traveled, but those rules lasted only a month. There was so much to do in New York City and so little to offer Giulia in Baltimore, so I headed to Manhattan for five or six weeks straight, just as excited to see her as I was to get out of Baltimore.

Amtrak was far too expensive to sustain on a teacher's salary. I eventually discovered the Chinatown bus, a network of buses that drive from Chinatown to Chinatown along the eastern seaboard for only $20 one way, no matter your destination, $35 round-trip.

I always brought grading and reading to do, but I almost never did it. Instead I purchased a Discman to give the long rides a soundtrack, and the songs I listened to became my protective cocoon as I shuttled back and forth from my loneliness in Baltimore to the blur of New York. I burned matching CDs for the two of us—Belle and Sebastian, Sufjan Stevens, Nada Surf, Death Cab for Cutie—so she could listen to the same music at work.

After a few months of traveling to New York, I noticed that my Discman was still on full battery power. Pretty impressive, I thought. Before long, I was obsessing over the batteries. They were magic. We were magic. The fall became winter, and we ice-skated in Central Park. Winter became spring, and we made picnics and watched weekend softball leagues. Through it all, the batteries remained full.

———

Summer came. I ramped up my grad school classes for the summer term and worked at my school's summer camp. Giulia was in her first summer of a full-time job, no extended vacation. We shifted our visits away from New York to Bethany Beach, the small coastal beach town in Delaware where I had spent every summer of my life. My parents had a house there, so Giulia and I could meet in Wilmington and we'd drive south from there for a weekend of sun, volleyball, and surf. We soon fell into the habit of going for long-distance paddles together, Giulia on a kayak, me on a paddleboard I borrowed from my friends who lifeguarded at the beach. We spent a few hours out on the water together each weekend, escaping from the trappings of life on land, exercising our bodies, talking, or simply enjoying the silence.

When the summer dwindled to an end, I knew it was time for us to get married. I needed more of Giulia. I didn't want the best part of my life to be confined to the weekends. I consulted one of her girlfriends about ring size and style. Labor Day weekend, our last weekend in Bethany Beach, I stuffed the ring inside a Ziploc bag and put it in the pocket of my bathing suit before we went out for our ritualistic paddle. After our paddle, as we floated out at sea a few hundred yards away from the shore, the waves rocked us as I pulled out the ring. She said yes.

It was ninety-six degrees on our wedding day, with 98 percent humidity. We married where we'd met, at Georgetown, in the iconic chapel on campus, and then had our reception at a nearby country club. We all cried and laughed through the toasts, and the dancing, and then after we cut the cake, I walked up to the microphone at the front of the room.

"Excuse me, everyone," I said, more nervous than I'd ever been. "I picked up the guitar a few months ago for two reasons. The first is that I want to sing my kids to sleep someday; the second is that I wanted my wife to hear her favorite song on her wedding night. I'm not very good, so bear with me, but Giulia, this is for you."

And then I clumsily began the off-tempo strumming that was meant to mimic the ukulele version of "Somewhere over the Rainbow," and I started to sing. I had practiced the song hundreds of times. I thought Giulia might cry when I sang it, but instead she walked out from the crowd and stood in front of me and rocked and swayed and sang along.

At the end of the night, and as the lights came up and the venue tried to shoo us away, the band put on a recording of me singing. All of our guests joined hands in a large circle around Giulia and me. We danced together in the center. It all felt like a dream.

Two days later, we flew to San Francisco to start our new lives. We rented the upstairs of a house ten blocks from Ocean Beach, the four-mile stretch of beach that is San Francisco's western boundary. I bought a new wetsuit and a new surfboard, as well as the prerequisite flannels and hoodies. I taught high school and commuted down the peninsula; Giulia worked in online marketing for a fashion company and scootered across the city.

Next we got an adorable little English bulldog—Augustus, Goose for short—who had so much excess skin that he had wrinkles on his legs.

Our families came out to visit our new California lives. We took my mother in-law to the LoveFest on Market Street, a rave-style parade that celebrated all things quintessentially San Francisco, and she couldn't stop laughing at the naked men in the parade. My parents were in town for Fleet Week, and we perched atop a view on Telegraph Hill and my dad put his arm around my shoulders and said, "You've got yourself a good life set up here."

Cas, Leslie, and the boys had moved to the Bay Area the same time we did, planting their roots in the dreamscape of West Marin, ninety minutes north of the city, in a haven of organic, crunchy living. We drove up there about once a month to spend the weekend hiking, gardening, eating good meals, and watching movies.

While Giulia was at first a bit wary of a couple who were noticeably older than us, and nothing like her hip friends in New York—Cas often picked up one of his sons as if he were a guitar while we rocked out after dinner—she quickly fell into the pack just as I had in Baltimore. We even adopted a few of their family quirks, and we began to blast loud music of our own after dinner to dance our way through doing the dishes together.

We made other friends in San Francisco, people who met us as a married couple. I made some buddies out in the water. Giulia had her work friends. And together, we connected with a group of young couples who were our age, some married, others living together, and we'd meet for potlucks and concerts and Frisbee in Golden Gate Park.

Chris, my closest friend from our group, wanted the group to go paintballing for his birthday, so we all drove off to Vallejo to shoot one another up in the woods. We were all first-timers, and terrible. The facility organized our group against other groups of people in various games. We lost the first five games well under the time limit. By lunch, we had learned how to at least last long enough to make it until the clock expired on the game, so we could tie.

Giulia wanted nothing to do with getting shot. She spent each game hiding behind trees near the back of the course, far from the action. She sat and did nothing and hoped no one would find her.

The last game was one-sided capture the flag. We were on offense, trying to steal the flag from a circular base that the defense guarded.

Chris and I planned a coordinated attack and steadily snuck closer and closer to the base. When we were about thirty yards away, a few of our teammates made a reckless move around the back of the base and the whole defense turned to fire at them. For the moment, the side of the base we were approaching was unguarded.

Out of nowhere, I saw Giulia. She had been following behind my slow creep, and with the defense distracted, she pounced. She ran at a full sprint right past me. I couldn't believe what I was seeing. She had essentially boycotted paintball the entire day, and now here she was, brazenly going after the flag.

Giulia grabbed the flag and barely slowed her stride as she turned and rushed back into the trees to escape.

The defenders realized what had happened only after she was already running off with the flag, and they collectively turned and aimed their paintball guns on her. Giulia was only a few feet away from me when they pulled their triggers. It felt as if it were happening in slow motion, straight out of a Hollywood movie. Pellets flew at Giulia and erupted in orange and green and yellow all over her back. She yelped and fell to her knees, the flag flying out of her hand as though it were spring-loaded. She stayed on her knees and they kept shooting, her body taking each shot, refusing to go down. I could hear her laughing and taunting the other team as they kept shooting.

I didn't think. I had to finish what Giulia started. I dashed out of my hiding spot and grabbed the flag from where it had fallen. I zigzagged off into the woods to avoid the onslaught of pellets that were now targeting me, the flag held triumphantly above my head. I made it to the referee and he rang the bell, and we won the game.

Giulia ran to greet me and we danced and hugged, her back an explosion of color, the welts already forming under her clothes, and the rest of our group circled around us in a frenzy of primordial victory, hooting and hollering and beating our chests. We had won our first and only game of the day, and it was all because of Giulia, the unexpected hero.

After a few years at her first California job, Giulia grew restless with the slow pace of career advancement in the company and traded it in for a more engaging and higher-paying job at a beauty start-up. Her new boss loved her. He promoted her from marketing manager to senior marketing manager within the first year. Giulia welcomed the challenge of finding an audience for an unknown brand, rather than tapping into a globally recognized label as she had at her last job. Giulia thrived and found herself not only honing her marketing skills, but branching out into other aspects of the business. At the holiday party, her boss pulled me aside to gush over Giulia's invaluable contributions to the company.

A year and a half into the job, the Great Recession hit. The company's funding dried up almost overnight, and they had to shutter its doors. Giulia, like everybody else, was told to pack up her desk and head home.

Giulia had never faced this kind of setback before. She took great pride in a job well done and believed that it guaranteed security as the reward. But now, all the hard work ended with the company closing up shop.

Giulia didn't know what to do with herself. Her work had been the center of her identity since I had first met her, and now she was without it. I kept telling her to take a break. There was no need to rush into another job. We had been married three years and had saved aggressively since the first day, putting almost half our paychecks into saving. San Francisco was still affordable back then, and we dreamed of owning a home. Her dad, Romeo, echoed my suggestion and encouraged Giulia to take a break. He looked back on a full career of too many long hours away from his family and told her to slow down, not rush, enjoy some time off; and besides, we were only a month away from my summer break, and my sister was getting married in Delaware.

We decided to drive cross-country for the wedding. We'd leave right after my last faculty meeting of the year: the two of us and Goose in our Honda Civic with sleeping bags, a tent, a laptop, and all five seasons of *The Wire* on DVD. It took some convincing, but she agreed. We gave ourselves three weeks to get across the country.

The trip was dreamy: $5 rotisserie chicken from Safeway, $5-a-night campsites with hot showers in Oregon, bears in our campsite in Wyoming. Along the way, we stopped at free Wi-Fi spots, and as I read, Giulia searched for jobs. True to form, she got an offer in only our second week on the road. They didn't care that she was traveling. Just be in the office after the Fourth of July.

Somewhere around Iowa I said that I was ready to have kids. By Indiana, Giulia agreed. We were twenty-seven. I knew that life wasn't supposed to be perfect, but this felt pretty close.

two

July 2009

───────────

I met Giulia at the door after her first day of work. I had been anticipating her return home all day. This new job felt special. She had certainly liked all of her previous jobs, but one was at a giant corporation and another at an unknown start-up. Now she was employed in a company with a reputation for being young, hip, and edgy. The company was, in a word, cool.

She came up the stairs and was as beautiful as I had ever seen her. Giulia had shocked me with her beauty from the first moment I saw her—her graceful poise, her classy style, but most of all her casual way with it all, a beauty that was flawless and effortless. She almost never wore makeup, but she had put some on for today, along with her most chic sweater and pants. Her cheeks had the slight blush of red from her scooter ride home across the city and into the cold fog of our neighborhood.

"How did it go?" I asked her enthusiastically, wrapping my arms around her before she could even get in the doorway.

"It was . . . good," she said, avoiding eye contact, looking beyond me into the house.

"'Good'?" I repeated. "What does that mean?"

"It was just the first day, Mark, there's not much to say," Giulia said. She scooched past me into our room to dump her stuff in our bedroom. "It's just, I guess, everyone is so smart and cool there."

"Nice. So you should fit right in," I said, flirting with her.

"No, but seriously. They are really smart. And really cool. . . ." Her voice trailed off. "I hope I can keep up."

I had known Giulia for nine years, and she had always exuded confidence. I could always count on her thriving at work. I'd seen her do so across four internships and two jobs. She left each one to glowing recommendations and even brighter opportunities. Even though I'd never seen her in a single meeting, I was certain of her work success, more than my own.

But this insecurity was new. I had seen her panic about that paper while we were in college, but that was supposedly because she was afraid her computer might crash and with it her work would be lost. It had nothing to do with her. This anxiety expressed itself differently, more personal, as though she were afraid she might not fit in.

"Well, it's just the first day," I said. "I'm sure you'll get the hang of it. It'll be great."

Giulia went to work, each morning taking a little bit longer to get herself ready, as if the right outfit or hairstyle would help her rediscover her confidence. I still had a month left of summer vacation, so I stayed at home and mostly futzed around the house. Our two-bedroom house was spacious for San Francisco but fairly typical of the Outer Sunset, where the extra space was written off by most, given the neighborhood's reputation as one of the foggiest places in the Bay Area and one of the sleepiest, most suburban-like parts of San Francisco. We kept the second bedroom for guests, but mostly in anticipation of turning it into a nursery. Our friends always wanted us to host dinner parties because we actually had enough space, compared with their hipper but much tinier places in the Haight or Pacific Heights.

The bedrooms were adjacent to each other at the end of a long hallway. The house revolved around an open-air atrium that cast natural light throughout all the rooms. Surrounding the atrium were our living room, dining room, kitchen, and hallway, which had the bedrooms at one end and the front door at the other.

The house always needed tidying because neither of us was especially neat, and Goose tracked sand back into the house, so there was always sweeping and cleaning to do.

Giulia and I talked and texted throughout the day as she struggled to find a sense of place at the new company. She needed me constantly for reassurance.

She called one day while I was eating lunch and reading a book. I could immediately hear the uncertainty in her voice.

"Hey, honey, would you do me a favor? I just sent you an e-mail I've been working on for a little while. It's to my boss, and I want it to sound, you know, just right. Can you read it and make sure it's okay?"

"Yeah, of course, no problem. What's it about? It is something sensitive?"

"Just read the e-mail, and let me know," she said impatiently. "Call me when you're done."

I logged on to my e-mail, found her message, and opened it.

Dear Jill

I wanted to follow up from our meeting about forecasting for the next quarter. As I'm still new to this company and position, I'm struggling a bit to keep up with the assignment. I hope this isn't a problem, and that we can find more time to talk about it.

Thanks

Giulia

"Did you read it?" Giulia asked hurriedly, in a whisper, when I called her back.

"Yeah, I read it," I said. "It's fine, Giulia. It's polite and totally fine. It doesn't sound like a big deal."

"You don't think it's too much? Like, I'm not capable of doing my job? I don't want her to think I can't handle this." She was impatient and cold, as though she were interrogating me.

"No, not at all, it's totally fine, Giulia. You should go ahead and send it." I tried to keep my voice calm and patient. I could sense that she needed support but also didn't want to be needy.

She sighed. "You sure? I worked on this for the last hour. I want to make sure it's right."

"It's a great e-mail, Giulia."

"Okay."

And then she hung up.

Giulia's calls became more frequent and more frantic. She forwarded me several e-mail drafts a day, most only a sentence or two. They took her hours to write. Her anxiety about what to say in an e-mail monopolized her day. She was assigned projects, and didn't know where to start, and labored all day over how to write an e-mail of a few sentences long to ask a question about the assignment.

"Come on, Giulia," I begged her over dinner, as she sat sullenly, picking at her food, not saying much. "What's going on?" I had been asking her this every day for a week, each time sounding more exasperated, and each time, Giulia shut down. She didn't say anything and kept her eyes down, so I filled the silence. I wasn't sure if she was unwilling or unable to talk about what was happening, so I doled out a litany of clichés. "Don't beat yourself up so much. That's the problem, not the work itself. You are amazing. Everything I've ever heard about you at work is how incredible you are."

She continued to sit quietly.

"You can do the work, I'm sure of it." More unmoving silence, so I continued with the positive affirmations. Whether or not they impacted Giulia, they at least helped to keep me calm and from slipping into frustration with her. "You have so much to be proud of. You're doing better than you think."

She didn't react to anything I said, but I couldn't stand the defeat of the silence, so I compulsively kept talking about letting bad thoughts go, being in the moment, staying positive, not giving up, all the weary platitudes. I cleaned the kitchen as she watched in silence. Only a few weeks earlier we had blasted music for our dishwashing dance parties, one of our favorite chores together. Now she was a nonparticipant, a silent, isolated spectator. Even our favorite songs couldn't bring her back to me. She sat and tolerated my lectures, stoic and poised to hide whatever thoughts were racing in her head.

With nothing else to do, we got ready for bed. I followed her into the bathroom and slowly rubbed her neck as she brushed her teeth and took out her contacts. When she finished, we got under the covers together and I cradled her body, my fingers caressing her earlobes, one of her favorite ways to be cuddled. I felt her breathing slow down and the muscles in her body relax, and I thought that maybe I had gotten through to her, with my words or my touch, and that she was calming down, and tomorrow would be better after a night of sleep.

But she couldn't fall asleep.

Three weeks into her job, I jolted awake in the middle of the night to hear Giulia shouting in Italian in a different room. I rushed out of bed to see what was going on. Giulia was in the kitchen, Skyping with her mom in Italy, who at nine hours ahead was in her midmorning routine.

"What's going on in here," I mumbled, squinting at the fully lit kitchen. It was two a.m.

Giulia craned her neck to face me. "I can't sleep. I'm just talking to my mom."

"Come on, Giulia, let's get to sleep," I said, waving vaguely at the camera. "You must be so tired. You haven't been sleeping well, let's go to bed."

Giulia's mom backed me up: Giulia needed sleep. Giulia protested but consented, signed off, and went back to bed with me.

In our bedroom, I pulled her close under the covers. I asked yet again what was wrong, trying to coax out the words that might help give shape to what was happening. I forced myself to be gentle, to mask any hint of frustration, but she still had nothing to say, as if accused. "I'm tired, I want to try and sleep, not talk." She was becoming too lost in the anxiety to step back from it to examine it.

I instinctively began to rub her neck and earlobes again, while whispering that she was doing a great job, and tried to get her to focus on her breathing.

The truth is, I didn't know what else to do. Her anxiety had been brewing for a few weeks now. Each day felt like a steady escalation of tensions, and I was losing my patience and energy. Her barrage of forwarded e-mails and desperate phone calls over trivial work matters was dominating my life. At home, she wasn't interested in dinner. At night, she was restless and agitated, and I didn't understand why she couldn't just relax and sleep. We downloaded guided meditations, lit scented candles, played the sound of waves. None of it worked.

In the quiet of the night, the only sounds in our room were a calming playlist, Goose's snoring, and my whispers to Giulia about how beautiful, smart, and competent she was and that life would work out like it always did. Through my affirmations, I felt helpless with worry. How scary this must feel to her: to lose sleep to the intensity of thoughts that you didn't have words for. But even my worries lost out to exhaustion, and eventually I drifted off to sleep, such a guilty indulgence. Giulia inevitably stayed awake as I slept, twisting and turning well after my whispers had quieted to nothing, and the playlist ran out of songs, and the only sound left was our snoring bulldog. As I slept through it, grateful for the rest, it left me empty inside when I awoke to see her eyes wide-open.

Four weeks into her new job, my school year started. I was teaching five history classes and coaching the varsity water polo team, which made it impossible to respond to all of Giulia's phone calls and texts.

Giulia continued to spiral into crippling anxiety. She began to call in sick to work. She even agreed to see a psychiatrist but was offended by the initial diagnosis of depression. Depression didn't happen to someone like her. This was just a minor setback. She'd will herself through it. The psychiatrist prescribed sleeping pills and antidepressants. Giulia had no intention of taking them. Regardless, she had the scripts filled at the local pharmacy and brought them home. When she set them on the table, she joked that I should make sure to hide the pills in the morning, because since she was so depressed, what if she took them all? We laughed, a bit uneasily. The idea of my *principessa* committing suicide seemed absurd.

That night we sleepwalked through the same failed ritual, more hours of trying to calm Giulia to sleep, to no avail. In the morning, I woke up late and rushed out the door to get to school on time. I completely forgot about the medicine, which remained on the dining room table where we had left them the night before.

I came home from work and Giulia was Skyping with her mom, who seemed to be glaring at me through the computer. I had no idea what was going on until Giulia said to me, "You left the pills out."

"I did?" I asked innocently.

"Yeah, you did," she said. "I asked you to put them away."

"Oh yeah, that's right, you did ask, I'm sorry I forgot," I said. "I was so rushed this morning, I forgot."

"Well, don't forget anymore," Giulia's mom said to me. "And hide them like she asked you to."

"Okay, I won't, I'm sorry, I just, you know, forgot. I'm always so tired, I was so rushed." I didn't think it was a big deal.

And we hung up Skype, and it wasn't until later, after dinner, as we were getting ready for bed, that I learned it was a very big deal that I had left the pills out. Giulia told me that when she woke up that morning, she saw the pills, and sat down at the dining room table, and stared at them, and then called in sick for the third day in a row. She sat with the orange jars and studied them. She shook them out into her palm to test their weight. She arranged them in patterns.

And she thought about taking all of them.

"But I wanted to call my mom, first," she told me as I listened in horrified silence. "I'm not sure why, I just wanted to talk to her. So I Skyped her, and told her that I was thinking of taking all the pills, and my mom begged me not to. So we kept talking. We talked until you got home."

"What time did you call her?"

"I don't know, maybe ten or so."

Which meant that Giulia's mom had stayed on Skype for six hours, stuck on the other side of a computer screen on the other side of the world, refusing to let Giulia hang up until I came home.

This changed everything. I asked Giulia to stay in our bedroom with the door closed, and I took the pills and went around the house for a few minutes, opening and closing drawers in each room to make as much sound as I could to make it hard for her to know where I hid them, the worst game of hide-and-seek I had ever played.

The diagnosis of depression and the prospect of suicide suddenly became very real. The pills no longer felt optional, and I insisted that Giulia take them as prescribed, and while supervised. In the morning, I'd take a dosage out of the bottles before returning them to their hiding place and bring the few pills back to her with a glass of water. I watched her take the medication. It was the same routine at night.

After the Skype call, Giulia's dad, Romeo, dropped everything and flew out to California. At six feet seven, with a mustache that he has had since he was sixteen, Romeo was a two-time Olympic water polo player and easily could have been the most intimidating person you've ever met. Instead, he was the complete opposite: gentle and mild. When I first met him, he was more nervous than I was.

When Romeo arrived, I breathed a sigh of relief. It had been almost a month of Giulia's faltering stability, and now I could go off to work and know that she was safe with family. She had unofficially put herself on sick leave and went to bed with little to no expectation of going to work the next day, so father and daughter spent their days together walking the beach; riding bikes; talking about work, and life, and balance, and happiness.

And nothing helped.

Even away from work, Giulia's anxiety grew. She went from restless sleep to no sleep at all. She stopped eating. The color drained from her skin. It was like watching her vanish right before my eyes.

One morning, when I woke up, Giulia sat calmly at the foot of our bed.

"I talked to God last night, Mark," she told me.

Giulia and I both grew up Catholic, but she wasn't what I would call religious. She almost never talked about God and rarely prayed. I couldn't hide the skepticism in my voice.

"Really?" I said.

"I did, and he talked back," she said. "He's never talked back before, but last night he did. His voice was so loud and clear. I thought it was going to wake you up."

"What did he say?" I asked.

"He said that everything is going to be all right. We are going to figure this out."

"Well, that's good to hear," I said for her benefit, but nothing about this felt good. Giulia had never talked like this before. I wanted to tell her how crazy this sounded, hearing voices in the night, but she seemed comforted by a reassuring message. I just listened.

"The little girl inside me is so full of life and wants to be free and feel love, and God is going to help that little girl find her way out."

"Good," I said again, no less nervously.

The next morning, when I woke up, Giulia wasn't sitting at the foot of the bed. She was pacing around the bedroom, mouthing thoughts to herself.

"Good morning, honey. How did you sleep?" I asked.

"I talked to the Devil last night, Mark," she said, speaking very loudly and quickly. "He said everything is *not* going to be okay. He said that there is no way out of this. I can't be saved. I'm not worth saving. We might as well just give up." She was very matter-of-fact about this, as if reading the weather forecast, but with a rushed intensity.

I jumped out of bed and pulled her close to my chest.

"Oh, honey. I'm so sorry."

"It's okay, Mark. I'm not sorry. Just stop wasting your time with me. It's not worth it."

"Giulia, you're totally worth it," I whispered back to her. "There is no Devil talking to you. It's just you and me."

"You don't know. You weren't there. The Devil is real and he's here and he's going to make me pay."

"I don't believe that for a second, Giulia," I said. Which was true. I tried to calm her with the same reassurances that hadn't been working for six weeks. I simply didn't know what else to say to my wife, so I stumbled through more meaningless affirmations.

"You are an amazing woman. You are doing such a great job. You don't have to pay for anything. You are going to be great and you're doing all the right things."

"But you were asleep! You didn't hear what I heard!"

Giulia was growing desperate for me to believe her, but I couldn't pretend anymore that hearing God and the Devil was no big deal.

"I didn't hear what you heard because the Devil isn't real, Giulia. He's not real. He's not tormenting you. This is all in your mind."

With that, Giulia exploded. "You don't believe me? That the Devil is here to get me? Fine, whatever, get out of my face. This is all going to be over soon anyway."

She pushed me away and stormed out of the bedroom. I heard her stomping around in the living room, mumbling to herself the whole way.

I left our room as well and crossed the hallway to the guest room, where Romeo slept. I woke him up and quickly explained what was going on. "I think we need to take her to the hospital," I told him. He agreed.

We went into the living room. Giulia glared at me and began

to beg her dad. "Papa, the Devil was here last night. You have to believe me. Mark doesn't believe me, but you do, right, Dad?"

"*Giulia, mi dispiace, povera Giulia,*" Romeo responded. Giulia, I'm so sorry, poor Giulia.

"Giulia, we need to get you some help," I said. "We are worried and don't know what to do. We want to take you to the hospital."

"No! Don't waste your time. The Devil said I'm not worth it. They won't do anything there anyway."

"Please, Giulia," Romeo said. "We want to get you help to feel better."

Giulia backed away from us. "Leave me alone!" she shouted as we slowly approached her, cornering her in the front entranceway. "It's not worth it! Stop wasting your time!"

Finally Romeo and I grimaced at each other, knowing what we had to do. He grabbed her around the legs, and I scooped her under her armpits, and we carried her down the hallway. She shrieked and reached out wildly for anything to hold her back and latched on to the hallway bathroom doorknob. I pried her fingers individually while she tried to squirm her body free. Romeo and I worked in silence, overpowered by the fierce sound of Giulia's resistance. I caught a glimpse of Romeo's face and saw that he was sobbing, and only when I saw his face did I realize how much I was crying, too.

We got her down the narrow stairs into our garage and into the passenger seat of our Honda Civic. Once in the car, she settled down, and we sped off to the emergency room, Romeo crammed into the seat behind Giulia. We didn't say anything, but we both wanted her to be within arm's reach. As we wound along Park Presidio Boulevard through Golden Gate Park, Giulia quickly popped off her seat belt and shoved open the car door. I swerved as I slammed on the brakes. Romeo and I simultaneously reached over to close the door and grab her before she could throw herself out.

I left Giulia and Romeo in the driveway of the Kaiser Permanente ER with the car idling and ran inside.

"My wife's having some kind of a breakdown!" I couldn't believe what I was saying. "She keeps saying that she talked to the Devil, and she tried to throw herself out of the car on the way over here."

"Okay, where is she?" the admitting nurse asked.

"Out in the car. Can someone come and get her? She won't get out of the car."

"I'm sorry, we can't do that. If she doesn't walk in here voluntarily, we can't drag her in." He was disinterested, as though he had said this to people a million times before.

"Then what do I do?" I asked, exasperated.

I had been in this waiting room before—for stitches to my head after my surfboard hit me, for an infected foot—and I knew it to be wide and spacious, but now it felt tiny and choking. I needed to get out of the room, out of the hospital, but I had to get Giulia out of the car first.

The nurse paused for a minute, to muster up some compassion for what he had to tell me. "You have to call the police. Sit in the car with her, explain her behavior to the police. They will show up and arrest her, and they will walk her in the door. It's probably going to take a while. And she's going to be in handcuffs."

I rushed back out to the car and told Giulia that if she didn't come into the hospital, the police would come and arrest her and make her go. She resisted for almost fifteen minutes. I had 911 punched into my phone and my finger hovering above the "Call" button before she finally agreed and got out of the car, Romeo holding her arm as she pushed herself out of the seat, me grabbing her other arm once she was out of the car, so that she couldn't break our grip and slip away from us.

The admitting nurse interviewed Giulia in a triage room that was no bigger than a closet. I sat with Giulia and let her answer.

"Have you been feeling stressed lately?" the nurse asked.

"The Devil tells me to quit," Giulia said.

"Okay, does that feel stressful?" the nurse asked.

"It doesn't matter, the Devil says this is all pointless so it doesn't matter if I'm stressed or not."

"But it matters to me," the nurse said, "because I want to help you feel better."

"There is no feeling better," Giulia said.

Eventually I stepped in and told the nurse everything. The new job. The escalating anxiety. The loss of sleep, appetite, and weight. The dozens of ways we tried to get her to sleep. Her dad flying out from Europe. The sick days. The obsessive fixation on God and the Devil. The absence of mental illness in her personal and family history. The startling intensity. The fear, the fear, the fear.

The nurse stepped out and left us in the closet. They had wheeled in a portable computer for the nurse to take notes, and the quiet hum of the screen was the only noise between us. We had no idea what was coming next.

Just as I realized that they had shoved us out of sight into a tiny triage room because it was the best way of hiding Giulia from the rest of the waiting room, a different nurse ushered us into a full room. This new nurse took Giulia's vitals and asked her many of the same questions, and I launched into my explanation a second time. Then a third time, when the ER doc came and ordered Giulia to be injected with Ativan to calm her down. The first hour was a blurred shuffle of people, and I told as much as I could to each one, in the hope that they could make sense of what I couldn't understand. Then we waited—and waited and waited—for the mental health worker who was on duty that day.

We sat quietly, Romeo and I, disoriented and unsure of what to say. Giulia became increasingly groggy as the Ativan did its job. The hospital posted a security guard outside our door, an older man who slowly eased into his chair. The precaution felt ridiculous.

The social worker finally arrived, after five hours. Giulia was now fully under the influence of the Ativan and groggily rolled her head in the direction of the social worker when she walked in. The social worker asked Giulia the same questions the nurse and the ER doctor had asked her.

"Have you ever felt suicidal?" the social worker asked Giulia.

"No," she answered, barely whispering the words.

"But she did try to throw herself out of the car on the drive over," I said urgently. I needed the social worker to see the full picture, and Giulia clearly wasn't painting it. "And earlier this week, she spent all day contemplating an overdose on sleep medication. A psychiatrist prescribed them, and Giulia asked me to hide them. I forgot to hide them, and Giulia spent all day looking at the pills, tempting herself to take them."

"If you wanted to take them, what stopped you from taking the pills, Giulia?" the social worker inquired.

"I called my mom. She talked to me. I didn't take them."

"So you didn't take the pills because you talked to your mom," the social worker reiterated.

"Yes," Giulia said.

"Okay then, well, that's a good sign. Giulia, you're not doing so great, but you're going to be fine," the social worker said. "You stopped yourself before because you talked to someone. That's a good thing, and a good sign that you're going to be fine."

The social worker was trying to calm down Giulia, but it was having the opposite effect on me. I was completely unconvinced by this optimistic spin. "Are you serious?" I asked, shocked. "She might not have taken pills, but she's talking about the Devil."

The social worker ignored me and focused back on Giulia. "I'm going to write a prescription for a different sleeping pill and a better antidepressant, and you all can go home," she concluded.

"Really?" I asked. "A sleeping pill and an antidepressant? She's already been prescribed those and they didn't do anything. What about the voices?" I was incredulous that the social worker wanted more of the same approach. There had to be something else, some wunderpill that would quiet the voices and chase away the fear. Surely there had to be.

"Yes, everything's going to be fine, these medications should help," the social worker said, reassuring us. "She just needs sleep." She turned her attention back to Giulia, who had been silent through the whole exchange. It might have been the Ativan, but I think Giulia had been resigned to the fate she thought the Devil had sealed for her.

"I want you to make a contract for safety with your husband," the social worker said. "That means you two make an agreement that you will be safe. If you're ever feeling like you might hurt yourself or hurt someone, you have to tell Mark about it. It's clear that he wants you to feel better and keep you safe. Don't act on any suicidal feelings, tell Mark first, and he can get you help."

We all nodded, waited in line at the pharmacy to fill Giulia's new prescriptions, and drove home.

After six hours at the ER, we felt that we were being shooed away with nothing but a different prescription and a contract for safety. I was hoping for more guidance from professionals whose help we needed. Or at least a different type of medication, one that would deal with these new obsessions with God and the Devil. Maybe this was the only help they could provide. But I felt abandoned all the same.

I needed something to latch on to, so I treated the contract for safety like a reaffirmation of our marriage vows. When we got home from the hospital, I got a pen and a journal and went off to the beach with Giulia and Goose. Romeo stayed back to call Mariarita.

It was a beautiful day, with a clear blue sky, light winds, and casual waves that broke hundreds of yards out in the low tide. We sat in the sand and repeated promises we had made to each other throughout our relationship and wrote them down in the journal: to be open and honest with each other; that we loved each other, and our love was so strong we could get through anything; that we would keep each other safe if we felt scared or alone.

Then we rolled up our pant legs and waded out into the shallows of the water. I pulled out my phone and snapped a picture of Giulia—"This is what you looked like the day you beat this thing," I said to her as I took the picture and she tried to smile—and then we dipped our hands in the water to rinse them. The waves lapped in against our legs, leaving trails of foam. I scooped up a helping of the ocean and poured it into Giulia's hands, and she did the same to me. I then washed her face, and she washed mine. We didn't say a word but flowed on intuition as we rinsed away the horrors of the day. I focused on her smile, *bello come il sole*, and tried to erase the jarring memory of forcing her into the car as she resisted.

"I'm sorry I scared you today, Mark."

She sounded like herself. Not slurred by the Ativan, not agitated by the voices she was hearing. Just Giulia.

"It's okay, Giulia. I'm sorry I haven't been patient with you."

"Through sickness and in health, Mark. That's right now."

The water calmed us down. Giulia stopped talking about God and the Devil, stopped talking about giving up, stopped talking about being scared. We instead somehow found optimism that the worst was over, we had survived the ER, and things were going to work out, like they always did. I needed to believe these things to be true, so I let them be. Giulia unexpectedly jumped onto my back and let me carry her, piggyback style, out of the water. With her on my back, I felt the lightness of relief. We turned our backs to the sea and splashed through the waves to the dry sand, where Goose was digging for rocks.

Even though you're not supposed to turn your back on the sea.

Mariarita arrived the next night. She pretended to be happy with us all together, but her worry was palpable. I alone couldn't help Giulia. Romeo hadn't stopped things from escalating either. It was now a full-court press, all three of us in the house to love Giulia back to health.

Mariarita saw motherhood as her life's work. She bragged that her children never ate a single frozen meal in their lives and every dinner was home cooked with fresh ingredients. She printed up e-mails that Giulia wrote to her and made them into a scrapbook. Her world was Giulia and her younger Pietro.

When Mariarita met me when I was eighteen, she absorbed me into her care as well. One summer I visited the family in Italy and fell asleep on the beach for a few hours, and Mariarita spent the afternoon readjusting the umbrella over my head so that I didn't get sunburned.

When Giulia and I married, I nicknamed Mariarita "Suoc," short for *suocera*, Italian for mother-in-law. She loved the name and wore it proudly in front of her friends.

Suoc was now here, in full mama-bear mode, and wanted to sleep with Giulia, so mother and daughter settled in the guest room. Romeo slept in our bed. I took the couch.

I collapsed in the living room but took a little while to drift off. With Giulia's parents there to help, I should have felt relief, but instead I felt like I had been exiled to the couch. "Let the adults handle this." I tried to see the situation as Giulia's parents might have: their little girl was in crisis and needed support and protection. Her young, surfer-dude husband meant well but wasn't equipped to do the job. Look what had happened with leaving the pills out, after all. I had to admit that I didn't have a clue about what to do, but that didn't stop me from feeling defensive and petulant.

Eventually, I drifted into the first solid night's sleep I'd had in six weeks.

Then, at seven a.m. the next morning, Romeo jolted me awake.

"We need to go back to the hospital," he said.

I jumped up, pulled on pants, and found Giulia pacing around the guest room, her mom upright on the bed, eyes wide-open and full of tears, shaking her head in disbelief. Her terror was obvious.

"Mark, the Devil was here last night. But don't worry. I protected my mom. I protected you. I protected all of you guys. I stayed awake and the Devil is still here but can't get you because I am here." Giulia was babbling. "I need to get out of here. It's over, and worthless to fix things."

This time Giulia didn't fight getting into the car or resist going into the ER. We drove back to the same Kaiser Permanente ER and went through the same admission process with many of the same people from two days before. A nurse hooked Giulia right back up on an IV drip of Ativan. After thirty minutes, she began to settle down in the hospital bed. Suoc sat at the foot of the mattress, Romeo took the chair, and I sat on the floor, my back against the wall. We were all lost, silent, sunk in our own worlds. None of us could do anything. Over the past six weeks, we had steadily ramped up our attention and focus on Giulia, Skyping and praying and meditating and holding her in our arms, but we hadn't helped her. It was almost as if her slide into psychosis was inevitable and that no matter what we did, she still had no appetite, couldn't sleep, heard voices in the night, and remained fixated on heaven and hell.

The steady beep of Giulia's heart-rate monitor lulled me into an uncertain sleep while slouched on the floor. When I woke up, I told Giulia about the dream I'd just had, one I'd been having for weeks.

In the dream, Giulia and I walked together, hand in hand, and the surroundings changed rapidly—my childhood in Tokyo, Ocean Beach, our freshman dorm. Everywhere I had ever been, we now walked together, as if the entire span of our separate lives had been predestined to bring us to where we stood together.

We didn't know where we were going, but we were looking for something. It was urgent that we find it, but I didn't know what it was. All of this uncertainty had derailed our plans, and in going from place to place, and year to year, it was as if we were sifting through the past to find where we had gone wrong, so we could get back on the path we had always been on. Each time I had this dream, like I just had sitting on the hospital floor, I woke up before we found what we were looking for and where we had gotten so lost.

I explained the dream to Giulia, with her parents in the room. It was the first of dozens of intimate conversations between husband and wife that would occur in full view of family and medical professionals. "I know what we are looking for in my dream. We are looking for peace, and we are looking together. You must feel very alone right now. I do too, Giulia. I'm scared, too. But we are actually standing side by side, always holding on to each other. Can't you see how beautiful that is? We will find this peace, Giulia. We might feel awake in a daze, but soon we will find our peace."

Giulia paused for a long time to process what I'd said.

"Mark, I am the Devil," she whispered through the fog of Ativan.

The on-call psychiatrist was tall and serious and spoke with efficient purpose. But he brought no good news.

"Giulia needs to be admitted to the psych ward for treatment," he said.

I knew that this was coming, that this was the inevitable next step in the process, but it still felt surreal.

"There's a complication," he added. "Here at Kaiser, we don't have a psych ward. We have psychiatrists who treat people in the ER, and who do outpatient care, but we don't have an inpatient facility."

"So where is she going?" I asked.

"We don't know yet," he confessed. "When we admit a patient through our ER, we call the other hospitals in the area to see who has an open bed."

"What if no one has an open bed?" I asked.

"Then we wait," he said.

More waiting. Was this how every mental health crisis was handled?

"It could be a long wait," he added.

He turned to leave, and I stopped him.

"How long do you think she will have to be in the psych ward?" I asked, my voice cracking with desperation.

"It's tough to say," he said. "At least overnight, possibly several nights."

"Will they be able to get her better?"

"I wouldn't be sending her there if I didn't believe that," he said.

I lost track of how many hours we waited. Suoc and I left the ER to get some food for lunch, hamburgers and milkshakes from a place across the street that I had always wanted to try. But not like this.

Romeo called the airline to try to change his flight back to Europe, since he was supposed to leave the next day. He hung up in frustration when they kept asking him for his confirmation number and he kept saying that he didn't have it because we were in the emergency room. We all napped.

After hours of waiting, four people appeared in the hospital room, and my world erupted. Everything seemed to happen at the same time. It all felt out of reach, and the best I could do was hurry to keep up. The four people loaded Giulia onto a stretcher to wheel her into the ambulance for transport to a hospital on the other side of the city, where they had an open bed. Suoc went in the ambulance with Giulia, and I sprinted three blocks to the parking garage to get the car, Romeo chasing behind me. The ambulance was already out of sight by the time we pulled away from the ER, so we sped across the city to the hospital on our own. I screamed about not being able to find a parking spot, and I slammed the door shut in fury once we found one. I left the keys in the car and raced back to get them, then dashed off to the hospital lobby. The receptionist saw us panting and somehow understood and told us what to do. "You need to go to the third floor. There are four elevators, and only the one on the far left stops at the third floor. Get on that one."

There were other people waiting for the elevators. I walked to the fourth one and pushed the button and waited uncomfortably. Another elevator opened and the people around me asked if I was going up and I didn't know how to tell them that I had to ride the special elevator because my wife was being admitted to the psych ward, so I said nothing.

The elevator eventually arrived and slowly creaked up to the third floor. The doors opened, and I stepped off into a new world.

The entirety of the walls were glass windows, and almost all the blinds were pulled. The waiting room was about eight feet by ten feet, the floor a bland, greenish tile, with a few beaten-up vinyl chairs sagging along the perimeter. Mariarita was collapsed in one of the chairs, hair disheveled, hands clasping each other for something to hold on to.

She had just landed the night before. She had cried so much already that now her body shook but no sounds or tears came out.

The waiting room was an enclosed fortress in the middle of the ward. Chaos swirled around it. The only bridge between the fortress and the chaos was a single glass door.

No one greeted us in the waiting room. No warm, comforting smile, no pat on the hand. Instead just those glass windows with blinds pulled, a few signs printed on white paper, hastily taped up.

VISITORS ARE ADVISED THAT THEY ARE NOT PERMITTED TO BRING ANY OF THE FOLLOWING OBJECTS WHEN THEY VISIT A PATIENT:

weapons
sharp objects
drugs
alcohol
cigarettes
cameras
anything with drawstrings (sweatshirts, shoes)

PACKAGES MUST BE CHECKED AT THE NURSES' STATION AND OBJECTS IN VIOLATION WILL BE CONFISCATED.

VISITING HOURS ARE FROM 7–8:30 PM. SATURDAY AND SUNDAY THERE ARE ALSO VISITING HOURS FROM 12–1 PM.

NO FORMER PATIENTS ARE ALLOWED TO ENTER AS VISITORS.

There were a few open gaps in the blinds, which offered a glimpse into life on the third floor. I could see flashes of people walking past, but not Giulia. The only unimpeded view was from the glass door, in the far corner of the room, so I went over to look through and see more of what I could.

Directly across from the doorway was the nurses' station, a stout counter at least twenty feet long. Several people sat at the station, all looking down at paperwork. I knocked at the door. A few nurses looked up, then returned to their paperwork. No one moved.

I craned my neck to the left to the end of the nurses' station, and I saw Giulia. She was sitting in a chair across from a nurse with a clipboard. Giulia was in the hospital robe that they had given her in the ER, her glasses on, her shoulders held upright in a perfect balance, as if she were balancing a textbook on her head. I tapped on the glass again, louder. I wanted to reassure Giulia that she was okay, that the people were there to help her. She looked up, saw me, and looked away, returning her focus to the nurse at her side.

I sat back down.

"What's going on, Suoc? What happened?" I asked my mother-in-law.

"Nothing," she replied with her thick accent. "They brought her up here while you parked the car and now we're here. What can I say."

"What did the nurses say?"

"They didn't say anything to me. They took Giulia inside and closed the door and that is it. Nothing." Suoc lowered her head.

I felt so much of everything and had so much to say, but I didn't know where to start, and no one was listening to me anyway. *She*

doesn't belong here. You take care of her or I'm going to sue you for ev-
erything this hospital is worth. Give her the best room. She doesn't like
heavy carbs with her meals. If any of the patients even tries to touch her,
I will fucking kill them.

My heart raced, my fingers twitched, my stomach hurt. My sa-
liva tasted bitter, as if I were going to vomit.

I walked back to the glass door to look at Giulia's new world.

A pale, gaunt man with thinning gray hair and a jean jacket
hovered near Giulia. He looked to be in his late forties, and his
movements were painfully slow. We made eye contact for a flash of
a second, and I was terrified of what he might do to my wife, the
two of them locked away from me on the other side of a glass door.

An older Chinese woman raced by, pacing furiously, swinging
her arms in exaggerated circles. She talked as she walked to no one
in particular, and no one listened to her. I was scared of her, too.

There was a big guy in his twenties, well over six feet tall and
probably more than 250 pounds, with frumpy brown hair matted
as though he had been lying in bed for days. He shuffled in and out
of view, his pants sagging underneath his hospital gown, revealing
the top of his bare ass. He saw Giulia, and saw me at the door, and
flashed me a confident smirk. He scared me most of all.

What the fuck had we done? Where had we taken Giulia? This
place was full of crazy people who would rip apart someone like my
sweet, beautiful wife, who let me remind you wasn't crazy at all. She
just hadn't slept. She was stressed out. She just needed to sleep.

Finally, one of the nurses stood up from her seat behind the
station and walked over to the glass door. She surveyed all the
patients to make sure they were at least six feet away, a rule that
wasn't posted in the waiting room but I eventually learned. She

inserted one key into the doorknob and then a second key into a lock on the wall. With two keys in place, the door buzzed, and she pulled it open and stepped briskly into the waiting room and slammed the door behind her.

I jumped up to meet her. Suoc and Romeo stayed on the chairs behind me, overwhelmed by the expansive gulf between their refined Italian language and this American nightmare.

"What do you want?" the nurse asked coldly.

"Uh, what do you mean," I said. "We just dropped off my wife, Giulia, she's there talking to a nurse, and uh, we, uh, have some—"

"I know you dropped her off. So what do you want?" she repeated.

"Well," I said, taking a deep breath. "What is going to happen? This has never happened to us before."

The nurse rolled her eyes, irritated. "Your wife is clearly psychotic and delusional. She has been brought here on a 5150 and so—"

"A 5150, what does that mean?" I said. "And what's psychotic?" I thought of psychopath, and psycho killer. Did they think she was going to hurt somebody?

"A 5150 means she's been involuntarily checked in here, and so she needs to stay at least seventy-two hours, as required by law." She brushed off my question about psychosis and stared at me, signaling that I wasn't going to get any more out of her.

"When can we come and visit her?"

"The visiting hours are posted," she said, not even bothering to answer my question.

"I know, but it's so short, only seven to eight thirty p.m. Can't I visit her during the rest of the day?"

"No."

"But that's too short," I said. "You don't understand."

"Your wife is here on a 5150, that's what I understand," she lectured me. "She has certain rights, and you have certain rights. You've obviously had a long day. I suggest you go home and come back tomorrow to visit her."

"But can we go and see her room?"

"No, we need to process her and get set up, and that is best done alone, away from the family."

I didn't like being called "the family."

"But I want to see the facilities. Is she going to get meals? Will you take good care of her? What will she do all day? Can I call her? What's wrong with her?"

The nurse had no time for this. "I have to get back to work. Come back during visiting hours."

I started panicking. "Wait, please. Please. You don't understand . . ." I was croaking. "Please. Can I at least say good-bye to her?" I wanted to take it all back, go back to the emergency room, to the social worker who said that Giulia could come home, to the waves and the ocean that were supposed to wash this all away. But now Giulia was locked in and I was locked out and I couldn't even say good-bye. "Please. Just let me say good-bye to her."

If she had to stay there, I at least wanted to go to Giulia and hold her hands and look her in the eyes and kiss her forehead and tell her to be strong and that there is so much love in the world that will lift her up out of this darkness.

"Please," I begged. "Please. I didn't say good-bye to her."

"It's up to her," the nurse said, finally cracking. "I'll go ask if she wants to talk to you. But she has rights. Otherwise, we'll see you tomorrow."

The nurse crossed back into the other world and I stood at the door, my hands and face pressed against the glass. Giulia watched me. She sat so still and upright, trying to hide her fragility. The nurse approached her and asked her something as she gestured back to the door where I was peering in. Giulia shook her head no.

three

September 2009

———

"Get out of here!" Giulia shrieked as she pointed at us. "It's not safe! You need to leave!"

Suoc and I stood in the doorway to Giulia's bare room. It was our first visit. We had dropped Giulia off the day before and spent every minute of the past twenty-four hours waiting until we could come back. Now we were here, to see the inside of the psych ward, with our beloved Giulia in it, and she was screaming at us to leave.

Giulia sat upright on a twin bed that was stuffed back in the far corner of the room, her blanched blankets a heap around her. The tile floor and the walls were the same color, a white so insignificant that it was practically a noncolor. She still wore the hospital gown they had changed her into at the ER, the blue faded after years of use. Next to her bed was a bedside wooden table, with two chairs nearby, and that was it. The room was otherwise empty, useless, colorless space.

Giulia's door was just a few feet away from the nurses' station. I learned later, when they moved Giulia to another room, that this room, always within eyesight and earshot of the nurses, was for the most vulnerable patient.

I was distraught with impatience to see some type of improvement after a night in the psych ward. I was also anxious to assess the conditions of the hospital and, most important, to see how Giulia had handled her first twenty-four hours alone. I had been calling the hospital every hour on the hour, but the only report I had gotten was that she had been in her bed all day and refused to engage with anyone.

Instead of the improvement I was hoping for, Giulia was worse— more agitated, more intensely delusional. "Stay away from me!" she continued to scream.

I still didn't know how to engage with her outbursts, so I resorted to calming, gentle assurances, as if trying to soothe a scared child.

"Hi, Giulia, it's good to see you," I gently replied over her loud warnings.

"Get out! The Devil is here and he wants you. You need to leave now!" She was hysterical with fear. I looked over my shoulder back at the nurses' station, and the two nurses working there were watching us intensely. Visitors were not allowed in patients' rooms, but since Giulia had just been admitted yesterday and hadn't left her room, we had been granted an exception.

"Honey, it's okay, there's no one to get us," I said slowly as I fidgeted in the doorway and forced a smile to hide my racing anxiety. "We're just here to see you." I paused and tried to shift the conversation to the condition of the hospital. "How are things going? Are you doing okay in here?" I instinctively took a step forward, to be closer to her, and Giulia exploded.

"Don't you dare come near me!" she screamed. She was uncontrollable with a fear that something was going to happen to us.

I retreated back to stand shoulder to shoulder with Suoc in the narrow doorway. We stood in helpless, defeated silence. I could hear Suoc's heavy breathing, the first I had really noticed of her since we'd stepped onto the elevator up to the third floor for our visit. I was so focused on seeing Giulia, I had almost forgotten that Suoc was there. We were practically holding each other upright in the doorway, both of us consumed with love and fear for Giulia.

After a minute, I mustered up the courage to try something.

"I've got an idea. What if we take those two seats and put them over here, by the door? That way we can talk to you but you don't have to worry about being so close."

Giulia didn't respond, which I interpreted as a tacit agreement. She nervously watched as I scooted into the room and slid the chairs away from the bed. The farther back I pulled them, the more her body relaxed.

"Okay, this works. We're here, and we're fine. You don't have to worry."

Giulia leaned back against the headboard. We sat down. Suoc fidgeted at a loose string that dangled at the cuff of her sweater.

"So, Giulia, tell me about your day," I said. I was dying to know what she'd done all day. "Are they treating you well here? Do you like the nurses?"

Giulia continued to have no interest in the day-to-day.

"I did bad things and the Devil is here and I need to go down in order to come back up. I don't know why he picked me but he did and that's all there is to it."

She took a long pause and looked at us pleadingly. "I don't understand why you guys are involved in this, too. Everyone wants to gather me in a big circle, and shame me for what I've done. You all know about my faults and now I have to suffer for them and you both are part of it."

"*Dai, Giulia, non è vero,*" Suoc responded in Italian. Come on, Giulia, it's not true. "Mark, do you know about this?"

"I don't know about this, but what I do know is that Giulia is a very good person who has friends and family who love her and care for her a lot."

But Giulia kept on insisting. The conversation continued this way, volleying back and forth between two irreconcilable realities. On one side, Suoc and I were trying to stay calm and be in our reality, so we could confirm our love and faith in healing. On the other, Giulia spastically prepared for some apocalyptic showdown with the Devil.

Giulia grew intolerably frustrated by our inability to understand her. She rolled onto her back, pulled her knees toward her chest, and chanted, "*Voglio morire, voglio morire, voglio morire.*" I want to die, I want to die, I want to die. At first she hissed through her teeth, then she started shouting, "*VOGLIO MORIRE, VOGLIO MORIRE!*" in an aggressive roar. I'm not sure which scared me more: listening to my wife whisper her death wish or scream it.

A nurse barged in and recommended we take a break, so we stepped out into the hallway. I had called them all day and they had reported the same thing: Giulia hadn't left her bed and wouldn't talk to anyone. She spent the whole day on her side, staring at the wall. Which was certainly worrisome. But now she was in a fury, and the nurses weren't impressed. "Perhaps you are making her more agitated by being here," the nurse said. I somehow convinced her to let us stay.

From the doorway, I asked Giulia if I could come close to her for ten seconds. Just ten seconds. We could test to see if the Devil really was contagious. She had barely conceded before I snuck in and stood by her side. After a few seconds, I left.

Giulia watched in shock.

"You're not dead," she declared in disbelief. "And I'm not dead either. Why?"

"Because we love each other," I said.

"We do, don't we."

"Yes, we do. And that is stronger than this."

She sat in uncertainty for a while and then looked back with an entirely different expression—fragility, helplessness, desperation.

"I'm scared, Mark."

"I'm scared, too."

I pulled my chair up close to her bed and held her hand. We didn't talk much, but at least we were together, and she was calm. We somehow managed to stay thirty minutes past the close of visiting hours, and Giulia took us to the cafeteria, where food had been laid out. I had a piece of cake. It was delicious, and I considered going back for seconds but decided that wasn't a great idea.

I kissed Giulia on her forehead before I left, feeling victorious. I had convinced her out of her reality and back into mine, if even for a moment.

The first few days of Giulia's hospitalization, I spent almost every waking hour on the phone. I spoke with the nurses at the hospital, asking for updates; with the social worker who had been assigned to Giulia's case; with her doctor's voice mail (he never picked up, but that never stopped me from calling); with friends and referrals about what might be going on, in order to have second, third, fourth, and fifth opinions; and finally with family, reporting whatever I learned.

With every call I made, I grew increasingly agitated at the inflexibility of the mental health system. I understood that the mentally unstable needed protection, but the system didn't understand that my wife didn't need protection from me. I was there to help. Of course I was there to help. But so many rules and loopholes stood in the way.

For starters, I was technically not allowed to speak to any of the nurses or Giulia's doctor. Romeo and I had been parking the car when Giulia was processed by the psych unit, her mom by her side. When asked whom the doctors would be permitted to speak with, Giulia looked at her mom and said, "Her."

Suoc was unenthusiastic with the prospect of being the main point of contact. Her first language was Italian, and she was hesitant in English. Her fundamental suspicion of psychiatry didn't help. The American nurses, speaking in technical language about psychosis and delusions, were intimidating. But, no matter. Since Giulia hadn't signed off for me to speak to the hospital staff, legally, no one could give me information about her status or care. Still, I badgered them with phone calls hourly. A few nurses caved to my entreaties and answered my questions, but they were uncomfortable with it. The doctor insisted that I get Giulia to sign a note giving me permission to receive information on her behalf. She couldn't even acknowledge our reality, how was she supposed to officially grant me permission to speak to her doctor?

Another frustration involved the prescribed medication. The psychiatrist had seen Giulia within a few hours of her admission and had prescribed sleeping pills and a medication called Geodon, a fairly new antipsychotic that was known to help control the hysteria, paranoia, and delusions associated with a psychotic break. But on a 5150, it was up to Giulia to decide whether to take the prescribed meds or not. She refused the medication.

Logically, this made sense. The law protected patients from taking any unwanted medication while in the seventy-two hours of a 5150. This not only respected the rights of patients—an important development in a long history of abuse against the mentally ill—it afforded a "wait and see" approach that worked for the common occurrence of people who were in there because of drug overdoses.

In Giulia's case, however, I felt like this was lost time toward her recovery. Her psychosis was related not to drugs, but to anxiety and an absence of sleep—at least that's the theory I had pieced together. She didn't need a seventy-two-hour detox from drugs, she needed the opposite: the right drugs, and right away. The law that was meant to protect Giulia instead seemed to be letting her get worse.

After the three days expired, things would become more complicated legally. The doctor would have to either discharge Giulia or upgrade her 5150 to a 5250, a fourteen-day hold. In the fourteen-day hold, Giulia would be offered the same medication as before, but now if she refused, she could be forcibly injected, even if it was against her wishes.

I learned all of this from the Internet and from the piecemeal conversations I dragged out of the nurses, who were still not permitted to talk to me in those first days.

On the third day, the hospital was going to have a hearing where the doctor presented his case to a judge, to see if Giulia's 5150 should be upgraded to a 5250. I asked if I could attend, and they said sure. I still wasn't technically allowed to speak with any of the nurses, but I was allowed to go to the hearing. It was going to be on Thursday at ten a.m., almost exactly seventy-two hours after we had brought Giulia to the ER.

For some reason I thought I needed to dress up for the hearing, so I wore a shirt and tie and arrived at nine thirty. I buzzed the ringer to the nurses' station.

"Can I help you with something?" she asked, poking her head through the door. "It's not visiting hours until this evening."

"Oh, I'm not here to visit," I said. "I'm here for Giulia Lukach's hearing. I was told it was going to be at ten a.m."

"Oh right, yeah, actually that already happened. The judge was running early, so they finished about a half hour ago."

"But they said ten. I'm thirty minutes early." I was in disbelief.

"Well, it's done already. You can come back tonight to visit."

"Wait, wait, wait, I'm not leaving yet—" I grabbed on to the door handle that was on my side of the room so the nurse couldn't close the door on me. "Can I at least find out what happened at the hearing? I mean, come on."

"Okay, wait a minute." She closed the door and went back to the nurses' station.

I sat in the waiting room, fuming with frustration at the bureaucracy of the mental health system, picking at my stuffy shirt and tie. I had wanted to be there. Suoc and I both adamantly agreed that Giulia was looking worse than when we brought her there, so there was no way that she should be coming home. What if the doctor hadn't agreed?

After a few minutes of shuffling through paperwork and speaking on the phone, the nurse at the station came back into the waiting room and sat in the chair next to me.

"The judge signed off on the doctor's request," she said. "Giulia has been upgraded to a 5250."

"So she has to be here another fourteen days?" I asked.

"Yes, kind of. If she's ready to come home sooner, then of course she'll go home earlier."

"What if she's not better after fourteen days?"

"Then we do another hearing, with another possible extension." A heavy silence followed, as I thought about how long two weeks were.

"So now this means that Giulia can't refuse her medication, right?" I asked.

"Right," the nurse said.

"So did she get her medication?" I pressed.

"I'm not supposed to get into the details, since Giulia still hasn't signed off for you to speak directly with us."

"Oh, come on, please," I begged her. "Give me a break. Please. I came out here for a hearing, I got here early and I still missed it, the least I can get is a little update."

The nurse looked at me uncomfortably. "She got her medicine this morning, right after the hearing," she said quietly.

"Did she take the medication voluntarily?" I asked.

"I can't tell you that," she said timidly. "I shouldn't have even told you that she had medicine."

"Please, this is a nightmare, just please work with me here," I said, exasperated. "Can you at least tell me if she took the pills by herself?"

"She did not take the pills by herself. But she got her medication."

I knew what that meant. I closed my eyes and imagined three

nurses walking into Giulia's room, offering her pills, knowing she would refuse them, and then holding her down as they rolled up her hospital gown to expose her thigh for an injection. This was what a 5250 meant. And I had showed up early, in a shirt and tie, to argue that Giulia needed the 5250. But the image of it, the nurses pressing on her body, Giulia tensed and yelling and resisting whatever way she could, and them injecting her anyway, and knowing with certainty that it had happened, felt so tragic that it eclipsed the anger that had been boiling over.

"So that's that," I said quietly, breathing deeply to hold in the tears. "Can I go see her?"

"I'm sorry, but it's not visiting hours." The nurse gently patted my hand and then went back to work. I sagged into the already sagging chairs, completely overwhelmed by the layers of emotions that buried me into my seat: grief, fear, rage, more grief.

In the perverse dystopia of the psych ward, this was progress.

The world outside the hospital became its own maze. Giulia had worked at her new job for only six weeks, and she had called in sick for the past two weeks. She hadn't accrued enough days to file for a medical leave. I spoke with her boss, who put me through to their outside HR rep. The rep presented us with two impossible options: either they fire Giulia from her dream job or I quit it on her behalf. Either way, Giulia's job was over. It was just a matter of how it looked on her employment record.

Meanwhile, my work reluctantly introduced me to the Family and Medical Leave Act, which granted me upward of three months off as a caregiver. I took sick days for the first few days of Giulia's hospitalization but returned to school for a day to see how it felt. A friend had convinced me that maybe the course work and students would be a distraction.

It was a disaster. I zombied my way through my classes. I needed only fifteen minutes of my first period to know that I was going to be filing for an extended leave. During water polo practice, I hid my tears behind sunglasses, and I told my team that I was going to be taking a lot of time off.

On the car ride home from my last day at school for three months, I called back the HR rep and quit for Giulia. This would be better for her résumé in the long run, because otherwise the job would have to tell any other companies that they had fired her for work abandonment.

Within the course of five minutes, without talking to Giulia, I had quit her job and taken three months off of mine.

On the third evening of Giulia's hospitalization, I was able to convince her to sign the paperwork that allowed me to speak with her nurses and doctor. Finally.

The next day I called each hour, as usual, but this time I got full reports. Today, Giulia was obsessed with a fear that she didn't have a heartbeat. She left her room but always had her palm placed on her chest, looking for her heartbeat. She began engaging with other patients, to ask if she could feel for theirs. But she never found hers.

"Mark, I can feel your heartbeat!" It was a tremendous relief for her to feel my pulsing chest when I visited her that evening. "But I don't have one."

"Sure you do, Giulia." I pressed my palm up to the chest of her increasingly bony frame. Pounds evaporated off her as she continued to not sleep or eat. Once I felt the beat, I tapped along with my hand on my thigh.

Uncertain, she put her hand on top of mine, to verify.

"I don't feel it. No heartbeat."

I continued to tap the rhythm. She reached back to my chest.

"There's yours. I can feel yours. But I don't have one. I told you I'm not in this world."

"Mark, you need to fight for Giulia," my mom warned me over the phone.

"I know, Mom, I am fighting," I said wearily.

I had started to call my mom nightly as soon as Giulia was hospitalized. I needed to talk to someone, and as long as I can remember, my mom has been a soothing presence in times of crisis. When I was a little boy and constantly getting sick with asthma and allergies, I was rushed to the hospital a half dozen times in panics of blue-faced wheezing, but I don't remember feeling scared because my mom was able to maintain such a cool head and stroke my cheek to reassure me that everything was going to be all right.

I tried my best to model my mom when I visited Giulia and put on an ironclad mask of calm and confidence, even though I was quivering with fear on the inside. After each visit, exhausted by the effort, I needed to talk to my mom so I could put down my guard. My parents had moved back to Japan after twenty years away—we had lived there for six years when my siblings and I were in elementary school—and the time difference made it perfect for me to catch her while I lay awake unable to sleep and she was getting started with her morning. Each time we spoke, we inevitably ended up brainstorming what to do next and how I could be more proactive in supporting Giulia.

"I know you are fighting, Mark," she said to me that night. "But you don't know what it is to really fight. You are trusting and you give people the benefit of the doubt, which is wonderful in most situations, but not this one. This is your family. This is your wife. She is in the hands of professionals and you have to let them do their job, but you have to fight like hell for her. Just like she fought for you."

My mom was referencing when I had been the one hospitalized, a year prior, with acute pancreatitis. Giulia visited me one morning as a nurse was changing the sheets of my bed. The nurse had to roll me from side to side to accomplish this, and my latest dose of morphine had almost worn off. I was racked with a pain that a female doctor told me is the closest that men can experience to the pain of childbirth. I was gasping, "Ten, ten, ten," to indicate that I was a ten on the pain scale. The nurse was focused on changing the bedsheets.

"Stop!" Giulia screamed. "He's at a ten, he needs medicine. Stop moving him!"

"I'm almost done here," the nurse said as she shifted me around. "Just give me another minute."

"Get off of him!" Giulia stormed out into the hallway and kept screaming. "Get this nurse off my husband! He's at a ten and this moron is changing his bedsheets!"

Other nurses intervened. I was given morphine. The sheets were changed later. The nurse apologized to both of us, in front of the doctor. Giulia's loyal-to-a-fault protection of me became legendary in our family. Now my mom was insisting that I be just as fierce in my loyalty.

———

After a week, Giulia started to engage more with her surroundings. She came out of her room more and went to the group therapy sessions that were in the TV room, chairs temporarily pulled into a circle for patients to share their experiences. Sometimes they worked at tables on art projects, which Suoc and I encouraged by bringing boxes of crayons and a sketchbook so Giulia could continue to work outside of her scheduled art time. At our nightly visits, she'd show me some of the artwork she had made. Her first drawing was a brightly colored living room—rainbow couch, happily patterned rug, pastel-teal walls. On one of the walls, Giulia had drawn a dark picture frame, and inside the frame she had written, "The Devil wants me to fail."

She also discovered the patients' phone just down the hall from her room, which she used to call me. Dozens of times a day she called, with not much to say except any variety of how psychotic she was, how scared she was, or how much she loved me.

She was powerless in the psych ward. She ate when she was told to, showered while supervised, got to go outside for only thirty minutes a day on a depressing patio, took her meds—and if she didn't, she was pinned down by orderlies to have the medication injected into her hip.

The phone was a rare opportunity for a small display of power, a way to choose how to interact with the world. I told Giulia that if she wanted me to visit, all she had to do was call, and I would come. Every morning, she called and asked me to visit, just as I had anticipated. I couldn't conceive of not visiting her.

Then one day, she didn't invite me. Although she had called several times that day, she had never said anything about wanting to see me. I hadn't asked her either, but by six thirty p.m., I was lost. Was I really supposed to *not* visit? I jumped on the Vespa and motored off to the hospital.

I signed in and went to Giulia's room, where she lay on her side, looking at the wall.

"Hi, honey," I said to her back.

She slowly rolled over, saw me, and rolled back to the wall. "I didn't invite you here today."

I had grown pretty good at talking at Giulia rather than with her, so I brushed off her comment and rattled off some of the stuff I had done that day. But she just rolled back over and said, "I didn't invite you here today."

So I sat at her doorway in silence. I had nothing else to do. My entire life revolved around these visits. When I wasn't in the hospital, I was on the Internet researching, on the phone seeking advice, on the beach by myself, watching the ocean, crying. I had nowhere else to go, so I watched her breathe. I counted the square tiles on the floor. I waited.

About twenty minutes into the silence, Giulia rolled back over for a third time and said in the same deadpan tone, "I didn't invite you here today."

I continued to stay in the doorway. I thought I was making an important, positive statement: I wasn't going anywhere.

The ninety minutes of visiting hours wound down, and with only a minute left I broke the rules and tiptoed up to her bed. She heard me approaching and rolled onto her back. I leaned down and broke another hospital rule by kissing her on the forehead. "I love you, Giulia. I'm glad I came to visit you today."

She looked me in the eyes and said again, "I didn't invite you here today."

———

Sometimes I visited Giulia with Suoc, and sometimes I visited by myself. Either way, I almost always found a parking spot on the same block, one street over from the hospital entrance, near a restaurant with big glossy windows. After a half dozen nights of parking in the same area, I looked inside those windows and saw the beautiful hostess who worked there smiling at me. I hesitated from my hustle to the hospital, startled to catch her eye and her broad smile, and then put my head down and kept going for my nightly visit.

The next night, she was there smiling at me again. This time I gave her the slightest smile in return. The following night, the same woman, the same welcoming smile.

To her, I was probably a guy who lived in the neighborhood, on his way home from his job, and from the way she smiled I could tell she was hoping I would come inside, chat, maybe exchange phone numbers. She couldn't possibly know that I was parking in the same spot to visit my psychotic wife on the third floor of the hospital, the floor that needed a special elevator for access.

But each night, the hostess was there. I returned the eye contact, never lasting more than a fraction of a second, but that moment of connection through a restaurant window was my one escape from hell. It wasn't a hell of my own creation, but one I got sucked into, so it became my hell. This was my moment of rebellion.

I looked through the window and saw in a flash an alternative: a charmed life full of joy and laughter. I knew that life well because I had been living it with Giulia. I looked into the hostess's face long enough for it to blur into Giulia's, and I was so full of rage that this life had vanished. I was mad at Giulia, and her illness, and the nurses and doctors, and then mad at myself for becoming a resentful husband longing for an escape, an escape into a life I thought I already had.

I never went inside to say hello. I never even paused long enough to break my stride. I always broke eye contact first, put my head down while stuffing my feelings back into the pit of my stomach, and rushed down the street to the hospital.

No one understood what was going on with Giulia. She had shown no hints of instability before this breakdown, yet her psychosis was unshakable. The daily dosages of medication contained a variety of antipsychotics: Geodon, Seroquel, and Depakote, in addition to mood stabilizers to slow down her continued paranoia of religious doom. While I theorized that Giulia was in some sort of a breakdown owing to stress and sleeplessness, no one on the medical team definitively knew what caused it.

After a week, the lead psychiatrist at the hospital called for a family meeting. He didn't invite Giulia, and I didn't think to include her either. She was still so lost in her delusions and easily agitated. The doctor had approached Giulia on several occasions to talk about plans for recovery, but she aggressively shut him down every time he brought up the topic. This meeting would be with the family, but not with the patient.

Romeo had since returned to his job in Europe, and Suoc was intimidated by such an important discussion in a foreign language. So I went alone. I brought my laptop, so I could act as a stenographer and report back on the conversation.

I didn't tell Giulia I was coming. The meeting was during off-visiting hours, and I didn't want to disrupt her sense of the routine. Giulia's social worker met me at the glass door, and we tiptoed off to a back office, but Giulia saw me when she rounded a corner and smiled, so we stopped to say I was there to talk to her doctor, and I would be done in just a few minutes.

Giulia's social worker had been remarkably compassionate with me and tolerated my multiple calls a day to her. She was the one person who seemed to recognize how difficult this was for me, too. She led me into an office that felt like a faculty room at an elementary school: large round table in the middle of the room, with art supplies stacked to the ceiling on shelves along the wall. "For art therapy," the social worker explained.

Giulia's doctor joined us, as did the Kaiser case manager, who would ultimately be the one to facilitate her discharge out of this hospital and into Kaiser's care.

After introductions, the doctor began.

"Giulia's most pervasive symptom, as we all know, is psychosis," he said. "Psychosis is associated with several severe mental illnesses, and Giulia is not a textbook case of any one of them. She has had no symptoms until now, at age twenty-seven, which makes schizophrenia and borderline personality disorder seem unlikely. She has also never been manic before, which would make bipolar feel equally unlikely."

I already knew all of this. I had been researching these illnesses online relentlessly, and I looked for every possible reason to exclude Giulia from one of these life-altering diagnoses. I held on to hope that her affliction was something else. Giulia simply didn't fit neatly into any of the categories I'd read about. Surely, I told myself, there was another answer. Surely hers was a momentary and singular setback. I wouldn't dare believe anything else. I had been leaving messages on the doctor's voice mail almost every day, deluding myself that I could convince him that Giulia was different.

"Based on which medications she has reacted positively to, and which she hasn't, my working diagnosis is that Giulia is an extremely rare case of schizophrenia that has not displayed itself until adulthood. The technical term for what she is exhibiting is schizophreniform, which is basically the early stages of schizophrenia. That's what I suspect right now. Giulia has schizophrenia." His voice was steady and low.

The first time he said the word *schizophrenia*, I thought I must have misheard him. But he was clear with his final assessment, which felt like a death sentence. Our normal life together disappeared with a single word: "schizophrenia" dislocated my heart. Giulia would never be the same. Schizophrenia meant that the psychosis would come back to haunt her countless times for the rest of her life. She would never again be able to truly trust her own mind. She'd probably never be able to return to her career or her dream of becoming a marketing director by age thirty-five or having three kids. With one word, I had lost my wife and gained a lifelong patient. I put my head down and sobbed. I had tried so hard to stay cool in my interactions with the hospital team, but I couldn't anymore.

Because I was sobbing, I didn't hear Giulia knocking at the door or see the doctor get up to open it a crack and tell her that we weren't ready to talk with her yet. Nor did I see as she insisted and pushed the door open. I didn't know she was there until I felt her hand on my shoulder, and I looked up and saw the worry in her face.

"What's wrong, Mark?" she asked me tenderly. "Why are you crying?"

I ached with sadness, but I gulped it all down with one swallow.

"Nothing's wrong, Giulia," I said, forcing a smile, my eyes stinging with tears that I pretended she didn't see. "We were just talking about you coming home, and how you just need to take your medicine, and that we are all so proud of you."

Everyone else nodded in agreement.

After the meeting, I returned to San Francisco's four-mile stretch of beach. Ocean Beach gets relentlessly hammered by all sorts of weather, wind, and waves, which makes it perfect for getting lost. I walked Goose in my bare feet with my hood up to hide the sadness I wore on my face.

A friend of mine told me that I had to do just like they say on the airplane: I had to put on my oxygen mask and take care of myself first, before I could put on Giulia's. The first three days of her hospitalization, I barely slept or ate, and when I did, it was to binge on junk food. I felt like hell and was sinking into helplessness. I tried to talk myself into how, to be Giulia's protector, I had to be rested and clear. If I didn't put on my mask first, I would pass out, and then I'd be no good to anybody.

The waves looked fun enough, double overhead with a slight onshore wind, plenty surfable but far from perfect, which meant that the lineup wouldn't be too crowded. I went home and got my wetsuit and board. I'd loved to surf as a kid on the East Coast, and when we first moved to San Francisco, I was able to surf regularly for the first time in my life.

I paddled out that day to try to quench an existential thirst, throwing myself into the ocean to grapple with the implications of Giulia's psychosis. I paddled hard, pushed myself under waves. I wanted to feel their lash on my back and hear their rumbles above me. Ocean Beach is notoriously brutal. On big days, it can take upward of an hour of relentless paddling to get out to the lineup, and the surf was big that day. I happily swapped out one form of suffering for another.

Once past the breaking waves, I sat on my board, floating peacefully. Coldplay's "Viva la Vida" played over and over in my head, which was odd since I'd prefer to have any other music in my head rather than Coldplay. But Giulia loved the band, and especially that song, a staple soundtrack for our nightly dishwashing dance parties. Those carefree days felt buried and removed, but I couldn't shake the song.

It's about a king who had everything and then, in a flash, lost it all. A man who used to rule the world. That just about summed it all up for Giulia and me. We'd been so charmed, and we both lost everything.

Strangely, it's a sad song that doesn't sound sad. It's almost celebratory, and I didn't understand why until now. I had been jealously guarding my role as Giulia's husband. I hated the situation but liked the power and responsibility of being the one talking to the doctors. I liked coordinating the calls. I wanted to be at the center of her recovery. I was her king, right? If there was a key that would unlock her madness, I would find it.

As I floated on my board, I thought most about the surprising conclusion the king comes to at the end of "Viva la Vida": he doesn't even really want to be king after all. It's too much pressure to rule the world. Control is an illusion. Trying to maintain it is crushing.

I paddled out past the breaking waves into what felt like the open ocean. While I always thought I had faith, that day in the ocean I faced its enormity, and I dove in. I let go of Giulia and released her into the currents. I couldn't control what happened or how long it would take to get better, but I didn't feel afraid. In that moment, at least, I felt relief. I didn't have to rule the world anymore. I never had ruled it anyway.

I heard a soft puff of air and glanced to my right to see two dolphins swimming together. They were within arm's reach. They swam right under me and then popped up again on my left side.

I watched them swim away and I thought of how vast and terrifying the ocean is, and I resolved that if they could stay together, so could we.

My sister, Cat, flew in from the East Coast that afternoon. I went right from surfing to the airport to get her. That night we went together with Suoc to visiting hours. Cat wanted to visit her sister, which is what she called Giulia. The two had dropped the formality of "in-law" before Giulia and I had even gotten married.

Giulia greeted us at the glass doorway, her sketchbook close to her chest. She had been waiting. She was still in her hospital gown, even though I had brought her a few outfits to wear. She wore her glasses, and the grease in her hair gave away that she hadn't showered in a few days. When she saw Cat, she acted as though she had been expecting her, too.

Giulia led us off to a room that had unofficially become "our place" for visits. We had run into the challenge that during visiting hours there weren't many places to go. We weren't allowed in her bedroom, the cafeteria was too crowded, and the TV room was too dominated by the TV. A week into her stay, a nurse took pity on us. It was the same nurse who had patted my hand in the waiting room the day I missed Giulia's hearing. I think the nurse realized that the best way to deal with a spouse who showed up to everything early, armed with fifty questions, was to make whatever little accommodations were available. She had led us to an unused sitting room with a few couches that was locked, except that she was there to unlock it. And now we had a place to go to when we visited.

Giulia sat us three visitors down on a small, vinyl couch that creaked under our weight. We sat shoulder to shoulder as Giulia pulled up a matching chair across from us. She moved slowly and with control, and once we were all settled, she opened up the sketchbook.

"I have been working on this so you can finally understand what I have been trying to say to you," she said. "I haven't explained to you how many angels I have seen. You three, you are angels. You're on the list. But not me. This explains everything."

She handed us the book, and we looked down and collectively gasped in awe. The page was an explosion of bright colors, almost too bright to look at. The first page was a list, just as Giulia said, of all the people she considered angels. The three of us were on the list, at the top. The rest of the family members were there, too, along with other friends and colleagues who had touched our lives. Several of the names were circled and reinforced with accompanying colors, some traced and retraced so many times that Giulia had almost torn through the paper.

The next page was a poem, a rambling confession of guilt for how throughout her whole life, Giulia had been too selfish to return the love she was given.

None of us knew what to say. It was alarming to see so much self-loathing, but there was so much gratitude in her journal as well.

I broke the silence.

"Giulia, this is so beautiful and so lovely of you to write, but none of that poem is true," I said. "I have known you for nine years, and I have felt loved by you. You have certainly given back the love I have given you."

Suoc chimed in, "*Amore, questo non è vero, come ha detto Mark.*" This is not true, as Mark said. "*Sei una persona bella, come il sole.*" You are a radiant person.

But Giulia was not hearing any of it.

"I know you don't understand," she said. "But that's because you haven't seen what I've seen. That's why I wrote it down, so you would finally understand."

She turned her attention to me. She took my face in her hands and looked directly into my eyes.

"Mark, you're a wonderful husband. I'm so lucky that we met, and that you chose to love me. And now it's time for that to end."

She was saying good-bye.

"I know it will be sad, but you are too strong and beautiful to dwell on me. You need to move on. You deserve all the best in the world. I love you, Mark, and I want you to be happy."

She was calm and resolved as she talked me through this. I tried to listen without hearing, half there, and half hiding behind an insistence that this was not real. It was real that we were sitting in the visiting room of a psychiatric hospital, and Giulia was very sick, and she anticipated that she was going to die soon, but she was in a safe place. She wasn't going to die. This was not the good-bye that she believed it to be.

She kissed me on the forehead and then moved on to Cat. "I never had a sister before you. I love you, Cat. I only wish we could have grown up together, like real sisters." Cat hadn't said much of anything yet, she was so overwhelmed by the visit, and her face was so filled with tears that she had no response.

Giulia then addressed her mom. "*Mamma, mi hai sempre detto: fai tutto con amore, e hai ragione.*" Mom, you always told me: do everything with love, and you're right. "*Stò facendo questo con amore.*" I'm doing this with love.

She came back to me for one final declaration.

"Mark, promise me that you will be happy."

"Giulia, I already am happy. You are my happiness."

"Mark."

"Giulia."

She kissed me on the lips, then moved to get up.

"I love you all. And now you can understand. You can understand why."

She walked out of the room, and we trailed after her. We hugged her at the nurses' station, and she hugged us back. She left us standing there, and just before entering her bedroom, she looked over her shoulder and kissed her hand to wave. It was her final salute.

We went home and went to sleep, drained by the overwhelming visit. Giulia's evening was not as straightforward. I later learned from her that after we left, she brought the book to the nurses' station and tore the pages to shreds. She left them scattered on the floor for someone else to clean up. She then crawled into bed and tried to hold her breath long enough to suffocate herself. I don't think the human body is capable of choking itself, but Giulia tried many times that night. She lay back in her bed and held her breath as long as she could. Her body inevitably revolted and gasped out for a deep breath of oxygen. Discouraged, Giulia panted until her breathing once again became normal and steady. Then she regathered her will to die. She tried it again, and again, and again, and again, until morning.

One night at dinner, after our regular visit, Suoc said to me, "This is worse than if Giulia had died."

I didn't say anything.

"The person we visit every night is not my daughter, and we don't know if she is coming back."

I was silent, but halfheartedly agreed. Every evening I ripped open a wound that I'd spent the whole preceding day trying to patch up.

I did all of this grieving with my mother-in-law as a roommate. She planted herself in our house and had no intention of leaving. I was coming unglued, and I started to wonder just how long she would stay in San Francisco.

Suoc and I had always gotten along in the past. She was fun to talk to and a great cook. Whenever she visited, she left our house cleaner and more polished.

Now, with her daughter in the psych ward, Suoc immersed herself in the doting and fussing. She didn't know anyone else in the entire state of California besides me and Giulia. She reorganized our pantry, then our pots and pans. She swept daily, sometimes several times a day.

The creature comforts felt stifling. When she swept, I saw it not as a help, but as a judgment that our house wasn't clean enough for her. She did the laundry and ironed everything, down to my boxer shorts and socks, and I burned defensively at what I assumed was disdain at the way that Giulia and I lived.

Most challenging, we took different approaches to Giulia's uncertain state. I asked some questions of the medical approach to fixing Giulia's psychosis but was generally trusting. Suoc was outright hostile, and I felt uneasy with how literally she took Giulia's delusions. She wanted to analyze and interpret them ad nauseam. I was inclined to take the doctors' advice: acknowledge the delusions but not focus on them. My conversations with Suoc on the way to and from our evening visits to the hospital became more intense.

Finally, one drive home, I'd had enough.

"Sorry, Suoc, but this isn't working for me anymore," I said coldly, my eyes on the road. "I need my space to handle this my way. I appreciate all the help you are doing, but I need to be left alone. I can manage the household like I've been handling it for the past three years of marriage to Giulia. If I feel like eating an entire pizza in front of the TV and want to leave the box on the coffee table for a few days, then that's fine! It's my home, where I should be able to live by my rules, but I'm feeling like an outsider in my own home."

Suoc pouted in silence. The rest of the drive home neither of us said a word. We got home and she went straight to her room and closed the door. The next morning, I found her sitting quietly at the kitchen table. With no emotion in her voice, she told me, "I bought a ticket to New York. I'll stay with a friend from when we lived there. My plane leaves in a few hours."

I insisted that I drive her to the airport, which she allowed me to do. We hugged stiffly at the curb, and then she was off. I felt guilty, but I needed my space. I needed my home back. If Giulia and I were going to rebuild our lives, I needed Suoc to quit ironing my boxer shorts.

The doctor extended Giulia's 5250 after the first fourteen days expired. However, we all agreed that she was looking a little better. Her outbursts were becoming less frequent, and after her third week in the psych ward, they were almost gone. She was more predictable, less explosive. Our visits were more typically conversational—the weather, updates about friends and family, little to no talk of religious delusions. We still mostly went to our little room, "our place," but some days we strolled the halls of the psych ward in our restlessness, past barred windows and faded framed prints of impressionistic paintings that no one looked at.

"That guy kissed me," she whispered to me on a walking visit as we passed a patient.

"What?" I asked, wheeling around to get a look at the guy.

"He kissed me today. He came in my room and kissed me on my face."

"Really." I stopped walking and turned to see the figure disappear into his room. He slammed his door shut.

"Yup."

"Well, that's weird," I said. I took a deep breath and focused on keeping my cool, then changed the subject. "Goose has been really enjoying the beach lately. We've been staying for hours, and he couldn't be happier, although of course he misses you."

Giulia smiled. She always loved to hear about Goose. She asked me repeatedly if I could bring him to the hospital. I brought her a stuffed animal bulldog instead.

This was Giulia's twenty-second day in the hospital. I knew the routine. When I'd signed in that night, I'd chatted with the nurses as I always did, to get a rundown on the day. No one had said anything about another patient coming into Giulia's room, a clear violation of hospital policy, and kissing her on the face.

Of course, there was the possibility that Giulia was making this up. While she was doing better, she still had her moments of delusions.

I kept the rest our visit light, but I was tired, and Giulia was tired. After three weeks in the hospital, we were at a loss over what to say. I understood why some families just watched TV together when they visited.

At the end of visiting hours, I gave Giulia a kiss of my own on her forehead and then marched over to the nurses' station. "What happened to Giulia today?" I asked, banging my hands down on the counter loudly.

"Uh, what do you mean?" asked one of the nurses behind the counter.

"I mean, what happened to Giulia today?" I repeated. "Because she told me something. And I want to hear it from you."

All three nurses were now looking up at me nervously. They looked at one another and back at me, and finally the charge nurse, the woman who had so rudely shooed us away on Giulia's first night in the hospital, the woman I had desperately tried to win over to my side over the past three weeks, stumbled her way through a response.

"Well, there was an incident today. It involved Giulia and another patient. None of us were here when it happened."

"Yeah, I know there was an incident. Who the fuck kissed my

wife? What the fuck happened? And why didn't anyone tell me about it?" I demanded.

"Uh, well, yes, from my understanding, yes, another patient went into Giulia's room and kissed her."

"Yeah, I know! But not because any of you said anything to me. You left it up to my delusional wife to tell me about that. I have tried so hard to be nice to you all, and to work with you, and you don't tell me about this? This is fucking ridiculous. What do you know that I don't know already? What does it say in her file?"

I'd grown savvy enough to know that the file was sacrosanct. Everything and anything was in that file—how well Giulia slept, how much she ate, if she took her pills, how often she shit, everything was in that file.

The charge nurse trudged over to the file cabinet, flipped through the file, and came back empty-handed. "It doesn't say anything in Giulia's file."

"What the fuck do you mean it doesn't say anything in Giulia's file?" I was losing control. I had mourned plenty over the past three weeks, but I hadn't yet raged. The adrenaline felt good, compared with the dull emptiness of grieving for someone who was still alive.

"It doesn't say anything in her file," she repeated.

"You guys didn't make a record of a patient kissing another patient?"

"Well, we did," she said sheepishly. "But not in Giulia's file. It's written about in the other patient's file."

"What does it say?"

"I can't tell you that," she said. "You don't have permission to know the contents of anyone else's file."

"You have got to be fucking kidding me."

You have got to be fucking kidding me was one of Giulia's favorite phrases, ripe with condescension. I was delivering it in a way that I knew would make her proud.

"I am not kidding you," the charge nurse replied, gaining a bit of moxie as she sensed I was losing control of the situation.

"This is fucking ridiculous."

It felt good to explode at someone and to have a target for my anger. I had cried so much in the past month, but I hadn't yelled at anyone, because who was there to yell at? I finally had a situation that granted me full permission to air out my anger, to give it free rein to wreak all the havoc I had been feeling inside. This nurse had failed to protect Giulia, just like the nurse who had rolled me over even though I was at a pain level ten. Now it was my turn to protect Giulia.

"Let me get this straight. You're telling me I'm not entitled to know what happened to my wife? All I know is that some guy kissed her, and that's the best I'm going to get out of you fucking people?"

"Visiting hours are almost over," she said, desperate for something to say.

"There's thirty fucking minutes left in visiting hours," I spit back at her. "Don't try to kick me out. Take some fucking responsibility for this situation."

"You're clearly upset. Maybe you should head home so we can talk about this tomorrow after you've calmed down." She was starting to go on the offensive, sensing that I was on the edge. I didn't want to give her any reason to find fault in my behavior.

"This is a fucking disgrace." I stormed out of the hospital. As soon as I got home, I called the hospital and demanded to speak with Giulia's doctor, that night.

With nothing else to do, I Skyped my parents. It was four in the morning in Japan, where they lived, but they woke up on the first ring.

"What happened, Mark?" my mom asked.

I had grown up in a household of no swearing, but I explained the situation through tears and profanity. It felt so profane, I couldn't think of other words.

"Mark, you need to talk to the doctor," my mom said. "We need to make sure that this other patient isn't going to be bothering her anymore." My mom was calm with a mission in mind, which was exactly what I needed.

"I did call, I'm waiting for his return call."

"Okay, good," she said. "You should also—"

My phone rang, with a blocked number. Anytime someone from the hospital called, it was a blocked number. "Mom, Dad, I gotta go," I said. "I think that's him."

"Okay, good luck, you're doing a great job," my parents said, eternally encouraging and supportive. I hung up Skype on my laptop and picked up my phone.

"What the fuck is going on?" I demanded of the doctor. I still had some *fuck* left in me.

"Well, Mark, to be honest, this is the first I've heard about this as well."

His not knowing calmed me down, because the nurses would have called him if it had been an emergency. I gave them at least that much credit.

"Here's what I understand happened," he said. "There is another patient who believes he is God, and he offered some type of forgiveness to Giulia. She has been so set on being the Devil, and here was God, saying he would forgive her. She let him into her room, and he kissed her on the face."

"Did he try to touch her?" I screamed. "Did he? Did he fucking try and touch her?" I was raging again.

"No," he said, and I began to weep in relief. "We asked Giulia and the other patient, and both said it was just a kiss. An orderly walked by and saw the patient kneeling at Giulia's feet, and rushed in to break it up. We think he was only in her room for a few minutes at most. And he didn't touch her.

"We moved the patient to another room, and he is now under constant supervision."

I couldn't be mad at the God delusions, just like I couldn't be mad at Giulia for her Devil delusions. But I wanted Giulia out of the hospital.

"I am not certain Giulia is safe in the hospital anymore," I said. "I think we should talk about relocating her."

"Well, let me interrupt you there," the doctor chimed in. "Giulia has been in here a long time, one of the longest stays we have right now. We check in on patients every fifteen minutes, but we can't watch everyone all the time. To be honest, I can't believe nothing has happened up to this point. The group tends to take care of themselves, and protect each other, but it's still strangers in a confined space together." None of this was reassuring.

"What I'm getting at is this might signal that the hospital is not the best place for her anymore. We had been talking about Giulia plateauing in the hospital anyway, and she seems to be doing better on the medicine. She's not completely out of the woods, but she's much more stable. She's been here so long, and the psychosis seems so much more under control . . ." He was searching for words, uncertain of how to put this in a way that would make sense. "And so I think this is a sign that she's ready to come home, to a more comfortable and familiar environment."

And like that, as I still reeled with the shock of a patient kissing my wife, the doctor told me that Giulia was coming home the next day.

I listened to "Viva la Vida" on loop on the way to the hospital. I opened the glass doors to the psychiatric ward for the last time. I was grinning from ear to ear, eager to forget all the rites and rituals of taking the special elevator, signing in, having my possessions checked. I avoided the nurses. I rounded the corner to see if I could help Giulia with packing her stuff. She was out in the hallway, waiting for me.

"Honey! You're coming home!" I beamed as I saw her.

"Mark," she whispered as she leaned in close, looking wildly over her shoulder to see if anyone might be listening. "This is a big mistake. Lock me up forever. I am the Devil and need to be locked away."

My buoyant optimism skipped a beat. The doctor had been so convincing last night on the phone that Giulia was looking more stable, yet here she was, still psychotic and talking about the Devil, and she was coming home, where there was only me to take care of her. What was I getting into?

I brushed off my hesitations and said, "You're doing great, Giulia," because *she was coming home*. She could finally get out of this place.

We finished with the final packing of her stuff, but she was mostly done already. She had showered and put on her freshest clothes. After only a few minutes together, she had returned to a sense of stability and talked about how she couldn't wait to see Goose and take him to the beach.

We left her room for the last time, then walked together to the conference room, overstuffed with art supplies, for her discharge meeting. She signed countless forms. The only one I can remember made her promise to not purchase a gun for the next five years.

She would start an intensive outpatient program with Kaiser the next day, where she would get a new social worker, a new doctor, a new case manager, and who knew, maybe a new diagnosis, new medications, new therapies. But all of that would come tomorrow. For now, she was coming home.

With the paperwork signed and a paper bag filled with various medications, a nurse led us to the glass doorway, the one that had divided my world from Giulia's world for the past twenty-three days. I held on to her as we walked out into the waiting room, our first time crossing this plane together. She was weak from the weeks of inactivity and lack of sleep.

We got into the elevator. The special one I had ridden alone so many times.

I wouldn't let go of her hand. She blinked and beamed as we stepped into the fresh air.

"Wow," was all she said. "Wow."

"Giulia, you're coming home."

She glanced over at me. I saw some clarity in her eyes, a glimpse of the real Giulia. She looked back at the hospital, up to the third floor.

"I'm coming home. Let's get out of here."

four

October 2009

Our bulldog, Goose, sauntered through his days by following the sun from room to room. In the morning, he sprawled out on the hardwood floor of our main hallway, because the rising sun cast a warm sunspot through the large windows. By midday, he relocated to a different patch of sun, in the dining room, his body pressed up against the legs of the table. In the afternoon, it was the breakfast nook. These rooms collectively formed a ring around a central atrium in our home, a space we never really used but loved anyway for the light. Goose agreed and spent his days slowly walking in a circle, moving from one sunny nap spot to the next.

Our dog's patterns were predictable, so when I brought Giulia home from the hospital, I knew he would be in the dining room, loudly snoring with his tongue stuck out as he slept.

As we pulled into the garage and parked the car, I could sense Giulia's hesitancy. As much as she wanted to be home, she was scared. She kept looking at me, wordlessly seeking approval and validation. I led her up the stairs to our floor of the house and went right to the dining room.

"Goose, look who's home," I whispered to him.

Giulia stood back, watching for his reaction. He normally

greets family by pawing at the air, nipping at fingers and ears, his stubby little tail a spastic frenzy. This was the longest he had been away from her. I was nervous he might plow into her with his sixty pounds and knock her over in her fragile state.

But Goose understood. He saw her, walked up to her, and looked into her face with his big brown eyes. Giulia crouched down, put her arms around his floppy neck, and pulled him in toward her chest. He sat there with his head lifted high and welcomed her hug. I had spent so much time fretting how I would deal with Giulia, and here was our dog, in all of his simplicity, giving Giulia exactly what she needed: gentle and unassuming love.

We were home only a few minutes before we were back in the car to go to the beach. Goose dug at rocks, Giulia and I sat in the quiet of the day, a day as beautiful and warm as the day I took her to the hospital. A jogger ran by and Giulia jumped up in alarm.

"Why is she doing that?" Giulia gasped, her hands clutching her face as she backed away from the woman.

"Doing what? She's just running," I said.

Giulia rocked back and forth from one foot to the next, a side-to-side sway. Her lips puckered and unpuckered, her hands clasped tightly against her chest.

"This is not good, Mark. She's running from me. I need to stop it. This was all a mistake. It's not safe for me here." She continued to back away.

Since we were finally outside of the hospital and its no-touching rule, I walked up to her and put my arms around her waist. She leaned into me, her frame still so frail.

"Giulia, you're home. You're where you're supposed to be. You're back with me and Goose, back at the beach, where we belong, together." I looked into her eyes. They were blank, but searching through her confusion.

By then, Goose had abandoned his rock and had wedged himself between us, to sit on our feet.

"We love you, Giulia, we're so happy that you're home."

Giulia continued to fidget, but after a few minutes she calmed down and sat back on her beach chair. Psychosis waxes and wanes like the tides, and a passing jogger had triggered a fierce return of her disoriented, paranoid thinking. And then just as inexplicably, it faded away. The hospital hadn't fixed anything. It had only stabilized her, and not even all the way.

The first few weeks went much like our outing to the beach. Giulia was cautious of everything, desperate to feel comfortable and settled at home but trapped in uncertainty. The psychosis seemed like a bad fever that came and went at whim, and Giulia slipped in and out of it several times a day. Sometimes the psychosis had her fixated on religion, sometimes it was intense paranoia, or it might be delusions. Her body language became the visual cue of its return, with the rocking side to side, the puckering lips, the hands to her chest. For me, the transition from being with Giulia ninety minutes a day to all day, every day, was abrupt and demanding. I rarely left her side. The first time I did, to step into the bathroom on the first afternoon she was home, she walked out the front door and was halfway down the block by the time I got to her. I feared it was dangerous to leave her alone, to do whatever she might want, like listen to the voices that were in her head.

Thankfully, there was IOP, the intensive outpatient program at

Kaiser, intended as a step-down program from her time in the hospital. On Monday, Wednesday, and Friday mornings, nine a.m. to twelve thirty p.m., Giulia attended group therapy, one-on-one meetings, and "classes" such as cognitive behavioral therapy, art therapy, or dance.

IOP afforded me ten hours a week when I didn't have to be vigilant about Giulia's care. I kept my running shoes and surf gear in the back of the car, so when I dropped off Giulia, I sped back to the beach for a bodysurf. If the waves weren't cooperating, I'd park the car at the base of the Cliff House and change into running clothes and head up the hill to the Lands End Trail, a stunning urban trail that wound along the northwest corner of the city. I loved IOP for providing the rare opportunity to detach from Giulia.

The true merit of IOP was not necessarily in the therapy it provided—which Giulia tolerated but mostly rolled her eyes at—but rather in the regular contact with psychiatrists. In outpatient care, most patients see their psychiatrists infrequently, no more than once every few months. But Giulia was seeing these doctors three times a week, so they could closely monitor the impact of their ongoing experiment with antipsychotics and antidepressants, in the pursuit of the magical cocktail that might heal Giulia. I was learning that psychiatry, and the prescribing of medications, is more art and guessing game than science. She was discharged on the antidepressant Lexapro and two antipsychotics—Geodon and Zyprexa. Although she had taken the Geodon throughout her twenty-three days in the hospital, the doctor from her hospitalization hastily added Zyprexa to the mix in her last few days at the hospital, since it has a reputation of being one of the most potent antipsychotics.

Giulia had initially refused to take her medication in the hospital, but she hated the alternative—nurses pinning her down to inject medication into her hip. She eventually began to take the pills of her own volition while in the hospital, although she frequently voiced her displeasure with taking them. She knew that if she wanted to be home, she had to take the medication. But she still hated the medication, especially Zyprexa.

That pill in particular became our biggest sticking point. I had researched the side effects of Zyprexa once the doctor had prescribed it and knew what might be coming: acne, increased appetite, weight gain, lethargy. As with all psychiatric medications, there was the worry that it might make her more suicidal as well.

The side effects hit hard. The acne came, as warned. Giulia gained almost sixty pounds in a matter of two months. She had gone from alarmingly thin to the heaviest she had ever been, in only two months.

Worst of all, the Zyprexa slowed her down. Giulia moved as if she were walking underwater, and she thought that way, too. She had a hard time with open-ended questions. "What do you want for dinner?" I'd ask. She'd pause to process. I learned to rearrange the questions so that she could answer with a straightforward yes or no.

"Do you want chicken for dinner?" I'd ask.

Pause. She'd stall for a long time.

"Yes."

I had observed her sluggishness in the hospital, but those visits were only ninety minutes long. Long enough to notice, but short enough to forget in the avalanche of all the other worries at the time. While she was at home, there was no forgetting. The side effects were everything. Every step, every minute, was tainted by side effects, a life in forced slow motion, an engine stalled with no signs of a restart.

But the Zyprexa was working. Giulia's racing delusions had slowed down, along with everything else. Her outbursts of clasped hands and worried rocking back and forth were gone. The medicine was doing its job.

Giulia had a hard time seeing it that way. Zyprexa only meant side effects to her. If given the choice, she would have stopped the medication immediately, and she made that clear to everyone. So the doctors ordered that I watch Giulia take her medication, to ensure that she swallowed the pills. She later told me that she had mastered a technique of concealing her pills under her tongue or in her lip, even when I made her open her mouth to prove that she had swallowed.

The pills caused additional tension because Giulia, still a suicide risk, couldn't have direct access to her prescriptions. I changed up hiding spots almost daily. I first hid them in the pocket of a jacket hanging in the hallway closet for a day, then in a box of cereal, and then behind our DVDs of *Arrested Development*. It got to the point where I would forget where I put them and had to search for them myself, while trying to conceal the hiding spots in the first place so Giulia wouldn't be clued in on where to look for them in my absence.

Zyprexa became the symbolic representation of the impossible choices that mental illness brings into relationships. Giulia wanted all of the Zyprexa, to kill herself, or none of it, which would probably usher in a relapse. She wanted nothing to do with the prescribed dosage. But the current dosage seemed to be helping her, even though the side effects were brutal.

We never discussed a plan. I didn't see any other choice except to follow what the doctors told us to do. We had to keep her out of the hospital and her mind free from the torments of psychosis. We developed our silent, sad routine. Giulia sat on our bed and waited with the bedroom door closed as I dug a few pills out from the hiding place du jour. When I returned I handed them to her with a glass of water and we avoided eye contact. After she drank them down, I checked her mouth. I began to see her mind like an old television set, one with a dial you had to turn to change channels. She had gotten stuck between channels, and all that was broadcasting in her mind was crackling white noise, which drove her mad and scared me to death. The medicine was like turning down the volume. The channels might still be stuck, but at least the set was no longer spewing the deafening static. The volume had to be lowered until the channels could work again.

There was relief, but a potent sorrow in this. With the volume down, Giulia's entire life was on mute. She wasn't psychotic, she wasn't delusional—she just kind of wasn't.

Our days also fell into a routine. Our life was like a lazy Sunday afternoon, on repeat, ad nauseam.

Wake up.

Walk the dog at the beach.

Go to yoga, or play tennis, or ride bikes, or some other wholesome activity, all of which we did slowly and delicately, under the haze of Giulia's medication.

Eat lunch.

Walk the dog again.

Do an art project, or read, or watch a little TV.

Dinner.

Medicine.

Bedtime.

IOP mornings helped—I loved my surf sessions—but there was almost no variety. We rarely saw other people. We became just like Goose, shuffling around in circles, trying to chase the sun spots in this new existence. But there wasn't a lot of sun. We mostly trudged through fog.

The medications knocked Giulia out early, by around seven p.m. She fell asleep almost as soon as she lay down, whether on the couch or in bed. Her sleep was motionless and dreamless, the collapse of a hurting mind that wanted to be rid of itself. When she finally woke twelve or thirteen or fourteen or even sometimes fifteen hours later, she had barely moved.

After Giulia fell asleep, my nights were filled with a thick loneliness. I spent all day with Giulia, our lives stripped down to the barest essence of survival, but at night the rest of the world crashed back in on me. I paid bills, I e-mailed updates to our parents, I sat uneasily with my guilt over leaving work, my worries about where her illness was going to take us, my frustrations with no companionship, no sex, no job, no life. I couldn't go anywhere or have anyone over.

I turned to the Internet, the baseball playoffs, television. Netflix stream had just been invented, so I binge-watched *The Office* and *Lost*. I used the TV narratives as conversation pieces with Giulia the next day, so I had something to talk about. The TV and the

Internet gave me something to occupy my attention, but best of all, they asked nothing of me in return. I could turn off the TV or log out of social media and walk away without anyone needing me.

About a month in, I couldn't handle these nights anymore. I was wound too tight with anxiety and grief to sit on my couch all night. Giulia was so heavily medicated that she didn't move in the night, let alone wake up, so I started to go running. I usually set out around ten p.m. I tiptoed down the street in my bare feet with a headlamp on, crossed the dunes, and hit full stride once I got down to the hard-packed sand of Ocean Beach. I ran from one end of the beach to the other and back again, music blaring at full level in my earbuds, my headlamp turned off to run in the darkness. I sometimes saw figures blur by in the dark, other night wanderers who came to the beach to empty themselves of feeling. Low tides were the best: the ocean retreated back into itself and left an expanse of glistening wet sand. It was like running on a mirror held up to the universe. I foolishly ran while looking up at a sky reflected below my feet and begged and pleaded to the world, *Please get us through this mess.*

Giulia's psychosis faded after a few weeks at home. I credited the Zyprexa. But she wasn't better yet. In the wake of the psychosis lay a crippling depression. As the depression settled in, Giulia often said to me, "You don't know what I went through in the hospital. I can't live after that. I can't make it."

Yes, she had tried to throw herself out of the moving car on the way to the hospital, but that felt like a side effect of her psychosis. I didn't understand true suicidality until her psychosis was gone. Without the delusions, suicide was almost all Giulia thought about. It was one of the few topics she brought up unprompted in conversation.

We took one of our countless family walks on the beach on a morning when the fog was particularly beautiful. Ocean Beach is usually cursed with a high fog and a stiff wind. This morning, the wind was absent and the fog coated the ground like a dense, magical mist. We couldn't see more than ten feet in front of us. Because it was such a low fog, we could see the sun above us, through the fog, desperate to punch through. The light illuminated the fog in a way I had never seen, and it felt as though we were lost in a blinding, gold pixie dust.

The moment was too beautiful to wallow in the slowness and sadness of our lives, so I chased Goose and ran in circles around Giulia. I took the golden fog as an excuse to refuse to let our lives become nothing but heartache. I flirted with Giulia by kissing her cheek and pinching her butt as I raced around her.

"Mark, I need to ask you something," she called as I whizzed by.

I circled back to her, my forehead wet with sweat and fog, my heart rate up, eyes alive and feeling good, dammit. "What is it, honey?"

"If someone kills themselves, do they still get a funeral?"

I stopped in my tracks.

"What was that?"

"If someone kills themselves, do they still get a funeral?" she repeated. "Because I know if you kill yourself you go to hell, but do they let you have a funeral? Because I'd want to have a funeral, for you guys. I'd hate for you to not at least get to go to a funeral for me."

"Well, we don't have to think about that stuff, Giulia," I said, "because you're not going to kill yourself. You're going to make it."

Giulia took a long pause, then said, "God is a fuckup."

I slumped beside her, my feet now heavy. We turned around and walked back to our car in silence.

When we crested the sand dunes, Giulia said, "Mark, will you let me kill myself? You don't know how unbearable this is. If you cared for me, you would let me kill myself."

I ached at this definition of caring. Giulia was asking me to love her in the way she needed, which was to let her end her life.

"I do care for you, Giulia, but I don't want to lose you."

"What if we make some sort of deal?" she tried to bargain. "Like how about a month from now? You let me kill myself in a month. Sound good?"

I shook my head. "I don't think so."

"Six months?"

"Nah."

"Okay, fine, one year. You let me kill myself in one year."

At a loss for what else to do, I agreed. "One year. Okay. I can do that. If in one year from now, you still don't feel any better, then fine." I didn't really agree, of course. I instead lied to her and pretended that she only had to make it through the year, and then it would be over. She believed my lie and was gleeful about it. Now she was the one skipping across the top of the dunes as I plodded back to our car.

Our families asked constantly what they could do to help. But what was there to do? They called and e-mailed, but they were spread all over the country and the world. It's not like they could drop off dinner or swing by to keep Giulia company for a few hours so I could step away.

Cat and her husband, Alex, came back and spent the weekend with us. My brother Matt and his wife, Grace Ann, did the same thing a few weeks later, and then it was Giulia's brother Pietro's turn. There was more laughter in our house when we had guests, but as soon as they left, the pall of depression blanketed our home once again.

So they continued e-mailing me and calling me. "What can we do?"

Managing family became an additional challenge. They looked to me for direction, but I didn't have any. I didn't know what I was supposed to be doing, let alone what our parents in Japan and Italy could do. Giulia and I both came from families of problem solvers, so I knew they were talking among themselves and constantly brainstorming how they could be more hands-on to help us. But the prodding efforts of well-intentioned support felt suffocating. Of course, it would have felt even worse if they'd treated us as though everything were normal, but we were all in a lose-lose of helplessness.

I went to the Internet for advice and found a post on a forum with a few suggestions for what families can do from afar. It encouraged small, steady reminders of care and concern, with no expectations of a response. I forwarded it along to my mom, who put a plan in action. The e-mails slowed down—enough for me to know that they were there, but they otherwise accepted that they had to wait for me to call them rather than the other way around.

The frequent calls and e-mails were replaced by the slower art of letter writing. We began to get letters in the mail. Roughly once a week, a letter from a different family member showed up, a beautiful, thoughtful reflection on why they valued their relationship with Giulia. The letters were accompanied with photos—my dad sent a photo of Giulia and him at the marathon I ran in Washington, Matt sent a picture from the wedding. We hung the letters up on the fridge and put the pictures throughout the house, and I often found Giulia reading them or staring at the photos, the slightest hint of a smile sometimes on her face.

These gestures helped. This was our families doing it right.

The first time I left Giulia alone at home, awake, was mid-November, almost two months after her discharge from the hospital. Two months of always keeping her in sight. But at some point we needed to let the space return into our relationship, to detach each other from our intense codependency.

That morning we had a lovely, leisurely bike ride across the Golden Gate Bridge into Sausalito to each lunch. The ride back out of Sausalito is mostly uphill, and Giulia was drained when we got home. She definitely needed a nap, so when my friend Austin texted me about going surfing, I figured I'd give it a shot. Giulia had been in good spirits all day, it had been a pretty good week. I'd have to leave her alone at some point, so today was the day.

I loaded up my car with my board and wetsuit and left, hesitant but optimistic. We'd spent the day together outside and active, with no talk of suicide, no medicated stares. She'd be fine, right?

I suited up with Austin near his house, and then we hoofed it over the dunes and paddled out together. The wildlife was a frenzy of joyful activity—dolphins burst out of the faces of waves, sea lions popped their heads up to see who was in their ocean. Austin and I swapped off one fun wave after another.

As I hosed down afterward with fresh water outside of Austin's garage, I felt genuinely happy. It had been a good day. If we could string together a few more days like this, I'd be okay, and Giulia might start to come out of her haze.

When I got home, Giulia was sitting still at the dining room table. She didn't say hi. She instead said, "Don't worry about my medicines tonight. I already took them."

At first, I was more confused than panicked. "What do you mean? You don't even know where the pills are." I didn't remember where they were currently hidden—either behind *Infinite Jest* on my bookshelf or in my toolbox. I was still changing the hiding spot every few days.

"I found them," she said quietly. "I actually took more than I needed. When you left, I found the Zyprexa and put a big fistful of the pills in my mouth."

"Oh shit, oh shit, oh shit," I gasped, now fully panicking. "Did you swallow them?"

"No, I spat them out." She was calm and matter-of-fact about all of this. "I spat them out in the garbage disposal."

I raced into the kitchen and there they were, as promised, about twenty cream-colored pills of Zyprexa, dissolving in the bottom of our garbage disposal.

"Giulia . . ." I was becoming frantic, hyperventilating. I didn't know what to do or say.

"Don't worry, Mark, I didn't swallow any. Not the first time, or the second time."

"The second time?!?!?" I felt like I couldn't breathe.

"The second time I didn't swallow any either. I spit those out into the garbage."

94

I ripped the trash can out from under our kitchen counter and tore through the messy contents.

"Not that garbage can," she yelled to me over the commotion I was making. "The one in the bathroom."

Once again, she was telling the truth. A few dozen pills were in the bathroom trash can.

I went to the bedroom and started to pack a bag for her, not thinking, just acting.

"What are you doing, Mark?" Giulia stood in the doorway, glaring and accusatory.

"I'm packing your bag. I have to take you back to the hospital."

"No, Mark, please don't do that. I can't go back there. Please. I didn't take any pills, I promise. I spat them all out."

"But you tried to overdose, Giulia! Twice! I wasn't here to stop you, I left you and you found the pills and almost took them!"

"I tried, but I didn't do it. I have chances to do it all the time, but I never do. I spat all the pills out."

I was still racing, grabbing clothes from the closet and throwing them on the bed, unable to look at her, my hands shaking as I tried to fold up the clothes I had picked out.

"Mark, please calm down and listen to me," Giulia insisted.

I stopped and looked right at her. "I wasn't here to make sure that you were safe. And I can't always be here, always by your side. I need to make sure that you're safe."

"I am safe," Giulia said firmly with emphasis. "I didn't swallow any. I had the chance, but I didn't do it. I spat them all out."

She had a point. Between the garbage disposal and the trash can, I'd recovered what looked like four dozen pills. A bottle held only fifty, so maybe she hadn't actually ingested any.

I put down her clothes and went to the computer to research "Zyprexa overdose." Symptoms were rapid heart rate, slurred speech, possible coma, and death. I put my hands on Giulia's chest to feel her heartbeat, just as I had done in the hospital to prove to her that she was alive. It thumped along at a normal rate. Her speech was not slurred. She was alert. And the pills added up.

My head spun as I tried to make a choice between two impossible options. The first was to reopen the trauma of the hospital by taking her to the ER. Her parents would probably fly back out, she'd be on lockdown for another seventy-two hours—back to square one, after two months at home. The second option was that we stay at home, I monitor her heart rate, and trust her, and try to stay calm as the possibility of a drug overdose hung in the air.

I asked her over and over again to please tell me the truth, promise me that she hadn't swallowed any of the pills, and she never wavered in her response. I finally relented and put away her clothes, and we went into our normal routine. I nervously checked her heart rate every twenty minutes or so, each of us hating the other for having to do this. When she fell asleep, I continued to check her pulse, laying my hands against the softness of her neck to feel the steady beating.

The next morning she woke up, and we went to IOP together to tell her therapist and psychiatrist what had happened, and they both agreed that we had done the right thing. I left IOP and went to see my friend Paul, who lived only a few blocks away. Paul is one of the friends who gets it and doesn't try to talk you out of problems when they can't be talked away, so we filled the time by picking up guitars and strumming away the hours of IOP as I tried to forget my wife's suicide attempts.

I still don't know if those classify as genuine suicide attempts. She had stopped herself. Twice. She had the time, the space, and the means to end her life. She had tried to write a note but didn't know what to say, so she skipped that step. I had to give her credit for stopping. She still had enough fight in her to spit out the pills.

Eventually I had to return to work. When I first filed the paper-work for Family and Medical Leave, three months felt like an eternity, and no way would Giulia need that much time to get back on her feet.

But Giulia was not showing signs of improving. She plateaued in a lethargic depression. She constantly complained about the Zyprexa, so her psychiatrist switched her to Risperdal, another antipsychotic medication. These medications are not fast acting but instead take weeks to reach full effect. At times I felt like Giulia was a subject in a medieval science experiment—this drug didn't work? Let's increase it, or decrease it, or replace it, or add something else to supplement it. Sorry you're suffering through depression, psychosis, and miserable side effects while waiting to see if it works.

But I refused to lose hope. The Risperdal was a welcome break from the Zyprexa. Giulia was less sluggish, and her rapid weight gain slowed down. She was more spontaneous in conversation; she said more than just "yes" and "no" and rarely paused before an-swering. It had been more than two months since she had exhibited any sign of psychosis. Progress. Finally.

We flew to New York City for Christmas, where Giulia's whole family was waiting to see in person what I was describing over e-mail every night. It had been almost three months since Romeo and Mariarita had seen Giulia, and they were eager to see the signs of improvement I had been reporting over the past few weeks. My parents had seen Giulia only through Skype and were desperate to see her and help out.

In New York, Giulia cried for a full hour upon seeing her parents. When they returned to their hotel, she cried for another hour. In the morning, she woke up crying. I had never seen her cry so much.

"Talk to me, Giulia, tell me what's going on," I begged her as we dressed to meet her parents for lunch. She didn't respond.

"It's been going so well, what happened? What changed all of a sudden?" I prodded more. She still didn't respond.

We left my brother's apartment, where we were staying, and began the walk up Park Avenue to the restaurant. I continued to pester her with questions. Finally, with the restaurant in sight, she turned and told me.

"I stopped the Risperdal because I hate it so much. I've been doing better and hate the pills and didn't want to be so drugged around my parents, so I stopped it."

She spun back around and continued to walk to the restaurant and was visibly crying. I rushed up to her and asked, "You stopped all of the Risperdal? All six milligrams?" It was a maximum dosage, one that she should have slowly tapered off of over the course of a month. I was still giving her the medication each night and watching her take it, but clearly she had found a way to dispose of the medicine. With such an abrupt stop, she was in a free fall of withdrawal.

"Yes," she said through weepy tears, and was walking back again toward the restaurant as I stood still in shock and concern.

And before I had time to respond we were in the lobby, Giulia's parents embracing her through her convulsing tears, and we pretended not to mind the looks from strangers.

Giulia got back on the Risperdal, and I went back to work. My parents came out for their first visit since Giulia had been hospitalized. I was still Skyping with my mom on an almost nightly basis, but she hadn't been able to get away from her job in Japan until I was on the eve of returning to my own job. I eased into the comfort of having my parents around the house. My dad had to return for work, but my mom stayed on for another few weeks. I didn't realize until my mom was around how much I had needed her physical presence and not just our nightly calls. She gave me the space to pull back from my devotion to Giulia's recovery. I dreaded the day my mom would have to leave.

Around this time, Giulia's suicidal obsession shifted. A common misconception of suicide is that someone will try any available method, but studies show that the suicidal tend to fixate on one method at a time. It's not like if you take a gun away from a suicidal person but give him a rope, he will immediately hang himself. It's the exact opposite. It's all about one method, and if that method isn't available, the person's suicidal focus can falter.

For a long time, Giulia had focused on a drug overdose, since it felt the most accessible. A friend in IOP told Giulia that very few drug overdoses successfully lead to death, so she abandoned the idea of an overdose. She instead fell into the allure of the Golden Gate Bridge, one of the most iconic suicide spots in the world. With its four-foot-high railings and lack of any type of safety net, it's shockingly easy to hop the fence and fling yourself into the churning bay below. More people have killed themselves at the Golden Gate Bridge than at any other place on earth. Straddling the edge of the Western world, with stunning views of San Francisco, the bridge stands as a destination spot for suicide.

For Giulia, the Golden Gate Bridge was easy. We lived close. I was back at work. And my mom was gone.

One day while teaching, I looked down at the floor and didn't see the carpet of my classroom below me. Instead I saw my feet balanced on the rusted orange bridge, the bay a swirling two hundred feet below. I could even feel the wind. I had already dreamed about Giulia's suicide. Now I was hallucinating about it, in a classroom full of high school kids.

One day I came home from work and found Giulia sitting on the carpeted floor in our guest room, Goose sprawled next to her. I could instantly sense that something was wrong.

"Hey, honey, is everything okay?" I asked.

She didn't say anything in response.

"Giulia? You okay?" I asked again.

"I guess." She sighed. "It's just—I can't figure out what I'm going to do with the Vespa key."

"What do you mean? What would you have to do with the Vespa key?"

"I mean, when I drive to the Golden Gate Bridge, I'll probably take the Vespa. When I park it, what should I do with the key? If I leave it in the scooter for you, someone will probably steal the scooter. But if I bring it with me, and they don't find my body after I jump, you'll lose the only key we have to the scooter."

She looked at me pleadingly. "What am I supposed to do with the Vespa key?"

Giulia's psychiatrist added lithium to her chemical cocktail, not because he suspected she had bipolar disorder—they still didn't quite know what she had, maybe schizophrenia, but maybe not—but because a recent study showed that lithium augmented the benefits of antidepressants. The combination of lithium, Risperdal, and Lexapro didn't have any noticeable impacts on her mood and instead left her in the most stilted and zombified state yet, her arms frozen stiff at her sides, her fingers spread apart, her lips pursed, drool sometimes lingering at the corners of her mouth. It was awful.

Giulia's least favorite side effect was the weight gain. She stood in front of the mirror, slow and wavering, and poked at her expanded waistline and grimaced. She didn't fit any of her clothes anymore. She had to buy a whole new wardrobe, and she hated how her new clothes fit. I stood behind her and told her that the weight didn't matter, she was still so beautiful, but she didn't believe me.

Fortunately, weight gain felt like something tangible where I could help. I coached soccer, swimming, and water polo. I was clueless about suicide, but I had plenty of ideas for how to get active and lose weight.

I searched for "gym" in Google Maps to find the one closest to us. Living way out on the western fringe of San Francisco, in an unpopular middle-class neighborhood, we didn't have many options. All the fancy gyms were across town, like the one Giulia had previously belonged to when she scootered across the city to her job. I was surprised to find any gym at all, let alone one only a mile away and that had group classes like "cardio-kickboxing" and "Body Sculpting." Giulia loved classes at the gym. Best of all, it was only $10 a month. I signed us up over the phone without even visiting.

Fitness USA turned out to be lovably horrendous. It was in the basement of a strip mall, next to Hollywood Eyebrows, and it was covered in wall-to-wall bright red carpet. The walls were mostly mirrors, with the occasional flash of blue paint intermixed. There seemed to be no organization to the arrangement of the rusted machines. It felt like an abandoned set of *American Gladiators*.

The gym members were almost exclusively old Asian people, which made sense since our neighborhood was mostly filled with old Asian people.

We tried the "cardio-kickboxing" class. We were the only white people, the only people under the age of sixty. I was the only male. Even our teacher was an old Chinese woman. After the first fifteen minutes she ran out of moves, and we spent the next sixty minutes recycling and reshuffling the same moves over and over. She played a pulsing, tacky playlist of jock jams on full volume, and for seventy-five minutes Giulia and I danced, writhed, air-punched, and flailed, surrounded by Chinese and Filipino grandmothers. We loved it.

Our teacher often stopped in the middle of an exercise to watch us, point, and laugh. I didn't mind her laughing at me, because I was laughing at myself, too, a surfer from the neighborhood at a gym class where he clearly didn't belong. Our teacher coughed out commands that we couldn't understand and we had to do our best to pantomime along with her. She sometimes wore a T-shirt that proclaimed, "Don't worry, I won't hurt you." Everyone in the class adored her, especially me.

The aerobics class was perfect. I smiled throughout and felt the glow of endorphins as I sweated into the bright red carpet below.

But as much as I loved it, I couldn't watch Giulia. In aerobics class, her slowness was most on display, as if she had to move underwater while the rest of us got to dance free and light like children reveling in a sprinkler on a hot summer day.

At night, I started a mantra that we said to each other before falling asleep.

I'm getting better.
You're getting better.
We're getting better.

I realized, of course, that Giulia might not get better. She could get worse, or plateau, and forever be a shadow of herself, trapped in a medicated fog. But I refused those options.

Along with the aerobics, I kept up my night running. Sometimes I went during the evening, while Giulia prepared dinner. During one especially glorious sunset, I pounded through the sand and noticed that someone had written a message: *When it is done we will walk where the road meets the sun.* I liked it. The promise of walking where the road meets the sun felt like an offering of redemption and grace. I wanted to be there.

As I kept running, I forced myself to imagine Giulia's suicide. I had been in therapy since the first week of Giulia's hospitalization, and my therapist had long encouraged me to address the very real possibility of it. Not as a nightmare or a hallucination, but as a possible outcome. Giulia might still do it.

My feet were light on the sand, the air crisp and cool, and I saw it. Park the Vespa, bring the key—who are we kidding, Giulia would never leave the key and risk the Vespa getting stolen—walk shoulder to shoulder with the tourists along the sidewalk. No note, because she had tried and failed to write a note before. Stop to take a photo of a couple who ask for it. Get out far enough to the middle of the bridge so it was high enough to ensure fatality. Wait for a lull in nearby pedestrians and then up and over the railing, clumsily. Both feet on the last remaining beam, hands holding on to the railing behind. Pause long enough to look down and embrace the finality, but not long enough to have someone run up and stop her. And then off. Out. Free.

The impact is instantly fatal for almost all who jump off the Golden Gate Bridge—only a few have survived, most famously a teen who realized midfall that he didn't want to die and tried his best to brace his fall with the angle at which he hit the water. He broke a lot of bones but did not die. Many bodies are recovered, but not all. After impact, Giulia's life and breath would be ripped out of her by the coldness of the San Francisco Bay. Immediate, painless death.

But Giulia would not be done. Not quite. She would still be in my life, in both her presence and her absence. Her clothes, her possessions, her hair in the drain of the shower, even her smell on the blanket she wrapped herself in every night.

Her absence would be everywhere. I would miss her in everything. I would tell people about her and keep her alive in my stories.

She would not be done.

Her body, whether discovered or not, would join the land and the water and return to the elements, from dust you are and to dust you will return. Nothing dissolves into nothing.

We are never done, I realized as I ran through my grief, the grief for an imagined suicide that I was doing everything I could to prevent but had to accept regardless. *When it is done we will walk where the road meets the sun.* It was always done, and never done. We were already in the sun.

I stopped running a few blocks from my home as part of my usual cooldown. I usually dreaded these last few blocks, the threshold across which my adrenaline and endorphins wore off and the reality of caregiving for a suicidal wife returned. But tonight, I was completely at peace as I walked the last few blocks home and then up the stairs to my front door. I slept deeply that night and woke up the next morning at ease. I was neither anxious about the future nor resigned to Giulia's demise. I was alive in the present, and Giulia was alive in the present, which was all I could ask for.

Over spring break, we took an impromptu visit to Tokyo, to see my parents. My siblings and I had grown up in Tokyo, the blond gaijin who were cast to be in TV commercials and on soap operas. We had an amazing childhood in Tokyo, with its clean and safe subway system that allowed us to be independent years before American kids are able to get themselves around. As long as I had known Giulia, I had told her stories about our lives in Japan, and this was going to be her first time there.

My parents were thrilled to host us. The rest of my siblings and their spouses had been in Japan for Christmas while we stayed in New York, and my mom mostly repeated their itinerary with us.

We took the train out to Kamakura, a charming beach town famous for the Daibutsu, a gigantic statue of the Buddha. Kamakura had been the favorite destination of my siblings, and my parents were excited that Giulia and I were going to see it.

We left midmorning and arrived at Kamakura in time for lunch; we ate curry rice that warmed my belly and made me feel ten years old again. We found our way through the pleasant Zen gardens under a clear blue sky, a perfect chill in the air. We came across a large prayer wall, which held up dozens of prayer offerings written on wooden cards. Giulia stopped, pointed, and smiled.

Hanging in the middle was a prayer card that my family had written three months prior. The English writing stared out at us among the Japanese characters.

12–31–09
For our sister Giulia,
That she may recover with good health—mind, body, and spirit.
Lukach Family

Giulia beamed and posed for pictures, proudly holding up her prayer card, and I saw that prayers never end, either.

We continued along to a cave where pilgrims had been coming for centuries. You could see the markings of countless visitors in the walls and in the floors. Discovering the prayer card, in this sacred space, was too much for me. I grabbed Giulia and held her for a long, long time. The world spun around us, just like how our wedding guests had formed a circle and danced around us on that blissful night. I felt the embrace of the many people who had been in the cave before us, and the many who would come after us, and all the strangers we had never met, as if they were lifting us up and holding us on high so that we could gaze out over the world and stand together and realize that we were here now, in the gift of this present moment, and yes, life was hard at times, but doesn't it feel good to be alive?

Back in San Francisco, we returned to our routines. I worked. Giulia went to IOP, and took care of the dog, and attended art classes in Golden Gate Park. After work one afternoon, I scooped up Giulia and Goose and we drove down the coast to Montara, our favorite beach, for a hike.

We took a new route up a steep incline of Montara Mountain to a spectacular vista over the ocean. The trail up was slippery with loose gravel, and Giulia was tentative while getting to the summit of our little peak. We sat on the top, wind in our hair, Goose resting in my lap.

I foolishly hadn't factored her stiffness and sluggishness into our plans, and the walk down felt even more steep and dangerous than it had on the way up. Giulia nervously shuffled along the path, her feet occasionally slipping out beneath her.

"Are you okay, honey?" I called back up the trail to her.

"I'm okay. Scared, though."

"What are you scared of?"

"I'm scared that I might fall."

My mind flashed to a conversation I had recently had with Sienna, a friend of ours who had battled her own demons throughout her teens and twenties. Sienna used to sneak out of her house in the middle of the night when she lived in Santa Cruz and go swimming naked in the ocean, because she wanted to drown herself. But as the cold of the ocean overtook her, and the fear of sharks crept into her mind, her survival instinct always kicked in, and she sprinted back to the beach and climbed back into bed, wondering why she wanted to kill herself in the first place.

This might be Giulia's chance to scare herself back into living.

"Explain this to me, Giulia. You're scared you're going to fall, right?"

"Yes," she said.

"You're scared because you might get hurt, or even worse, you could slide down and even go over a cliff and die. And you're scared of that."

"I guess so," she said, only barely convinced.

"Don't you see what that means?"

Giulia didn't respond.

"Giulia, you want to live! Think about it. You're scared to fall because you're scared to die. That means you don't want to die. You want to live!"

She flashed an embarrassed, sheepish smile.

"I guess so," she admitted.

"Come on, no 'I guess so.' You know so. You want to live. Look at this place. We are on top of the world, and there is so much to live for, and you want to live for it!" I was bellowing, my voice echoing down to the beach below.

Her foot slipped, and her arms shot out to balance herself.

"Look! Scared! Scared to fall! My wife wants to live!"

She giggled at my buffoonery, my teasing of her suicidal feelings. We had cried about them for so long. It felt good to laugh at them.

"Giulia, this is your chance. Tell the world that you're alive. Celebrate in it. Be alive, and feel it."

"I'm alive," Giulia softly muttered.

"Bullshit! Scream it! This is your moment, Giulia. You want to live! Scream it to the world . . . you're alive! Fuck the illness. Fuck suicide. Fuck psychosis. Fuck the pills. You, Giulia, are alive. You are making it, one day at a time, one step at a time, you are making it."

I hadn't experienced the depths of depression on my own to understand that each breath Giulia took was a cry out for life. She didn't need to say anything to convince herself that she was fighting. But selfishly, I needed her words, as a validation that all the love and time I was pouring into her was making a difference. Still too young, inexperienced, and solipsistic, I hadn't realized that to give true love, you can't expect anything in return. I had been giving so much since the onset of her psychosis and feared that we might never return to a two-way affair of reciprocal care. What if she never got better? I wasn't ready for that. I needed to hear that she wanted to live for herself as much as for me.

"I'm alive," she called out with a little more vigor, but she could see in my face that I needed to hear it even louder.

She stopped and planted her feet firmly into the ground. She mustered all of her sadness and hatred for herself and her illness and focused it in her fists and her gut. She held her head high and screamed.

"I'm aliiiiiiiiiiiiiiiiiiiiiiive!"

Her eyes were wide and lucid, her fists balled up, her whole being a rejection of death as she called into the beautiful world.

"I'm aliiiiiiiiiiiiiiiiiiiiiiiiiiiiiiiive!" she shouted again, even louder.

"I'm aliiiiiiiiiiiiiiiiiiiiiiiiiiiiiiiiiiiiiiiiiive!" The third and final call was the longest.

We stood in silence and watched the glittering ocean, the swooping birds, the waving grass. She looked at me with tremendous pride and satisfaction.

"I'm alive, Mark. I'm alive."

five

April 2010

"Mark, if I kill myself, will you promise me that you will find a new wife so that you can still be happy?"

I sighed and leaned back into the couch next to Giulia, but I didn't respond. I didn't have an answer for her. I muted the television that we had been watching, and the flickering glow of the screen remained in our otherwise darkened living room.

I looked at her, into her anguished brown eyes, and held her hand, and said nothing.

I was tired from work, tired from worry, tired from spending so much time trying to convince Giulia why it was worth staying alive, tired from the frequent requests for updates from her parents, and my parents, and her doctors, so tired that I was getting angry at always feeling fatigued. I couldn't handle another conversation about suicide. There had been so many of them over the eight months since she had been hospitalized, and I didn't have anything left to get me through another agonizing night of convincing her why it was worth staying alive. My reserves of patience and compassion were grossly overtaxed, and all that was left in their absence was resentment.

With nothing to say, I sat in silence. Slowly, Giulia began to say more. "I can't ever come back from what I went through in the psych ward," she said nervously, a mantra I had heard hundreds of times and rebutted a hundred times. But this time I didn't say anything. I merely listened. I hated what I heard, but I also knew that at this moment she was safe, and we were together.

In the gaps between Giulia's sentences, I realized how rarely I let Giulia speak about what she was feeling. I treated her depression like a fire, and I was the extinguisher. I had to act quickly every time the feelings surfaced, lest the warning sparks grow into a destructive inferno. This was especially true when we were around others. I didn't want to put anyone through the awkwardness of her unexpected suicidal outbursts, so when we were with friends, which was rare, I mostly spoke on her behalf.

My first instinct when she was psychotic was to love her psychosis away. I took a similar strategy toward her depression. For the past eight months, I had tried to talk her out of her suicidality. Exhaustion finally beat me down into shutting up and listening to her.

"I hate myself so much, and I want to die," she said after a silence.

I said nothing. Her despair hung heavily in the room.

"God abandoned me," she said.

Again, I said nothing.

"I wish I had never been born," she said.

More silence.

And then she left me stunned.

"Thank you for listening to me," she said, grabbing my hands, pulling them up to her lips to kiss. "It's so nice to talk to you."

I realized then why people call suicide hotlines. The person on the other end of the line wasn't a therapist, wasn't going to prescribe medicine, wasn't going to try to convince the caller to feel differently, wasn't going to love the caller the way a family member would. The person on the other end of the line was going to listen without judgment or fear, an invaluable gift that the suicidal rarely receive.

She surprised me further by leaning in to kiss my lips. We still kissed on occasion, but only when I kissed her. This was the first time that she had kissed me since the hospital.

"Thank you, Mark," she said again. "I feel a lot better." She stood up from the couch. "Come on," she said, extending her hand. "Let's go make some dinner."

I squirmed in the high-backed felt chair. Giulia was in the chair next to me. IOP had finished for the day, and I had been called in for a family meeting. We sat in a big room with a few dozen chairs, a room where Giulia came three times a week for her group therapy. It was like all of the other rooms of all the other hospitals and outpatient programs: lifeless, white walls, no personality, no hope. Giulia's mental health team walked into the room.

Her doctor jumped right to the point. "We're not satisfied with the progression of Giulia's depression," he said. "She has been here for eight months. Most patients are in IOP for only a few weeks."

"What, are you saying this is her fault or something?" I asked defensively. My patience for following doctor's orders was also wearing thin. I had done everything they had said, yet we were still here.

"No, no, no, not at all," the doctor said. "This is not about fault.

It's just that the path we've taken, to try different medications, doesn't seem to be working."

"Well, what else is there?" Giulia asked. "Can I stop the medication entirely?"

"No," the doctor said. "This isn't about stopping the medication, either." He was now the one squirming, fidgeting with the pamphlet that I noticed was in his hands.

"Well, what is it?" I said.

"We would like you to consider ECT." The doctor extended the pamphlet for Giulia to take.

"What the hell is ECT?" I asked.

No one answered. I scooted closer to Giulia and looked down at the pamphlet. *Electroconvulsive therapy*, it blared across the top in bright blue letters.

"Electroconvulsive therapy?" I said, practically shouting. "Are you fucking kidding me?"

I had horrifying visions of electrical nodes glued to Giulia's skull, the flip of a switch, her body convulsing against leather straps.

"It's not what you think it is," the doctor said, standing up to demonstrate authority. "A lot has changed since *One Flew over the Cuckoo's Nest*. Patients barely even feel it. They say that their memory is a bit foggy for a few days, but that's it. It's a painless procedure, and it works like hitting the reset button."

"That doesn't sound too bad," Giulia said cautiously. "A reset button sounds pretty good to me."

I skimmed through the pamphlet. The procedure essentially induced a seizure, and while the science wasn't clear why it worked, it had a very high success rate for patients who battled chronic depression.

"Look, it's a big thing to consider," the doctor said. "We don't need to make a decision now. I just wanted to put the idea out there. But I do want to make an immediate change. I think it's time to take Giulia off Risperdal."

Giulia cheered. She hated all of her medication, but she especially hated the antipsychotics, which she felt were the biggest culprits for her weight gain and lethargy.

"Giulia has been on some form of an antipsychotic for a long time, and I'd like to see how she does without them. Her psychosis has been gone for months. She will stay on the lithium and the Prozac. If she does well without the antipsychotics, we might be looking at a different diagnosis as well. Let's give it a few weeks, and see how this new medicine combination works. We can regroup after that, and see if we want to further explore ECT."

We all stood up, shook hands, and I stuffed the ECT pamphlet in my back pocket. I wanted to be open-minded, but really. I hoped I would forget that the pamphlet was in my pocket and destroy the damn thing in the laundry.

Back in our aerobics class, the music pulsed and pounded. We punched our arms and stomped our feet into the offensively red carpet.

"Come on, keep punching, left, arm, left arm, left arm!" our loopy ancient Chinese teacher shouted out over the music. She was wearing our favorite shirt, "Don't worry, I won't hurt you."

Aerobics class continued to be as delightful as it had been the first day. We never spoke to any of our classmates, but almost all the old Chinese women smiled at us when we came into class, the tall surfer husband and the silent wife.

As usual, I tried to keep my focus on myself and away from Giulia, because the sight of her trying to keep up with sixty- and seventy-year-old women broke my heart.

But all the room's walls were mirrored. I tried to let aerobics class be something for me, a break from caring for Giulia, but inevitably my gaze drifted over toward Giulia's reflection, and I'd feel sad for her, and me, and us.

Today was different. I could see that immediately. All of the physical manifestations of her illness—the locked fingers, the pursed lips, the hunched shoulders, the slowness, the slowness, the slowness—were gone. She reached farther, stretched more, punched harder, kicked more vibrantly. She had stopped Risperdal, and now, at aerobics class, she was escaping the molasses.

The music kept pounding, the teacher kept shouting, the old women kept dancing, and I stopped moving. All I had at that moment was Giulia. I turned to watch her directly, not trusting what the mirror had shown me, worried that it was too good to be true. But the mirror hadn't lied. Looking at her, I could see that she was just as alive as her reflection. Her brow shone with sweat, a brilliant smile on her face.

She caught me watching her and yelled over her shoulder, "You'd better keep going, or you-know-who might actually hurt you, no matter what her shirt says!" And then she lifted her head and laughed at her joke, a natural, liberated laugh that was the sweetest noise I had ever heard.

Giulia was back. I turned back to our teacher, who stood with her hands on her hips and impatiently pointed at me to get back into punching, and I happily agreed and air-punched so hard that I thought I might throw my arm out of its socket.

Giulia's slide into psychosis had been unexpected and abrupt, but it was nothing compared with her escape out of depression. It evaporated before my eyes in an aerobics class, with wall-to-wall red carpeting, bad music, and elderly Chinese women.

"I'm done!!!" Giulia texted me a week later, after her final session of IOP. It was just over nine months since she had been hospitalized, which meant eleven months since she had first shown anxiety about her new job.

We went out to our favorite pho restaurant to celebrate, one we had discovered in the months after Giulia's hospitalization. It was our escape when I didn't feel like cooking, which was all of the time, and we sometimes ate there three times a week. Our favorite waiter gave us free appetizers like he always did. Giulia and I spent most of the night telling stories of the past nine months, and each one left us laughing at all of the absurdity.

"Remember when I thought that I was going to die when you visited me in the hospital?" she said.

"Which time?" I said, and she squealed in laughter, slapping her hands on the table and then clutching at her sides, which hurt with so much laughing. I was melting in my seat to see her laugh like this again, after such a prolonged absence.

"You know, when you got there and I thought I only had an hour to live, and spent the whole time counting down the time, and then, when it got close . . ." She couldn't even finish her thought, she was so hysterical in laughter at how she had gotten up and sprinted away from me as the hour finished ticking down and slammed the door to her room shut.

It certainly wasn't funny at the time. It was terrifying. We had spent an hour together as Giulia counted down what felt like certain death.

But for some reason over pho, we thought it was hilarious.

I took out my phone and showed her the picture I had taken the day before she was admitted to the hospital, frail and terrified on the beach, "the day you beat this thing," as I'd told her that day. And then I took a picture of her here, smiling over a steaming bowl of pho, her face full of confidence, her smile *bello come il sole* once again.

It was only at the end of dinner that we acknowledged all of the uncertainty and unanswered questions. Giulia was discharged from IOP without a firm diagnosis. They had more or less ruled out schizophrenia but didn't have a great diagnosis in its place. We had no clear explanation for what had gone wrong. It was probably related to a combination of lack of sleep, stress, hormones, and chemicals in her brain, but not even her clinicians knew what it was.

Which also meant that we didn't know if it would come back. Ninety percent of the time psychosis recurs. Ninety percent. The odds were troubling, but we buried the odds and focused on the memory of our charmed lives and convinced ourselves that Giulia would be in the other 10 percent. The working diagnosis, which felt jerry-rigged to fit the occasion, was "major depression with psychotic features," but in my mind, I just called it a nervous breakdown.

We also couldn't say what made it better. Medicine had helped the psychosis fade, but it also seemed to prolong the depression. All of the time Giulia spent in therapy must have helped, as did the friendships she forged through her recovery and the family who stood by her side. Right?

It all remained mysterious. The discomfort gnawed at us, but we willingly returned to laughing. We needed to celebrate for the night. Whatever it was, it was over. Done. Good riddance. Don't let the door hit you on the way out.

Our waiter came over with the bill. He laid it on the table and then said in his halting English to Giulia, "You look so happy tonight, and that makes me so happy."

"I know," Giulia said. "I am so happy."

I lounged on the couch in my gray lifeguard sweatpants, sand still caked to my feet from the dog walk earlier in the day, my hair oily and tangled. I had been ocean showering with a surf for the past few days, and I smelled like salt water and neoprene. The sweatpants were part of my lifeguarding uniform, back when I worked as a beach lifeguard at a crowded beach town in Delaware the summer before Giulia and I had married. I kept the sweatpants as a reminder of how strong and fit I had once been, when I used to swim and paddle miles in the ocean each day and do hundreds of push-ups and sit-ups a week. I multiscreened with the Giants game on TV and Twitter on my phone.

"Can you finish washing the dishes?" I yelled to Giulia, who was in our bedroom, also playing with her phone.

"Can you do them?" she called back.

"I cooked dinner. You know our rule, 'If you cook, you don't clean.'"

"Yeah, but seriously, that was a pretty simple dinner," she said. "Fried rice is easy to make, but it makes a huge mess."

"I did the grocery shopping for the food, too," I insisted.

"Well, I did the laundry today. Folded it and everything," she said.

"But you didn't put it away. I was the one who put the laundry away."

We went back and forth, tabulating our labors. This was a staple of our relationship, a competition over who had contributed more. Most of the time it was playful.

But I wasn't feeling playful tonight. I had cooked the dinner. I had done the grocery shopping. I had done all of that, for months. I had run our household by myself, for months. I ran her life, too. I had to. If it was up to Giulia, she would have stayed in bed all day or, worse, tried to hurt herself. So I planned her days for her: yoga, painting classes, volunteering at the children's day care at UCSF. I ran my life, too. I clung to my job. I drove her wherever she wanted to go. I sacrificed my entire life to her recovery. I wish I could say I wasn't resentful, but at that moment, with dirty dishes in the sink and Giulia justifying why she didn't have to do them, I hit my limit. I didn't want to get off the couch to finish the dishes. I wanted my no-longer-sick wife to do it.

"You know, Giulia, I did all the dishes, and all the cooking, and all the cleaning, and all of everything, for nine months." My voice grew louder with each word. "I know you were sick, but you're not anymore, and if it's okay with you, I'd love to get some goddamn help around the house!"

My outburst at Giulia hung in the air. It carried with it my own depression from the events of the past year. Now that Giulia was better, I'd hoped that it would be replaced with joy, but instead, resentment took up residence in my heart. Every evening I got home from work and changed into my gray lifeguard sweatpants. But I wasn't wearing them to do push-ups anymore. It was to sag into the couch and channel surf. On the weekends, if the waves were good, I'd paddle out to surf, but otherwise it was the same gray sweatpants, the same indent on the couch, the same pointless television.

I heard Giulia get up from the bed and go to the kitchen. I heard the water flow, the clank of dishes. She finished just as quietly and went back to our room, closed the door, and went to bed.

Every other week, I went to my therapist. She worked in a basement office decorated with small wooden statues from around the world, and her gentle voice sounded even quieter under the hum of a white noise machine that ensured our privacy from those in the waiting room. I loved her. She gave me the patience and reassurance I desperately needed.

We talked almost exclusively about Giulia for the month of her psychosis and continued to talk about her during the eight months of her depression. But as the illness subsided, the talk turned to me. My therapist wanted to know why I so badly wanted to be Giulia's hero. "The good news and the bad news is that you're not that powerful," she often told me. "But you sure do try and be powerful."

I wasn't too interested in understanding why I devoted so much of my caregiving to Giulia. To me, the answer was simple and cliched: love.

But I did want to know why I felt like such shit.

I had never felt so disinterested and lethargic before. I'm typically all energy, all the time. In college, when I sang for a ska punk band, I wrote a song called "Happy Here, Happy Now." Some of my bandmates joked that it should have been "Happy Here, Happy Dumb," because happiness is an easy target for adolescents to mock. I didn't understand at the time that happiness is a beautiful form of courage.

"Of course you feel like shit," my therapist said. "You've been through hell for the last nine months. It's about time you feel this way. You haven't had the chance yet."

I stared at her, puzzled.

"You keep saying that you took care of Giulia because you love her, but I'm not sure you really know what love looks like."

I recoiled at this suggestion. "What do you mean? I just sacrificed everything. How is that not love?"

"Sacrifice is a part of love, Mark. But might there not be more to love than just how much you sacrifice?"

I squirmed uncomfortably in my seat. I didn't know where this was going.

"Let me put it another way," she said. "It's like you've survived a tsunami, Mark. I'm sure you saw the footage from the tsunami that hit Indonesia. Entire buildings wiped out. People swept away. Horrifying stuff. It's not hard to imagine you and Giulia on one of those beaches. You were in bliss together, and then the wave hit. You grabbed on to a tree and each other and held on as the water pushed and pulled and tried its damnedest to rip you apart, but you kept holding on. For nine months, you held on."

I nodded. I hadn't dared watch the footage. I had enough nightmares.

"And then, just as unexpectedly as the wave hit, it receded. It's gone. You've made it, the two of you. You can stop holding on to that tree so tightly. You can let go of each other. You survived the tsunami."

"Exactly!" I said. "Which should feel good, right? So many people don't survive. Families are torn apart by mental illness. Ours wasn't. People kill themselves every day. Giulia didn't. So why don't I feel happy?"

"Look around you, Mark," my therapist said. "Look at the carnage: the demolished hotels, the uprooted trees, the crumpled cars. The realization that not everyone made it. The worst is over. But everything you once knew is gone. The love you had with Giulia, the way you once knew it, is gone."

She was right. Nothing was the same. Nothing could ever be the same. Our bliss, our puppy love from college, our charmed lives, it was all gone. Giulia's psychosis and depression would color the rest of our relationship. Maybe even my own happiness wouldn't come as easily as it always had. I would have to work for it and have the courage to do the work.

"If it's all destroyed, I guess we rebuild," I said.

"Exactly," my therapist answered.

"What does that look like?" I asked.

She didn't answer.

It was a blustery spring day. The wind howled and swirled the sand throughout our neighborhood. Sand drifts built up along the Great Highway. Even though we lived ten blocks from the beach, you could still feel the grit of sand in the air in our house.

We took Goose out to Fort Funston, a dog park that sat atop beach dunes a few miles south of our house. Fort Funston was one of our favorite walking spots, although we knew it would be miserable out there today. But Goose needed his walk, so we bundled up to brace the wind and the cold.

Giulia's phone sounded: a friend texted with a last-minute extra ticket to go to a concert in Oakland that night. Opening act went on at eight, headliners would probably be on at ten. Did Giulia want to go?

"You can't go, Giulia," I said, barely letting her finish all the details.

"What do you mean I can't go?" she said. "I want to go, so I'm gonna go."

"Be serious, Giulia," I said, shrugging her off.

"Be serious about what?" She put her hands on her hips.

"Giulia, you haven't stayed up past nine p.m. in almost a year. We don't live anywhere near a BART station, so you'd have to drive, and you hate driving the car. You don't know how to get there. And let's not forget that we're talking about you driving at midnight, or even later. This is a terrible idea. You're not going."

Giulia was furious. "But I want to go."

"Yeah, well, guess what, it's back to reality. I'm tired of sugar-coating life to you. You're better, so you can handle the truth. And the truth is, we don't always get what we want, and you don't get to go to the concert." I refused to budge.

I maintained a cold hostility, but Giulia was raging.

"You don't get to tell me what to do," she hissed.

"Yes, I do," I said. "I took care of you when you couldn't take care of yourself, and going to a concert tonight is not taking care of yourself." I was screaming now too, enraged that she couldn't see how bad an idea this was. "I'm sorry, Giulia, but I do get to tell you what to do."

"Thanks a lot, jerk." She stormed off into the wind and sand. I sat with Goose for a minute, burning from the wind and even hotter inside. She was better but was priming herself to make terrible choices, and if things went wrong, I would have to clean up after them. I finally tugged on Goose's leash to continue the walk, following Giulia's trail, but she was quickly out of sight.

Thirty minutes later, we were back at the car, where Giulia waited for us. I unlocked the door, and we all drove home in silence and spent the rest of the day not speaking. The concert came and passed. Neither of us mentioned it again.

I limped through the end of the school year, and as I promised, I quit. I had teary good-byes with the colleagues I had grown to care for, but I felt no remorse as I took down the maps and inspirational quotes from my classroom walls.

Giulia and I didn't have any plans for the immediate future, except for my brother Matt's wedding in Nashville. Beyond that, we didn't know when we would return to work, or what type of work, or even where. The wedding was our only concrete plan, and we decided to drive to Nashville, just as we had driven to Delaware the year before. Anything to try to re-create the spark of the past.

However, we had only four days to make it to Tennessee on a dry, dusty southern route. We beelined south to Barstow, California, stayed the night, and then turned east on the horizontal line that is I-40. What lay ahead was eighteen hundred miles of uninterrupted interstate.

I tried to find fun places to stop along the way, but Giulia just wanted to get to the wedding. She napped for long stretches as we drove through the heat. I pretended not to mind. But the road was long and lonely. I was behind the wheel for ten hours the first day, bored by the soundtrack within the first few hours, not interested in podcasts. I was left alone to be tormented by my thoughts.

I ran through all of the amazing things that my friends had done over the past year. One friend published a book. Another quit his job and started his own thriving business. A third launched a fresh-pressed juice company that was exploding in popularity. Our siblings all took big steps forward in their careers. It seemed that the past eleven months had been good to everyone but us. I couldn't imagine having a job right now, let alone kicking ass at one. When I felt the envy creeping in, I always tried to convince myself that there was no greater accomplishment than to give of yourself entirely in the care of someone you love. But here in the desert, Giulia couldn't even stay awake to keep me company. I was alone and miserable.

On a slow decline into a valley in Arizona, I saw off in the distance an eighteen-wheel truck that was climbing up the hill, miles away. We drove toward each other and I felt time slow down. I couldn't look away from the truck. The closer it got, the more I knew what was going to happen. A deer was going to run out onto the freeway and the truck was going to slam on the brakes. The sudden stop would send the truck into a wild tailspin, and it would skid across the highway into our lane with the loud groan of steel. It would be too late for me to react. At ninety miles per hour, we would smash into the sliding truck. The impact of the crash would kill all of us immediately, our bodies crushed under glass and metal, our dog thrown from the car into the rubble.

I fixated on the impending crash and gripped the wheel. I was sweating profusely, my tongue chalky and dry, so I cranked up the air-conditioning. The truck got closer and closer. I scanned just off the road for the deer that would trigger all of this, and I waited. I wanted to slow down, but I sped up instead.

The truck hummed along past us. No deer, no crash, just more empty road.

Giulia woke up with a start. "Why's it so cold in here," she mumbled as she turned off the air-conditioning. She fell asleep again in a few seconds.

I kept driving.

At our campsite in New Mexico, I couldn't sleep. We'd crawled into our sleeping bags around sundown. Giulia and Goose were both snoring, again within minutes. I ached with exhaustion, but no amount of reading or meditating could distract me from the certainty I felt was coming, the man lurking near the campsite with a gun. I had spotted him at dinner in town, sitting by himself in a restaurant booth. He and I had a second of eye contact, and then another, and it was in that second instant of connection that I knew he had picked us as his victims—young couple, full of promise. I looked over my shoulder when we left the diner and the man remained in his booth, but I knew that he had figured out where we were staying. Which is why I needed to be awake. I listened for the snap of a nearby stick, the crunch of footprints in the sand. Once he arrived, I knew there wouldn't be anything I could do to stop it. He would be armed; we were in a nylon tent. I planned to throw myself over Giulia's body as soon as I heard the gunshots, protecting her to the very end, but he would empty so many rounds into the tent that it wouldn't matter.

At two a.m., I dug into my backpack and took a sleeping pill that my therapist had suggested when I had been struggling to sleep in the thick of my caregiving. I hadn't taken one in months. I didn't try to stay quiet as I looked for it. I knew Giulia needed her sleep, but I wanted her to wake up so she could keep me company and tell me that my thoughts were nonsense, that everything was okay, to reflect back to me what I had done for her through her sleepless nights. She didn't stir.

I returned to my sleeping bag and tried to forget the man with the gun, who wasn't even real. I focused on how uncomfortable I was, lying on the desert floor. I fantasized about escaping. The next day, if we survived the night, I promised myself that I would pull over while Giulia and Goose dozed and hop one of the barbed-wire fences that lined the highway and walk into cattle land. I would climb the hills until I was too tired to walk any farther. Then I'd lie down in the hot sun and see what would happen. Maybe then I would fall asleep.

We made it to Nashville. My family was there, waiting for us, a giant ball of positivity. The Lukaches are a loud, enthusiastic group by nature—especially at a wedding. The festive spirit was amplified with the collective will to celebrate Giulia's return to health. "Giulia is doing so much better," my mom and my brothers and my sister and my dad kept whispering to me throughout the weekend.

I unloaded Giulia on my family. My mom and my sister took her to get their hair and nails done, and I focused on being my brother Matt's best man. I had put so much of myself into being a husband that I had neglected all other aspects of my identity. We celebrated his bachelor party the day before the rehearsal dinner, a group of guys at a Mexican restaurant to watch Mexico beat France in the World Cup. We nearly brought the place down with our cheers.

While there were moments of fun, I had a hard time fitting in.

These were the people I loved and I knew loved me, but their lives had kept spinning along as Giulia's and mine fell to shambles, and it hurt to see how fully they had lived while we suffered. I was mad at them, which was absurd, and I knew it was absurd, but that didn't stop me from feeling mad. I didn't get the inside jokes that my siblings told about *Saturday Night Live* skits, so I awkwardly interrupted. I wondered how many e-mail chains I hadn't been cc'ed on. My sister's husband, Alex, made a video from the Tokyo Christmas trip; everyone was in it except me and Giulia. The whole family piled into the living room the afternoon before the rehearsal dinner to relive that trip. When the video came to Kamakura, where they wrote Giulia's prayer card, I couldn't take it anymore. I stood up and stormed away from my family. I couldn't accept that their year had been so rich while ours had been lost.

The wedding itself was a welcome relief. Matt and Grace Ann met even younger than Giulia and I did, at age fourteen, and the perseverance of their youthful love reminded all of us in attendance how pure a joy it can be to love someone. Giulia and I danced together and raised toasts, and at one point while we sat around the table, we instinctively reached for each other's hands at the same time and had a quick smile and another shared memory to add to our repository.

The morning after, I went for a run with my older brother, Carl, and my sister, Cat, and as we jogged through Nashville, the conversation quickly turned to how much better Giulia was doing. Carl and Cat couldn't stop talking about it.

"I don't care how well Giulia is doing!" I exploded at them. "Of course I realize she's doing better. Will everyone stop telling me about it? And why doesn't anyone seem to care about how bad I feel?" I sprinted away from them and left them behind to muddle through my outburst in the swampy Tennessee heat.

"I don't think I want to go to Italy this summer," I said somewhere in Arizona, speeding back to San Francisco from Nashville.

"Why not?" Giulia shifted in her seat. "We always go to Italy in the summer."

"I know, but I don't want to go this summer," I said again. "I need a break from your parents." I'd had almost daily contact with them for nine months. Many of the conversations had been very difficult. We didn't always agree on how best to care for Giulia, and it felt at times like a turf war over who should have the final say: her husband or her parents.

"Well, that's really lame," Giulia said. A few minutes later, she reclined her seat even deeper and fell asleep.

I fumed through most of the drive home as Giulia slept. Me? The chauffeur to her cross-country nap, and I was the one being lame? Her disregard for my experience, one-liners that wrote me off as the bad guy, and an inability even to stay awake with me as I drove filled me with a dangerous rage that had me ready to punch through the windshield.

The outrage in the moment rested on the surface. Underneath lived a more existential rage that Giulia had gotten sick in the first place. She'd made life so hard for us. Everything that had been certain to us—our jobs, our finances, our goal of becoming parents—had evaporated. What would our lives look like from now on? I knew she hadn't done any of this by choice. But that did nothing to assuage my anger.

The time driving solo as she slept at least allowed me to calm down. I needed to talk to her, to try to explain why I was angry, so that I could get rid of it. When she woke up an hour later, I said to her, pleading, "I feel so angry, Giulia. I need to talk to you about what's going on."

"Oh, come on, Mark," she said back. "Can you please just lighten up? I think we had a serious enough year to last for a while. Just relax, would you?" She turned up the music and pretended I hadn't said anything, and my plan backfired.

When we got home, she bought a plane ticket to Italy. I wondered what to do with myself for the ten days she'd be gone. Whatever it was, it had to be something big. I needed to pull myself out of this sinkhole.

On a whim, I decided to bike down the California coast. I'd catch a ride to the Oregon border and then bike home, all 450 miles. I wasn't an experienced cyclist. I hadn't even changed a flat tire before.

But I have always been a fitness maniac. Happiness always included pushing my body and flooding it with endorphins. So I figured what the hell. Jump on a bike and see what happens, see if I couldn't lose my feelings out on the Northern California coastline.

Giulia wasn't thrilled at the prospect of my bike ride, but she didn't try to stop me. She worried that I pushed myself too hard physically and that at some point I was going to hurt myself. But she was headed to Italy, so there was nothing she could do.

I bought panniers for my bike and loaded them with rocks to get used to the weight I would be carrying—tent, sleeping bag, clothes, food, and water. The training rides hurt, and I liked how my legs burned under the weight of all the gear. I wanted this to be difficult.

The day before the trip started, I added an extra hurdle: I decided that I would take a vow of silence for the trip. I had spent the prior year writing e-mails to family, talking to doctors, calling Giulia. I was fed up with so much communication, especially right now. It seemed like whenever I spoke to someone—Giulia, my parents, even my therapist—I worked myself into a sour, indignant mood. I needed silence to defuse my resentment, which was too explosive to manage.

I took a note card and wrote on it: *For personal reasons, I have taken a vow of silence. Thank you for respecting this choice. I hope we can still enjoy each other's company.* I laminated the card and threw a reporter's notebook and pen in my pack for moments when I needed to write down details to buy food or reserve a campsite. Giulia was skeptical of my vow of silence, so I promised to e-mail her my location from my phone each morning.

My friend Thomas was a pilot and had been wanting to visit a friend in Crescent City, a working-class town twenty-five miles south of the Oregon border, so he flew me up to my starting line, and I clipped my feet into my pedals and began riding south toward my home.

I had only an hour until dark after landing in Crescent City, and I biked on a quiet, flat road to a campground that was perched on dunes overlooking a broad, windswept beach. I set up camp and ate a peanut-butter sandwich slowly as I watched the sunset. I crawled into my tent, used a flashlight to read *The Brothers Karamazov*, the only book I packed, and fell asleep.

My first climb out of Crescent City was a six-mile, twelve-hundred-foot incline through ancient, foggy redwoods. My body was focused, my spirits were soaring, and almost immediately I felt my agitation and depression start to slide away.

I intended to average 50 miles a day, to stretch the 450-mile ride over nine days, and I stuck to the plan the first day. I made it to camp by two p.m. I swam in the ocean, did nearly four hundred push-ups, read one hundred pages of Dostoyevsky, and was bored silly by sundown. I woke up the next day at five a.m., charged and ready to ride.

On day two I had already put down 50 miles by lunchtime, so I upped my goal. I rode another 40 miles, for a solid 90-mile day. The third day I did almost 110, and the fourth was 80. I loved every rotation of my bike chain. I pedaled silently through shockingly beautiful coastline, nothing to rush to and nothing to run away from. I biked along the Eel River, ate a dozen Reese's Peanut Butter Cups in the shade of a redwood, and took naps. A girl in Garberville offered me weed and then hugged me and called me a prophet when she read my laminated note card. A waitress in Klamath asked me if I was deaf.

Most of all, I loved my warm cocoon of silence. I crawled in and found peace. I dreamed and wandered through my mind in whatever direction I wanted. Of course I thought about Giulia, but I always tried to rein back into the present. I focused on the details of my bike, my route, my body. I'd never eaten my food so slowly or enjoyed it so intensely. Everything was now, immediate, and alive.

At the bottom of a hill I spotted a group of three riders at the top ahead of me, and I set the goal to catch them within the next five miles. I sped past the slower of the two riders at mile two, but the leader of the group accepted my unspoken challenge, and we ended up in a game of cat-and-mouse chase, bombing down hills at forty miles per hour and straining on the uphills. The race lasted fifteen miles and brought us to the town of Elk. I pulled to the side of the road, huffing and puffing, to catch my breath. He stopped about two hundred yards behind me.

I chomped on an apple and watched him as he paced and waited for his friends. After fifteen minutes, he jumped on his bike and rode back in the direction we had come from, to make sure that everything was okay with his friends.

I had spent all year just like that, pedaling through life at Giulia's pace. If I ever rode at my own speed and broke away from her, I looked back nervously, worried that something had gone wrong. I pitied the cyclist, just as I had pitied myself.

I finished my apple and got back on my bike to ride away from Elk by myself, free of the responsibility to look back with worry.

I liked to ride before breakfast, to work up an appetite. On my fifth day I pedaled 20 miles, then stopped for breakfast in Gualala. I checked the map I carried in my pack. I was only 110 miles away from home. I could be home that night.

The bike ride was taking a toll on my body. My knee ached constantly, my back was sore, my butt was chafing, and I was cold. I had hoped for sun and sweat, but instead I rode mostly through wind and fog. Each night I bundled up tight in my sleeping bag but couldn't shake the chill.

Fifteen miles after breakfast, I stopped for a snack in Salt Point State Park and to refill my water. I knew from the map that the stretch ahead through the Sonoma coast was going to be hard and the final leg through Marin harder still. The road was windy and dangerous, with steep, dramatic cliffs only a few feet from the shoulder.

I grimaced as I got back into the saddle of my bike. The pain was a deliberate intention of the trip. I could choose when to stop and when to start. I could control my suffering.

As I rode, I focused on how much my knee hurt, distracted from the pain in my back. Once the knee pain felt unbearable, I focused on the gnawing chafe under my butt. I did this over and over, transferring my pain from one area of my body to the next, and the next thing I knew, I was delicately balanced on the edge of the road. My bike had drifted as my mind wandered, and my wheels were centimeters from the drop-off.

As soon as I realized how close I was to the edge, my front wheel slid off the road. I tried to pull myself back up, but my bike responded by flipping forward. My legs and my gear rushed over my head. I heard the scraping of metal and flesh.

I lay in the gravel of a turnout for a few seconds, unsure if I had really crashed my bike or I had just imagined it. My feet were still clipped into my pedals. I crawled out from under my bike to assess the damage. My bike was mangled, and my stuff was strewn across the right lane. I tried to gather everything and drag it to the side, but when I reached forward with my right arm, I felt a hot pain in my chest.

I sat down and felt around my body to see where I was hurt. I found blood on my legs. There was a giant dent in my helmet. Any time I moved my right arm, my knees went limp with the pain. I felt a sharp, pointy bulge on the collarbone.

A few minutes later, a car slowed down and then pulled off into the turnout. A woman rushed out to see if I was okay. I nodded. She ran back to her car and I heard her on the phone. "This guy on a bike wiped out and he looks really hurt. He's all cut up on one side." Pause. "I don't know, he didn't say. Let me ask him."

She returned to hover above me. "Did you black out? Did someone hit you? Did you break anything? An ambulance is coming."

I reached for my notebook, the one I used to communicate through my vow of silence, and realized how foolish that was. The bike ride was over. I'd broken my collarbone.

I stared up at the fog above me. I could hear the ocean gently mocking me through the trees. I had tried to ride 450 miles to escape my anger, but I could feel it lying in the turnout with me, ready to pounce now that I had stopped pedaling.

The first word I said was, "Fuck."

It was a ninety-minute bumpy ride in the back of an ambulance from the site of my bike crash to a hospital in Santa Rosa. I called my parents. They called Giulia in Italy, who called me back after an X-ray confirmed that my collarbone was broken.

Giulia was pissed off. She hadn't wanted me to go on this trip in the first place.

"You always push yourself," she said. "I knew you were going to get hurt someday, and now you've done it, at the worst possible time. You're there, I'm here in Italy with my family, on the first vacation that I've taken after the worst year of my life."

"Giulia, I didn't mean to get hurt."

"Well, you did."

We didn't talk for more than a few minutes. She got off the phone to return to dinner with her family.

I reeled in shock at how Giulia reacted. Because I was hooked up to a heart-rate monitor, I could hear and watch as my heartbeat raced from my phone call with her. I focused on the numbers to will my pulse to slow down, but it only beat faster. I tried to put myself in her shoes, to understand why she had been impatient and dismissive with me—on vacation, a day's travel away, so what could she really do?—but I couldn't do it. My view was too clouded by the past year. I wanted some acknowledgment of my sacrifice. Lying in the hospital bed, feeling helpless and worn, I pandered to my hurt feelings of abandonment like a petulant child. I gave up on trying to calm myself down, or rationalize why Giulia had acted that way, and lay back in defeat and cried for myself.

"You don't know how important this bike ride was to me," I said to the nurse who had heard my tears and come to my bedside in alarm. She held my hand and looked at me with the pity I so craved. My collarbone was broken, my body bruised, the bike ride that was meant to heal me had instead made me more vulnerable than ever. Worst of all, this year of illness looked like it would forever shape how I interacted with Giulia in an uncertain future. My emotions were now set on a hair trigger. Anything short of complete empathy from Giulia sent me into a tailspin of insecurity. Broken and alone with my injuries, I needed Giulia to take care of me now. Instead, she chastised me and rushed off the phone to eat dinner with her family. Even before my bike crash, this cycle of reactions versus expectations was becoming the new currency in our marriage. I worried we were doomed to never return to a place of mutual compassion and patience. Lying in the hospital bed a world away from Giulia, I was consumed by my doubts.

Giulia called back a few hours later while I was trying to figure out how I was going to get myself home from the hospital, ninety minutes away from our house and unable to ride a bike.

"How are you going to take care of yourself with your arm in a sling?" Giulia asked.

"I'm pretty sure I can handle myself," I said.

"You're definitely going to need some help cooking, feeding yourself."

"Who can help?" I asked.

"I don't know," Giulia responded. There was an awkward silence, and then I stated what felt obvious.

"Maybe the best person to help take care of me is you, Giulia," I said.

"Me? I'm all the way in Italy. How am I supposed to help?"

I snapped back at her impatiently, "I just spent a year of my life doing nothing but worrying about you, thinking about you, and caring for you—"

"Oh Jesus, Mark," Giulia interrupted. "I hope you're not planning to hang this over my head for the rest of my life. I'm better now. Get over it."

We both hung up without saying good-bye. Thankfully, my phone rang almost immediately with a call from Giulia's friend Annie, who lived in nearby Petaluma. I had texted her that I was in the hospital in Santa Rosa. She came to pick me up and drove me the hour and a half to the city. I was still in bike shorts.

The next day, I woke up with my back aflame. Turns out I had crashed in a patch of poison oak. I felt even more hopeless.

six

August 2010

Giulia came home a week later. My poison oak was fading, my arm was in a sling, and we were a mess. We existed in different worlds. I submerged deeper into my depression, and she wanted nothing to do with it. I took long walks by myself in the fog, three to four hours at a time, listening to books on tape. I watched a lot of TV. I could easily plow through four hours of *Scrubs* in a single sitting.

Giulia stayed away. She felt entitled to enjoy her life and health now that she had it back. She was almost always out, anywhere that would take her from the rituals of her depression. She didn't want to walk the dog, or take art classes, or do aerobics at our goofy gym. Soon after she got better, we stopped going to aerobics class and then canceled our gym membership. Instead she started antiquing and hunting through vintage stores for clothes and spending money we didn't have on knickknacks for the house.

Neither of us worked. We had saved up for a down payment on a house before Giulia got sick but had spent the past year eating away at that. Home prices in San Francisco were skyrocketing, and our supposed down payment was dwindling with each month. Home ownership looked increasingly unlikely. I puttered around with a few attempts at freelance writing, but we didn't earn much money. It seemed like our self-assigned jobs were to avoid each other.

My therapist suggested we see a couples' therapist. Giulia's therapist agreed. They both recommended the same person.

Our new therapist was cheery and compassionate. As soon as we sat down for our first appointment, we launched into the messy, tense story of Giulia's illness.

We tried to be honest about the specifics. We both had a lot of anger, which wasn't going to be easy to unpack. I learned that Giulia called me "the Medicine Nazi" in group therapy. She had come up with the name with Marie, a friend she had made in IOP. Giulia also told me she hated the plans that I put together for her while she was recovering. Everything I did felt suffocating to her.

I wasn't ready to hear any of this. The rejection stung deeply. My efforts to help Giulia were felt by her as micromanaging and oppressive. I had been anticipating some sort of thank-you at the end of the long haul, but instead I got a resentful "no thank you."

I also spoke honestly, and it was just as hard. I shared with Giulia my moments of eye contact with that hostess near the hospital, when I had parked the car and indulged in a moment of escape to another life. Giulia was furious to hear this, reacting as though I had been unfaithful to her. I tried to explain that it was barely a second, and subconscious, but she didn't care.

The sessions were brutal. We both cried throughout them and left feeling worse than we had at the start. And we hadn't even come close to approaching the truly terrifying question of whether or not we could be mutual in our care for each other. While it was important for us to hear each other's interpretations of the past, it didn't feel like we were doing anything to heal the rift between us.

We were just ripping open very tender wounds and paying $180 an hour for it. We lasted only a few sessions and then unceremoniously dropped out.

My arm healed. I got back into surfing and running. The restoration of my physical health helped a bit, as did avoiding our biggest conflict. But we were biding time. We both knew something needed to change.

About three months after I broke my collarbone, Giulia surprised me by purchasing two tickets to see Sufjan Stevens in concert. Sufjan was one of my all-time favorite musicians. I had first discovered him back when I lived in Baltimore and spent many of those long bus rides up to New York listening to his music.

With all of our free time and free spending, it was our first date since our celebratory meal at our favorite pho place, more than four months before.

It was also my first chance to see Sufjan live, and I loved every minute of the concert. He played songs from his latest album, the weird, computerized *Age of Adz*, which I had been listening to on repeat for the past few months.

The last song of the concert was a twenty-five-minute opus called "Impossible Soul." Sufjan danced in fairy wings and neon clothes, and for the first time I really listened to the words. The song is about a relationship: the boy wants out, the girl wants in. The whole thing boils down to the girl reminding the boy, over and over again, of how much better off they were when they were together, or as she put it, "Boy, we can do much more together. It's not so impossible."

I had been struggling to articulate what exactly I wanted from

Giulia, and Sufjan gave me the language in "Impossible Soul." I needed to hear these words from Giulia. I was angry because I didn't feel loved. Whether my sense of abandonment was real or imagined, it was the reality of my experience, and I needed Giulia to tell me that we were better off together. But I felt like I couldn't ask for it. That would cheapen it. It had to happen on its own.

I left the concert euphoric. It had been an amazing show, but more important, it gave me a better understanding of how I felt and what I wanted. Giulia and I had suffered through her illness together, but we were trying to recover separately. We had to recover together. It shouldn't be so impossible.

I had missed the beginning of the school year, so there was no returning to work. Giulia futzed around on Craigslist, trolling for jobs, but neither of us was ready for a career again. We were still too shell-shocked from our traumatic year.

We decided instead to travel. That nest egg hadn't vanished yet, so why not spend it on a once-in-a-lifetime trip. We loved Ocean Beach, but it was where Giulia had gotten sick. We needed a change of setting. Yes, she had gone to Italy, and I'd had my bike ride, but we needed to do something together.

We toyed with going to one place for a long time or many places for a short time. Everywhere was an option. New Zealand. Indonesia. South Africa. India. The planning was fun, but it also showed us how much our roles had changed in our marriage. Giulia had always been the one focused on the details. I tended toward the spontaneous. But now I was the one who kept questioning the practicality of our ideas, and Giulia kept pushing them further afield. She wanted to be gone for a year; I thought about Goose, and having to give up our house and pack our stuff into storage, so I lobbied for only a few months. She wanted to be as off the beaten path as possible; I never wanted to be too far from psychiatric help, just in case.

We finally settled into the idea of an around-the-world trip for four months. We'd do a month in Indonesia. And then another month in Kenya, where friends had started a girls' school, so we could volunteer. And a whole bunch of little stops in between. We'd leave San Francisco at Christmas and be home mid-April, in time for me to apply for teaching jobs the following year.

We consulted her psychiatrist and stocked up on more medicine than we could possibly need. We packed up our clothes and sublet the house to a family we found on the Internet. We drove Goose up to Cas and Leslie's house and had a tearful good-bye.

We cleared security at the airport, and Giulia instinctively handed me her passport and ticket to carry. I had never carried the passports before. In all our previous travels, Giulia had carried the passports. We both knew she was the more responsible one.

This year of illness had changed us into different people, and we needed to relearn how to be together in our new roles.

We began our trip with two weeks on an organic farm in Bali. We had no Wi-Fi or air-conditioning, the perfect ingredients for living at a slower pace. We spent long, quiet hours together picking lettuce, cooking dinner, and sweeping away the ants that were everywhere. We then set out for four dreamy weeks of wandering around Indonesia, sleeping on beaches, eating banana pancakes, motorcycling around dusty roads, paradising.

Most of all, we enjoyed ourselves. There was no official declaration of a truce, but we gingerly avoided each other's triggers. It's as if we made an unspoken agreement that while we were surrounded by so much splendor, we shouldn't fight. All it took was avoiding certain topics.

After six weeks of carefree living in Indonesia, we jetted off to Bangkok, where we met Suoc. She had always wanted to come to Thailand, and our around-the-world trip offered as good an excuse as any. Compared with the beaches of Indonesia, Bangkok was unwelcome, polluted, and traffic clogged. We did some sightseeing the first day but were content to spend much of the time at the hotel, enjoying the continental breakfast and the air-conditioning.

Our second night in Bangkok, Giulia went into her mom's room to watch *Blue Valentine*. I stayed in our room to read a book. Giulia returned a few hours later, sat down on the bed, and burst into tears. I had no idea what was going on.

"What's up, honey, are you okay?" I asked, putting my book down.

Giulia kept crying, her hands covering her face. I laid my hand on her back and slowly rubbed to try to calm her down. "What happened?"

"Are we going to make it, Mark?" she asked.

"What? Where's this coming from?"

"I mean, is this relationship going to make it?"

I froze. We had spent all six weeks of our trip and many of the months preceding it avoiding any discussion of our relationship. With one question, the whole tenor of the trip changed.

"*Blue Valentine* was so sad, but it was really honest," Giulia said. "The husband and wife fell out of love. People do that all the time, but they pretend they haven't. In the movie, they were honest about it, so they separated." She started to cry again. "Have we fallen out of love?"

I hung my head. It was such a sad question to have to ask, and sadder still to try to answer. But hearing it said aloud somehow felt like a relief.

I had been silently wondering the same. The way we'd been treating each other suggested that the cracks in our relationship might be gaping chasms. Perhaps we had been too intoxicated with puppy love to notice them before, and it took the crucible of psychosis and suicidal depression to show us our relationship for what it really was. Or maybe our young love had been untested.

"What makes you think that we've fallen out of love?" I asked. I was afraid to answer her question, because I worried the same thing, but if I answered her, she would never unhear my uncertainties. I cowered in silence.

"A lot of things. We don't like the same stuff. You read your books and listen to your podcasts, and I watch my romantic comedies. You read the news and I watch the Oscars. I like wine and you don't drink anything. Some nights I wish we could share a bottle of wine together. Or go get a coffee. You don't even drink coffee. We don't even have that ritual."

"Those are small things," I said. "People don't have to like the same things to get along."

Giulia twisted her mouth skeptically.

"But you're right, we don't like the same things, and it would probably be easier if we did," I said quietly, my words tripping over themselves in an embarrassed mumble. "It would be nice if we could get our coffees together. Or surf together. Or play tennis. Maybe it would be better if whatever made us feel good individually could also make us feel good together."

She breathed deeply and then looked me right in the eyes. In college, we used to lie in bed and look into each other's eyes long after we had run out of things to talk about, and we would fall asleep that way. She hadn't looked at me this intently in years.

I looked right back, and I began to feel dizzy. In my periphery I noticed the corners of the room dissolving, and before long, the whole room had faded away. Only Giulia was left. Her outline shone bright against a nonexistent background. She was close enough that I could reach out to touch her, but my body had disappeared, too. I was nothing more than a pair of eyes, and I saw her under a microscope, but also from high up in the sky, ten thousand miles above.

I saw in Giulia all the impressions I had made of her over the course of our ten years together: a glamorous, ambitious rock star of a student; a businesswoman par excellence; a joyful, adventurous companion; a wounded, confused wife; a helpless, terrified patient in a psych ward. I tried to see through the layers of these impressions, to see Giulia for who she was and not who I wanted to believe her to be; but then she began to fade, too. I wondered if I even knew who Giulia was. Had I created an array of expectations for who she should be, canceling her out in the process? Everything became blurry, my head spun, and I thought I was going to faint.

"Mark, are you okay?" Giulia asked me, the concern noticeable in her voice.

Her words snapped me back into the room, sitting on the bed with her, and I reached out and put my hand on her hand.

"Yeah, I'm okay. It's just that question—it's the hardest question you can ask of a relationship. It made me dizzy just to hear you ask it."

"I'm sorry," she offered.

"Oh no, don't be sorry. It's important. We have to talk about this. We can't ignore our problems like we did for the last six weeks in Indonesia. It's a good thing."

"So what do you think? Are we going to make it?" she asked again.

"I don't know the direct answer to that. But, sitting here now, I realized that I have all these expectations of you. In our past together, I have collected conclusions about who you are and how you will react to things. Like, this question you're asking, if we're going to make it. I've thought about it dozens of times, but I never brought it up because I was afraid that if I did, you would freak out at me.

"I'm just as terrified as you are that our marriage might not work out. But I've never brought it up to anyone, not even my therapist, because I am afraid of the answer."

"But you gotta give me a chance to have the conversation with you," she said.

"Yeah, exactly. I think I know you so well that I don't let you actually be you. So now here we are, talking about if our marriage is gonna make it, and you're the one who brought it up. And we're not angry. I didn't expect this at all. Shows you what I know."

We sat in an awkward silence for a minute. "So what do you think? You're still not answering my question," Giulia said.

"I don't know, really. I just think it's important to realize that I have expectations of who you are, and you have expectations of who I am, and right now our expectations are stuck in a conclusion that we aren't going to be good to each other. I'm always imagining you as a mean Giulia even before you act, and I get so angry at you about it."

"But the truth is, I am pretty mean," Giulia said. "And you are, too. We aren't nice to each other, Mark. I used to spend so much time thinking about how I could make you happy. Now, I don't even try. You're right there, every day, but I don't try to be nice."

"Yeah, but maybe how we act is because we're preemptively reacting, if that makes any sense. It's like I *know* you're not going to be nice to me, so I don't try being nice to you first, because no matter what I do, you're going to be pissed off by it, so why try."

"I guess," she said.

"Yeah, I don't know. I'm not sure if this makes any sense. I'm just saying—we haven't always treated each other this way, which means we don't have to treat each other this way forever. We weren't mean to each other when we were eighteen."

"But there was a spark when we fell in love at age eighteen," Giulia said. "That happened in a moment. And honestly, I want that spark back."

"A spark isn't the same thing as loving someone, we both know that."

She nodded.

"In fact, maybe love, in the purest sense, is about being kind to someone with no expectation of how they're going to respond. They can ignore your kindness, reject it, or return it tenfold, but you just continue to be kind, and that is love."

Giulia's eyes filled with tears. "Well, we're not doing a very good job of loving each other, then."

"We're not," I said. "But who says we can't change it."

Our next stop was Kenya, where we lived even more remotely than we did in Indonesia. We stayed at the Daraja Academy, an all-girls high school that our friends started, the campus a potholed forty-kilometer drive away from the nearest city. The school was set in the chalky red foothills of Mount Kenya, a landscape that alternated between parched dry and drenched with floods. Elephants and zebras and even lions were regular sights in the area, and the fence around the campus was mostly to deal with animals instead of people.

The campus felt very different from any place we had ever been. The students had all been carefully selected from communities through partner organizations. Daraja was built to be a school for girls whose families otherwise couldn't afford high school, without which they probably would have either been married off or gone to work in a low-paying job. Instead, they were at Daraja. The energy of a school full of young women who were grasping on to education as their path out of poverty was contagious. There was a pride, an ambition, but also a fragility that you could sense everywhere.

Giulia and I helped around campus in a variety of ways: teaching, working in the office, cooking in the kitchen, even lending a hand for maintenance projects like fixing up the garbage pit. We worked hard, but we also had a lot of downtime. We lived in a rondavel on campus and spent hours at a time sitting together and reading and gently talking. We shared stories that we had learned about the girls and marveled at their courage and willpower. So many of them had lived such demanding lives. We talked ourselves into being more courageous about our own lives. We had been given so much compared with how little they had, but they fought and fought, so we should fight, too.

It was typical voluntourism, the juxtaposition of lives of authentic suffering as a means of contextualizing our own, but the gratitude it instilled in us was genuine. We made amazing connections with the girls, especially Giulia, who took part in a health class and opened up to some of them about her year of mental illness, becoming an instant confidante. For the rest of our time on campus, girls approached her to talk through the feelings that we would have called "anxiety" and "depression" but that they bottled up in shame.

We visited a nearby orphanage, run by a sister organization of the school, and spent most of the day doting over a six-month-old girl named Harriet. We were supposed to walk through the grounds and work with the grade-school-aged children, but we kept returning to the nursery to see Harriet. Giulia helped feed her as I watched, and I saw in Giulia a vision of parenting that I hadn't considered since our road trip to my sister's wedding almost two years before. When I changed Harriet's diaper, I caught Giulia watching me, and I could see in her gaze that she was seeing the same future in me.

In our last week, I got dropped off in the city of Nanyuki and ran the forty kilometers back over the potholed roads. I wanted to feel small against a landscape of enormity. I wanted to feel energized to a life of tremendous potential. I wanted to be alone and spend the whole time wanting to return to Giulia.

Bangkok was the spark, but Kenya was the slow burn, the daily, hourly, minute-by-minute opportunity to practice our focus on kindness toward each other, and we left the country transformed.

Our last day overseas, after four months away from home, was in Dublin, Ireland. I saw on the hotel map that there was a lighthouse at the end of a seawall, a few miles' walk from our hotel. We were tired of sightseeing. It was lightly drizzling, but it was the last day of our trip and we didn't want to stay in the hotel, so we bundled up like we did at home and went walking.

What looked like only a few miles on the map turned out to be much farther. It took more than two hours to get to the lighthouse. We walked slowly and calmly through the streets, holding hands and letting go throughout. We passed a giant beach with the tide so far receded that there were hundreds of yards of wet sand, the bay far out of reach.

The seawall jutted a mile into Dublin Bay, with the lighthouse at the very end. After a month in the dry heat of Kenya, it felt wonderful to be in the misty cold, surrounded by salt water, before returning to our beach living in San Francisco.

As we walked back from the lighthouse, Giulia took out her iPhone and started playing around on it. She spent the whole walk back on the phone. I was annoyed and walked ahead. Who does that—shatters the beauty of the last day of a long trip by isolating herself in her phone?

A few blocks from our hotel, I finally stopped to wait for her. She had fallen far behind me, well out of sight, but the route home was straight and easy, and after fifteen minutes, she arrived.

"Here, Mark, I want you to read this," she said. Her eyes were sparkling and looked wet, from the fog but also from tears.

"What is it?" I asked, agitated.

"Just read it. I had to write it now. I've been thinking about it for a long time and I had to write it right then and there, on our walk."

I took her phone and started to read. It was a blog post, for the travel blog we had been keeping for our trip.

Today marks a special day. It's our last day in Dublin, but more than that, it's our last day in a foreign city. Tomorrow we return to the United States, ready to embark on a new journey: our life back at home.

I know Mark tends to be the spiritual, reflective one on this blog, and I mostly just post pictures. But for my last post I want to make a special dedication to my husband. While we walked to a lighthouse, I reflected on the reality that I wouldn't be alive in this world if it wasn't for him and his unconditional love. I suffered from a major depression that stole from me my love for life, and I was suicidal for a very long time. I was hospitalized in a psych ward for 23 days. I describe this period of my life as "hell on earth." But Mark. Oh Mark. He was by my side every single day.

While I hold his hand today, everything feels different. We have been together since we were only 18 years old, for almost 11 years, but the love and admiration that I have for him today feels completely new.

This was never meant to be just a fun trip to get away and explore the world. This was a healing journey for the two of us. Getting sick changed everything . . . for the better.

I am a better person having suffered through a mental illness. I am a more loving daughter, wife, and I know one day mother. I wouldn't change a single thing. My past led me to today. I have a newfound love and appreciation for myself and my life. A new way of seeing the world and the people in it.

So my love, this post is for you. Thank you for being at my side in sickness and in health, through the good times and the bad, while we were lying on the beaches of Indonesia or with the beautiful girls at Daraja . . . you are my everything.

I'm looking forward to our many journeys in life. Holding hands, of course.

In other words, "Boy, we can do much more together."

seven

September 2011

———

We pushed our overloaded grocery cart out of Trader Joe's in the foggy September afternoon. "I'm really excited with the location I've picked for the new campaign photo shoot," Giulia said as we loaded up our groceries. "Getting the permits was a pain, but we're going to be shooting at the Palace of Fine Arts Theater."

"Where's that again?" I asked.

"You know, that cool park in the Marina that has the archways and columns and looks like it's from a European city." This was Giulia's second photo shoot at her new company at the job she'd found a few months after we returned home from Ireland. Although she hadn't worked in more than a year and a half, she fell back into her work routine as though she hadn't missed a day.

"The model is going to fly in from L.A. and I'll spend the day with her at the shoot, but I might need to ask you to take her back to the airport if that's okay?"

"Yeah, sure, no problem," I responded, enchanted by how firmly our lives felt back on track.

Giulia was positively buzzing about her new role, and now that she was back at work, I was sincerely trying my hand at a career in writing, working from the house on freelance projects, to mixed success. Some days were packed, others were completely empty. Not yet ready to return to a full-time teaching load and all the demands that meant on my schedule, I pieced together work in whatever way I could.

On the weekends we ran errands together, as we had done for three years before she had gone psychotic. Our lives felt like they were back in our control.

So much in our control that we were trying to get pregnant.

As we loaded the last bag of groceries, Giulia abruptly changed topics. "Let's get a pregnancy test," she said, an eager smile on her face.

"No, no, no." I shook my head. "We just started trying, it's barely even been a month. Let's not get too excited. There's no pressure yet. Let's be patient."

But Giulia wasn't listening. She grabbed my hand and pulled me along to the CVS next door to the Trader Joe's. I dragged my feet, but I was grumbling mostly for show. I had been looking forward to this for longer than I could remember. I envisioned fatherhood as my life's ultimate goal, something I learned from my mom, who always said that her true calling was to be a mother. Even when we were eighteen and newly in love, I talked to Giulia about wanting to have children together. Nine years and a psychotic episode later, Giulia's work felt good enough, our relationship felt good enough, her sleep felt good enough, and we both thought it was finally time. Her psychotic break had delayed this, and even threatened to take it away from us, but now we were finally here, "trying," an amazing euphemism for having lots of excited, joyful sex.

But I played it cool. I had to. The prospect of children and happily ever after felt dangerously fragile. We had consulted with

Giulia's psychiatrist, who had come around to the conclusion that her episode was a onetime thing. Giulia's magical combination of medicine was lithium and Prozac, and the big question was whether to remain on the medication or not. We read blogs and forums and consulted with specialists. There was no conclusive research about the impacts of these drugs on a developing fetus, so it became a matter of what felt most right. Giulia and I both believed that the ideal pregnancy was an unmedicated pregnancy, but removing all medicine felt a bit foolhardy to Giulia's psychiatrist. While the impact of medication on a fetus was unclear, a relapse of psychosis while pregnant would be devastating, to Giulia and our baby. We had to walk a fine line between taking care of Giulia's mental health and protecting the baby's developing health, and it wasn't clear if the medication would be helping one while harming the other.

We ultimately decided to taper off lithium, mostly because Giulia wouldn't be able to breast-feed on it. The salts in her milk would be too much for our baby's young kidneys. But Prozac, according to our research and the two doctors we spoke with, was commonly taken by nursing mothers, and while no study was able to conclude that it was completely benign, none had proven any ill effects, either. So we decided to slowly remove lithium but stay on Prozac. The taper worked wonderfully. Giulia continued at work, she didn't feel any more stress or struggle to sleep. So she stopped her birth control. A month later, she was dragging me around CVS to get a pregnancy test.

While I worried about the drugs and the possible return of psychosis, I was mostly playing it cool because I didn't want the "trying" to be stressful. We had friends who had tried for two years to get pregnant, and they readily admitted that it had been a very taxing two years. The last thing I wanted was to welcome another challenge into our marriage that could shake the foundation of our relationship. I didn't want Giulia to work herself giddy about dreams that might take several painful years to wither into impossibility. So I grumbled. I pushed for a conservative approach. I pretended I was in no rush. But deep inside, I was ready.

"I won't take the test," Giulia said, and she grabbed the package off the shelf. "I just want to have a few handy, just because. I won't take it for at least a week."

We paid, drove home, and unloaded the groceries. Giulia disappeared into our room as I arranged the food into the refrigerator and pantry.

I had just finished putting away the produce when Giulia returned to the kitchen, triumphant.

"I'm pregnant," she announced, arms crossed, bright smile on her face.

"No, you're not," I said.

"Yes, I am," she said, adamant. "I'm pregnant. I just took a test."

I couldn't believe it.

She pulled the pregnancy test out of her back pocket, and there it was, a bright purple plus sign.

"Oh, my God. You're pregnant." I barely whispered it. It was here. We were going to be parents.

"Yup," she said, her eyes full of tears and her smile as big as I'd ever seen it. "I'm pregnant."

Immediately the kitchen felt very full. It wasn't just the two of us in there anymore. There was a third person in here. And not just a person, but a life, a future collection of memories, passions, and talents, was now in the kitchen with us. My mind raced to images of Legos scattered on the floor, car seats, footie pajamas. We'd need to upgrade our Civic to something that could fit all of us—child and dog in the backseat, camping gear in the trunk, surfboards on the roof.

I leapt out of the chair and ran to her, lifted her up, held her, put my hands on her belly, empty of words, full of hope. Two years earlier, almost to the day, I had taken Giulia to the psychiatric ward. Now she was pregnant. We laughed and kissed and felt so fully and wonderfully alive and in love.

I put her down and then began to think of the details. The first thing I thought of was how to tell our families, and I surprised myself by wanting it to be our secret, at least for a little while. I wanted this celebration for us.

"Let's not tell anyone yet," I said.

"Okay," Giulia agreed, then sat down to the computer and logged in to Skype. She hadn't stopped smiling. She was acting on autopilot with so much joy, saying one thing and then doing what she instinctively had always wanted to do once she got pregnant.

"I'm going to tell my parents now."

"You sure? It's the middle of the night in Italy," I pointed out, wishing she'd wait but not really caring. If she wanted to tell the world, she should.

"I know," Giulia responded, her smile somehow growing as the phone rang. After twelve rings, Suoc answered. "Mom, I'm pregnant!" Giulia yelled out, and instantly Suoc wasn't groggy anymore, she was wide-awake and crying and shaking Romeo to wake up, and we all started to cry together at this gift, this reward at the end of such a long and hard road.

Giulia was right: some happiness is so big that it needs to be shared immediately. After a few celebratory minutes, we told Suoc and Romeo to get back to sleep, and then we called my parents and did the same thing all over again.

Giulia loved her pregnancy. She had always commented on how beautiful pregnant women looked; now, she was the beautiful pregnant woman. I had been waiting to become a dad for years, but I had no idea that Giulia's pregnancy was going to renew her capacity to love herself. Giulia was in love with her life as a pregnant woman, and it showed. A few times a week she took a photo of herself in the mirror and posted it to Instagram to document her growing belly, the outfits she purchased to flatter it, the smile that grew in proportion to our developing baby. I joked with her about taking so many selfies, calling it "peak selfie time," but that was because I once again felt the need to moderate my feelings. Her year of illness had made me more cautious in my optimism, but her exuberance was intoxicating and I let my worries slide to the side. She was sleeping well, thriving at work—the changes Giulia had been suggesting were making noticeable improvements to the company's bottom line—and, most important, in love with herself.

The night before the official ultrasound to find out the sex of our child, we went to dinner with three of our friends, three brothers. We ate at our favorite hidden Chinese spot and then drove to Polly Ann Ice Cream to load up on milkshakes. Watching the three brothers order, Giulia leaned into me and said, "It's a boy. Seeing them, I can tell. We are having a boy, and we are going to have a lot of boys."

The next day the technician confirmed Giulia's suspicion: we were having a boy.

I met a surf couple named Zach and Sachi, who lived in the neighborhood and had recently gotten pregnant. Zach and I became close quickly, and I shared with him the history of Giulia's hospitalization after one of our surf sessions. That night, Sachi called me. Turned out she had been diagnosed with bipolar when she was in her early twenties. She wanted to meet Giulia. She had questions about being pregnant with bipolar disorder, and how her doctors would holistically support both conditions. She didn't know anyone else who had been in the psych ward and then got pregnant.

We all met at Trouble Coffee on Judah Street, a hip spot with fancy toast that was at the forefront of an evolution in our neighborhood. The Outer Sunset was becoming unexpectedly trendy, and Trouble was one of the first places to set the cooler tone.

Giulia and I got there first and sat at the parklet in front of the coffee shop to wait for Sachi and Zach.

"How are you feeling about meeting Sachi?" I asked.

"Fine," Giulia said. "I mean, I guess I'm fine. I'm not sure what we're gonna talk about."

"There's plenty to talk about," I said. "Sachi is hoping she can learn from your experience a bit."

"Yeah, but I don't even know her. This is serious stuff to talk about the first time you meet someone."

"Yeah, that's true," I said. "But you talk about this kind of stuff with Marie all the time."

"That's different. I met Marie in IOP. We had to talk about it there. I've never met Sachi before. I'm meeting her for the first time, and we both know that we've been hospitalized, but that's it."

"If you're not comfortable, we don't have to talk about it."

"I'll see how it feels when they're here," Giulia said.

They arrived, we all got something to drink, and then we walked the few blocks to the beach. Giulia and Sachi were tentative, not sure how to start.

"So, how long were you hospitalized?" Giulia asked, finally breaking the ice.

"Um, about two months," Sachi said. She was shy, speaking to the ground. It was obvious she hadn't told too many people about this. "I was in a padded room by myself for a month of it."

"Wow, I can't imagine," Giulia said. "I was in there twenty-three days and that felt like forever. How long ago?"

"I was nineteen when it happened, so a while ago. I've been on medication ever since."

"Wow," Giulia repeated. "And now you're pregnant. Congratulations, how exciting."

"Yup. Just like you," Sachi said. They were warming to each other. "How's the pregnancy going?"

"It's great, I love it."

"No worries?"

"No worries."

And it began. Zach and I drifted back to let them talk and have their own space for a friendship based in shared trauma. That first morning on the beach blossomed into regular coffee outings and phone calls. Giulia and Sachi became a part of each other's support systems. In the years since Sachi's diagnosis, she'd acquired strategies for managing her stress and her disease, which included medication, therapy, and exercise. Sachi had much to share with Giulia for how to approach the three as an interconnected plan for stability. As for Giulia, she was a veteran of Kaiser's bureaucratic health system, and she helped Sachi connect with a great OBGYN and navigate some of the decisions around her pregnancy and mental health.

Giulia's concept of friendship was expanding. She had always made friends who were connected to work, which was the biggest part of her life; in college, she'd hung with the other business school kids, and since she'd moved to San Francisco, her work friends were some of her closest.

Her job was losing its centrality to her identity, so her friendship circle was drifting as well. Far more crucial was that she had spent twenty-three days in the psych ward, and the following eight months suicidal, and had survived both. There were many more people out there who had been through something similar, and Giulia was going to find them only if she talked about it.

Giulia and I shared the morning before she took the bus across the city to her job. She was no longer on the scooter because of her pregnancy. It was the first symbolic gesture that we were doing things not just for ourselves any longer, but for a family of three, and that gesture trickled down throughout our lives. Most important, it underscored the value of taking care of each other. We were doing this not just for each other, but to create a safe and harmonious home for our child.

In the mornings, we practiced kindness with each other. I chatted with her as she made her morning coffee and asked her about how her day looked and what time she might get home. She asked about my writing and didn't judge when the assignments were slow in coming. Our small gestures were unromantic but felt even more important than romance, because they were our daily practice of showing each other that we cared.

An underlying question we had to address was what our plan was once the baby arrived. I think we both knew where we were drifting—Giulia headed off to the office each day, while I busied myself with work and home care—but we hadn't said anything officially. Giulia loved her work, and I wasn't ready to be back in a school full-time. I was still a bit hungover from my year of caregiving and wasn't ready to resume responsibility for a group of teenagers. Besides, I could easily fill my days at home with the responsibilities of the house.

The crib arrived, and we converted the guest room into the nursery. We kept our guest bed in the room but pushed it off into the corner, to make space for the crib and the green glider Giulia had bought off Craigslist. It was snug, but it all fit. Goose watched in apprehension at what we were doing.

With the furniture in place, we lay on the guest bed together and finalized what felt natural anyway: Giulia was going to return to work after her maternity leave, and I was going to be the stay-at-home dad. I could write during nap time, but my main focus would be on the baby.

Goose jumped up to be on the bed between us. He rested his head on Giulia's belly, and with our decision made, we lightly dozed in the new room and drifted in and out of anticipatory dreams of the days ahead.

———————

My phone rang five minutes into the soccer game. I played goalie on a soccer team in a men's league in the city, and we had an eight p.m. kickoff ten days before Giulia's due date. I told the guys I needed to keep my phone handy, just in case. I stashed the phone inside the goalpost, and when it started ringing I ran off the field screaming that it was my wife and we were going to have a baby. I didn't even pick up the phone, I just knew. I sprinted to the sideline, grabbed my duffel bag, and kept running to the car, still in cleats, shin guards, and goalie gloves. Giulia had texted: "My water broke in the bath. It's happening!!!"

I sped home, showered, gathered up our overnight bags, triple-checked the new car seat, and dropped Goose off at a friend's. I couldn't wait to meet our son.

Giulia labored for twenty-seven hours, and with the final push, our son arrived. I held on to Giulia and there was Jonas, opening and closing his eyes, a brown tuft of hair on his head. He cried out to the world, and the nurses handed him to Giulia, and he was on her chest, reaching for her. I leaned into them and wrapped my arms around my family.

I fell in love instantly. I had been dreaming about this person since I'd first met Giulia in college, but those dreams disappeared and were replaced as Jonas became real, his own majestic person. I had been wondering who he was going to be, and now he was here to show me, and I knew I would follow him wherever he took me.

That first night Giulia rested and the nurses left us alone, but I needed to tell Jonas all of the important things immediately, so I stayed awake and whispered to him that the world is beautiful, and it is because of you, Jonas, and for you, Jonas, and you must care for it like it will care for you.

Nothing mattered to me as much as Jonas. I wanted to know everything about him. He gave us hints and clues through his cries and yawns and squeaks, and I read up on every small detail about infancy. Giulia and I spent hours discussing minute decisions that felt essential: cloth or throwaway diapers, video or audio baby monitors, which baby carrier, stroller, car seat, white noise app to help him sleep—everything. I lost sense of all other priorities. I dropped all writing projects, I stopped surfing. Everything began and ended with Jonas.

My obsession with Jonas made it easier to not worry about Giulia. Of course she was awake in fits and starts throughout the night to feed him, and I was up at her side to help with the diaper change and to coax the two of them back to sleep, and Giulia wasn't showing any signs of anxiety. Being with Jonas was like freebasing love, and we both inhaled deeply.

Our birthing class teacher told us that our baby would show his personality right away, and I searched for clues to understand who Jonas was. He broke out of his swaddling blanket and was happier when we were wearing him and swaying him, rather than still. We nicknamed him the Man in Motion, because the easiest way to calm him down was to take him for a walk in the stroller or rock him.

I was eager to parent Jonas and did everything I could, except the obvious: nursing. But even there, I was so amped on my desire to nurture that I threw myself into supporting Giulia, to comical results. Giulia had several bouts of mastitis, and I learned techniques to massage her breasts before, during, and after nursing. We developed a routine: Giulia settled into the green glider, Jonas in her arms happily eating away, and I stood behind her, working my hands into the mix to soften up her pain. It was tender and a beautiful moment and utterly ridiculous. The first time Suoc walked in and saw it, she muttered to herself, "This is *not* how it happens in Italy," and walked out of the room shaking her head.

When Jonas woke up at night, I fumbled awake to change his diaper before Giulia nursed him. We put him between us in bed, and Giulia curled up to him and dozed as he ate. I loved co-sleeping. We huddled together like a family game of Tetris, Goose at our feet as well. I lost track of the day and time because they didn't matter. Everything that mattered to me was in my bed.

I tried to wake up to the sounds of Jonas before Giulia did, so he and I could have each other to ourselves for a few minutes, to giggle and stare and wonder. I promised him all the things we would do together, the surf trips and baseball games and science fair projects, but he kept pulling me back to where he was, just a little guy with a full diaper and an empty stomach. I felt like I was drowning in something that was too perfect to have a name.

Giulia held four-week-old Jonas in her lap, her arms wrapped tight around his arms so he wouldn't squirm too much with the sting of his vaccination shots. The first one startled him, and the second and third induced pure terror. But soon the nurse was cooing, "Good job, Jonas, you were such a brave boy. You both did great as well," she added to us with a smile.

We spent the rest of the day around the house, forgoing our usual afternoon walk on the beach. I had read that babies were often tired after their first vaccinations, but Jonas seemed fine. He ate heartily as usual and was asleep by seven p.m.

But at eleven p.m. Jonas awoke in hysterics, his little arms aflutter in panic. I sorted through the folds of his pajamas to check his injection sites, and they were a little bit red and a little bit swollen, but only a little. Giulia and I held him together, shushing and whispering and telling him how brave he was and that it was okay, the shots hurt a little bit but it was going to feel better soon.

But he couldn't calm down. He kept crying. We blasted the sound of white noise from the speakers, we rocked him, we swung him back and forth the way he loved, we fed him, we did all the tricks that usually worked, but he wouldn't stop. He had never cried like this. We felt helpless. It was just a little pain from a vaccine, yet I was shaking to see our son act so scared.

Finally, after forty-five minutes, he collapsed to sleep out of exhaustion. I fell into the couched, completely wrecked.

"I don't know if I can do this, Giulia," I said. "I love Jonas so much, but there's so much bad that can happen to him. I can't stop thinking about it. I just . . . can't . . . I don't know." Now I was the one crying uncontrollably. I didn't get to what we both were thinking. The psychosis he might have to face. The suicidal depression. Who knew if he was destined to suffer the way Giulia had?

"I'm so scared that I can't be strong enough for him," I said.

"You can be strong enough for him," Giulia said. "You love him. That's strong enough."

I wanted to believe her, but I sat on the couch for many hours, long after she had gone to bed, awake to listen for more scared crying, thinking about Giulia's parents and what they must have felt through her illness, happening on the other side of the world in another language. I couldn't push the thought out of my head that the cliché might be wrong. Maybe what doesn't kill you makes you weaker.

Giulia took the legally allowed six weeks of maternity leave but wasn't ready to return to work. She had been in her job over a year, and she loved the work and the people, but the company had started to implode with internal drama when she went on maternity leave. She requested an extension of her leave, and they demanded that she return immediately.

Within hours of hearing that the company wouldn't grant her the time she needed, Giulia was online looking for other opportunities. She submitted her résumé to a few spots before bedtime that night. The next day, she told her company she wouldn't be returning. She wanted to be at a place where she felt supported as a working mom.

In the third time in as many years, Giulia was offered a promising position at a major international fashion brand. It was going to be the biggest position she had held in her career, at the biggest company. She went from unsure about returning to work to ecstatic. Jonas had just turned five months old when she dressed herself up for another first day.

The first morning of work, her alarm rang before Jonas had woken up. Giulia woke Jonas to feed him a few minutes before she had to leave. She forced herself to smile as we stood in the doorway and waved her off. I turned back into the quiet house.

Now what?

First up, to make lunch. I spent an hour steaming and pureeing butternut squash while singing to Jonas as he jumped in his bouncer in the kitchen. I packed up a bag to go out for a beach walk and realized when we got there that I had forgotten the food. When his diaper was dirty, I had five extra diapers in the diaper bag but no wipes.

It was a bumpy start, but I got the hang of it. We developed several staple activities—walks on the beach, of course, but also outings to the California Academy of Sciences in Golden Gate Park and story time at the library. I met another stay-at-home dad at Ocean Beach and latched on to him. His daughter was a year older than Jonas, but we both had dogs who needed walking, and more than that, we needed company from the isolation of being a stay-at-home dad. Even in a progressive city like San Francisco, moms often waved from a distance or chatted for a few minutes, but they never came too close.

In the in-between moments, I confronted boredom, which I hadn't anticipated. I had dreamed of endless shots of adrenaline brought on by his laughter and pushing him in a swing, but those high points were punctuated with lengthy stretches of tedium. Jonas wasn't crawling or talking yet, and the whole day was a running monologue in baby talk. When I took him with me to the grocery store, I imagined taking him through the fruit section and holding up all the different foods for him to touch and smell as I described them. Instead, the grocery store became more of an annoying errand than it had ever been, and I impatiently rushed through the store with him strapped to my chest.

My time home with Jonas felt weirdly similar to staying home with Giulia for so many months. There were countless, obvious differences between taking care of a newborn and supporting a psychotic and suicidal wife, but the caregiving had a similar tone. I was bored a lot. I second-guessed everything I did. I filled the boredom with reading various opinions to make me second-guess even more. I worried. I doted. I celebrated tiny signs of progress. A single smile made the whole day of microscopic care feel worth it.

Parenting Jonas wasn't chock-full of life-changing moments of connection the way I had anticipated, but I settled into it, reassured that this was exactly what parenting was supposed to be. I was having an ordinary experience. And after such a disruptive, atypical year with Giulia, ordinary was something to celebrate.

I aspired to make my first-ever homemade lasagna, and Giulia came home one night delighted at the effort. She left me to myself in the kitchen so she could spend time in Jonas's world for the fleeting moments they had together, and then we put him down for the night. We ate the lasagna together after he fell asleep, and we both brought up how this new routine felt so natural and successful. Giulia seemed to be adjusting well to the new gig. During her lunch break, she pumped while FaceTiming Jonas and me.

We heartily ate the lasagna after our different but equally full days, but most of all we savored this delightful sense of normalcy.

After a lengthy discussion, we decided to baptize Jonas. I had always found appeal in a devout sense of faith, so I was on board from the get-go, as long as we committed to making it real and not just a ceremony for show. If we were going to baptize him, I wanted to raise him in a home of faith. Giulia's delusions of the Devil and God left her with uncertain feelings about the Catholic Church, but the church ran deep in her Italian roots, and she couldn't ignore the tug of tradition.

We called up a priest from the high school that Giulia had attended in New York City and scheduled Jonas's baptism for the day after a friend's wedding that would bring us out to the East Coast anyway. I bought a new suit, my first since high school that wasn't from a thrift store.

We walked through the streets of New York, and Giulia looked like her old self, the self-assured, sassy, quick-to-laugh woman I had first fallen in love with. It had been eight years since she had walked so confidently down Lexington Avenue toward her new job, but now, as a mother and breadwinner, her radiant smile was hard earned, which made it only more magnetic. She had lost all the medicine weight through breast-feeding Jonas, and her restored figure gave her even more confidence. I found myself uncontrollably attracted to her, the kind of giddy fascination that had me shyly grabbing at her hand when we walked down the streets together, something I hadn't felt in years.

It was a glorious autumn morning in New York for Jonas's baptism, and the city looked as sparkling and promising as Jonas and Giulia did. Jonas had three different outfits for the day, and we changed him from one to the next as the day unfolded—the formal baptism outfit, provided by Suoc; the fancy party outfit, selected by Giulia; and the comfortable party outfit, picked out by me. My brother Carl hosted the baptism party, and we lounged around, feasted, and mostly doted over Jonas. Midafternoon, I proudly took off my blazer, covered my shirt and tie with a raggedy sweatshirt, and fed Jonas a mash of banana and avocado.

In a quiet moment during the party, Suoc pulled me aside. "This is the happiest I have seen Giulia since before . . ." She didn't finish her sentence. She was still struggling with what to call the thing that had happened to her daughter.

"I know," I replied. "Me too."

"*È bello,*" she affirmed. Behind Suoc's dark glasses I could tell that she was fighting tears.

"*È molto bello,*" I agreed, putting my arm around her. Giulia bounced Jonas in her lap, and he smiled and giggled at her.

Very beautiful.

eight

October 2012

It took Giulia six weeks to go psychotic the first time. The second time, it took only four days.

The Monday after Jonas's baptism, a weekend that glowed with the promise of everything falling into its right place for us, Giulia went to a company-wide meeting run by the president. It lasted three hours. Giulia called me the minute it finished. Her workplace was going to do a massive restructuring, and she was panicking. She had been at the job for only three weeks. Last one hired, first one fired—that was her fear. Since I stayed home with Jonas, she was our sole source of income and, equally important, her employment provided our health insurance. We had managed to stay afloat financially through the time off, and to travel by the grace of our savings, but now we needed to get serious again about our finances, especially since we had Jonas. The pressure to keep her job was real, and she stressed under the burden.

The night after the meeting, Giulia was a nervous wreck. She tried desperately to figure out what the restructure meant and what role she would play in it. She barely slept that night.

The next night, in the relentless churn of her mind, she concluded that the restructure was built entirely around her team, and it was actually an elaborate test for her, to see if she could hack it at this new company. The only way to pass the test was to realize that it was a test—to look behind the curtain and see the restructure for what it was.

The following morning, she e-mailed her therapist and her psychiatrist, who both wanted to schedule an appointment as soon as possible. But Giulia didn't want to miss work or miss a moment at home with Jonas, so she didn't make appointments with either.

This all felt eerily similar. Giulia fixated on something unreasonable—a company-wide meeting that she misconstrued as being all about her. She worried frantically about the impression she was making at work, in person and through e-mails. She called me several times during the day—not to check in on Jonas, but to try to sort through the barrage of thoughts haunting her.

But I figured we could handle this anxiety. We knew what to look for. Missing sleep was the primary trigger. The third night of the new crisis, in the blur of the middle of the night, I tried to convince Giulia that she needed to prioritize seeing her psychiatrist, and she might need to take more than just the Prozac she was on. Maybe she needed to go back on lithium or antipsychotics.

She wouldn't hear it. She insisted that this wasn't going to be a repeat of the last time, that she was in the lucky 10 percent who never had relapses, and the more we talked about it, the faster and faster she spoke, and the more she acted as she had two years before, and the more I feared that maybe she was on the verge of a relapse.

We couldn't agree on what to do. We both knew that meeting with her doctor would put her on a path lined with orange vials of pills. I believed that was the way to get her some sleep and keep this crisis from escalating further. Giulia doubted the efficacy of the medicine and instead dreaded a return to a sluggishness that eroded her sense of self. We hadn't talked about what to do if she couldn't sleep again. And now, in her restlessness and agitation, we couldn't agree on anything.

I eventually fell asleep as I always did, and Giulia stayed awake, but by morning she agreed she had to see her doctor. She scheduled an appointment for Friday afternoon.

I e-mailed Giulia's parents. Giulia had already Skyped them, and they were worried by how she was talking. But through my fear, I remained optimistic. We were still early in the process. Giulia was getting anxious and losing sleep, but we had experience. We knew which medications worked and at what doses. She'd had only three sleepless nights, after all.

That Friday morning, after a fourth night of no sleep, Giulia was standing in our room when I woke up to the sounds of Jonas sometime after dawn.

"I figured it out, Mark!" she declared. "I know what's going on. Heaven is a place on earth. That's the test. That's why they are restructuring. It's because heaven is a place on earth. And I figured it out! I need to tell everyone that I figured it out, and what a great thing to figure out. Heaven is a place on earth! I need to tell them all this, and then they will let me stay."

I knew then that we couldn't wait for her afternoon appointment. She had to see a doctor immediately. I changed Jonas into a new diaper and dressed him, and Giulia fed him and cheerfully talked him through her delusions as he nursed. I Skyped her parents and told them we had to go to the hospital. They were wide-eyed with fear. "Mom, Dad, it's such an amazing world because heaven is a place on earth! We are so lucky!" Giulia shouted over my shoulder to them.

I braced myself to get Giulia in the car. Romeo wasn't here to help me carry her this time. I hated the thought of Jonas seeing his mom scream and lash out as she had before.

To my surprise, when I told Giulia that we needed to go see the doctor right away, to get the right medicine, she agreed. She helped me pack up a bag of bottles and diapers. I buckled Jonas into his car seat, and Giulia took her seat next to him in the back, as she had done since he was born. She smiled and made baby faces at him.

We looked like a family off to a picnic.

Instead, we went to the emergency room.

We drove the same route—19th Avenue, across the park on Park Presidio, and then a right on Geary, to the Kaiser emergency room—and I couldn't shake the memories: Giulia and her parents in the car, Giulia trembling in fear of the Devil, trying to jump out of the car while we were in Golden Gate Park.

This time around, Giulia was elated. As I drove, I played lullabies for Jonas, and Giulia sang along. In between songs, she told him over and over how good this world is and how lucky we were. I frequently glanced at them in the rearview mirror and saw Giulia cooing at him and tickling his cheeks. This was nothing like the psychosis from before.

The wait to see a doctor was only five minutes. I think the triage nurse saw us—a frenzied, babbling mother and a five-month-old baby—and put us high on the priority list.

The on-call psychiatrist began by asking Giulia what was going on.

"Oh, nothing's going on except that it's great," Giulia said. "I figured out that heaven is a place on earth, and I'm so glad I finally understand that. It makes everything so much better. What a great place for our son to live in. And for all of us. We're blessed, and protected, because this is heaven. It's all so amazing!"

The doctor looked at me with raised eyebrows. "Anything you want to add?"

"Yes, please," I said. "She hasn't slept well the last few days. I don't think she slept at all last night. Three years ago something similar happened and she went psychotic and was in the psych ward for twenty-three days. She was obsessed with the Devil that whole time, and then spent almost nine months depressed."

"Yes, I know, I read her file," the doctor said.

"Okay, good, so you know her history. Then I'm sure you'll agree that this looks so much better. Look at how positive she is being. It's also only been four days. I think she's probably starting to slide into psychosis, but we're catching this so early, and it's so positive, we just need to get her back on her antipsychotic medication, and I think it'll all be fine. We know that she responds well to Risperdal and lithium. Let's just get her back on those, and she should be fine in a few days, don't you think so?"

"I'm not sure, but thanks for the explanation to both of you," the doctor said. "Giulia, do you mind if I go and talk to Mark in the hallway for a few minutes? It'll be real quick."

"Of course," Giulia agreed. "Take all the time you need. Jonas and I are fine in here."

I stepped into the hallway, anticipating that we were going to talk about the logistics of having Giulia at home and the signs to watch out for.

In the hallway, the doctor's demeanor changed immediately, from patient and gentle to firm and matter-of-fact.

"Giulia cannot go home," she said. "She has to go to the psych ward."

"No, no, no, no way," I said. "We've done this before. I know what I'm doing. It's going to be fine. We just need Risperdal."

"No, you haven't done this before," she said. She wasn't cold, but she wasn't budging. "You have a five-month-old baby at home. Giulia can't be home like this. It could be unsafe."

"It's not unsafe, I promise you." I began to panic. "Giulia has never once tried to hurt anyone while psychotic or depressed. She would never hurt Jonas."

"We can't take any risks," the doctor said. "Besides, look at her. She's too unstable to be around your son."

"Don't take Giulia way from us," I begged. "We need her. Please don't take her away from us."

I had so much to think about at once but couldn't find a thought to land on, and they all rushed at me: the sadness, Jonas, the logistics, the fear, her parents, my parents, the wobbling of my knees, her job, our insurance. I thought I was going to throw up.

I had genuinely, and naively, believed that they were going to let me bring Giulia home. I had worked so hard to support the mental health process. I figured that somewhere in her medical file it must have been written, *Husband is an ally, you can trust him, he will follow whatever you say*, but they were still going to rip her away from us. She wasn't even that bad. I felt betrayed by the system I had worked so hard to support. It was as though the doctor were telling me that I couldn't handle this, that's why Giulia had to go to the psych ward. I felt like I was betraying Giulia.

The doctor put her arm on my shoulder. I was crying by now, loudly, out of control.

"I'm a mom, too, Mark," she said to me in almost a whisper. "I would never want to take a mother from her child. But I can't let Giulia go home in this condition. I can't do it as a professional, but most of all I can't let it happen as a mother. This isn't good for your baby."

There was nothing I could say to convince her. I looked into her eyes in defeat. "How long is she going to be in there this time?" I knew that there was no way she could answer.

"I don't know," she said. "But we have to go tell Giulia."

I nodded. We went back in the room.

Giulia was still all smiles. She had Jonas in his arms, and the two were deadlocked in love with each other.

"Are you okay, Mark?" she asked when she saw me. "Are you crying?"

I forced a smile as I walked up to her and Jonas. "I'm okay," I lied.

"Giulia, you're going to have to go to the hospital," the doctor said. "Just like you did a few years ago. I don't know what hospital, I have to call and find a bed for you. But that's the plan."

Giulia looked at her, then back at me, and then at the doctor again. Remarkably, the news didn't upset her.

"Okay, if that's part of God's plan, then that's okay," Giulia said.

"In the hospital, they are going to give you antipsychotics," the doctor said. "Those medications are not good for Jonas, so you won't be able to breast-feed him while you're taking those medicines." This was another sucker punch.

The doctor was too upset herself to sound professional. "Do

you want to feed Jonas one more time?" she asked, her voice quivering.

"Yes, of course I want to," Giulia answered. "I love Jonas." She was so calm and unafraid. I began to cry again. "It's okay, Mark," she said to me. "Heaven is a place on earth."

The doctor quietly left our room and began the process of finding a place for Giulia. On the way out, she encouraged me to leave after Giulia finished feeding Jonas. He had already been in the hospital long enough, she said, and had seen enough with his impressionable eyes. Someone would call me once they knew where Giulia would be going.

Giulia pulled Jonas to her breast and told him how wonderful everything was as he nursed. She told him she had to go away, but that it was going to be okay, and that she loved him, and that Daddy would take good care of him.

By the time Giulia finished nursing, the doctor had returned. She took Jonas out of Giulia's arms and handed him to me, and we drove away.

I couldn't bear to sit in the house, so I packed up Goose, Jonas, and our beach gear and went to the beach. I always went to the beach for answers.

I set up the collapsible tent to shade Jonas and propped him up on a blanket surrounded by toys. Goose dug at rocks in the shallow water. I walked away from them. I didn't want Jonas to hear me cry more than he already had. I sat down fifty feet away and dug at the sand around my toes and wailed, grieving for Giulia yet again.

Ten minutes later, I collected myself and walked back to Jonas. As I approached him, I couldn't make out the difference between what was a memory and what was happening now. There was the beach day three years ago when I took a picture of Giulia and told her that she had beaten this thing. And only a few days ago I was out on the beach just like this, as a normal stay-at-home-dad— Jonas under the tent, Goose digging at rocks, me waiting for Giulia's FaceTime from work.

And then there was now. Giulia wasn't going to FaceTime, and she wasn't coming home that night. I was terrified of the present, so I kept trying to think I was somewhere in the past. I had supported Giulia when it was just the two of us. I had managed to get the swing of parenting. But I didn't know if I could care for both, Jonas and Giulia, simultaneously.

I slid under the tent and sat beside Jonas. I didn't say anything to him because I didn't know what to say. He was five months old. What do five-month-old infants even understand? I wanted to assure him that it was going to be okay, but I didn't honestly know. I wanted to explain to him that Mommy would be back, but I didn't know how long she would be gone. I wanted to tell him that I loved him so much and promised to protect him. But could I really protect him?

Jonas pawed at me and rattled and gnawed on his toys while I watched silently.

Then my phone rang. It was Suoc.

"What happened?" she asked.

"It's done," I said. "They kept her. She is going back."

Suoc erupted, wailing. We didn't stay on the phone long. She said she would come to California as soon as she could and then hung up.

Jonas and I returned to our silence. I lost track of time: how long since he had eaten or napped or how long since I had eaten.

My phone rang again. This time it was Jaimal, a surf buddy who lived just over the dunes from where Jonas and I now sat. "Do you want to catch some waves?" he asked. I hadn't even noticed the surf conditions. I told him that I had just dropped Giulia off at the ER.

Ten minutes later, Jaimal came running down the dunes toward us. He hugged me and sat under the tent with Jonas. I stood to pace outside.

"I still don't know what hospital she's at," I said in agitation. I checked the time: four p.m. We had left Giulia at the hospital three hours before.

"They'll call you when they know," Jaimal said.

"I hope it's not the same one as last time," I said. "And that she takes her medicine right away, and we don't lose those seventy-two hours like we did last time." Jaimal knew many of the details of Giulia's first episode from our frequent talks in and out of the water.

I rattled off questions: which hospital, how long would she be in there, who would be her case manager. I didn't want to repeat all the hiccups of her previous hospitalization.

When I paused, Jaimal asked, "What about Jonas, Mark? I know you're worried about Giulia. Of course you are, we all are. But you've got this beautiful little boy here."

Jaimal shifted his attention to Jonas. "You're such a sweet little boy, Jonas, you're surrounded by love, aren't you?" I hadn't spoken directly to Jonas since we got to the beach. "Let's talk about him for a few minutes."

Jaimal was right. Last time around I put all my focus on Giulia, abandoning every other part of my identity. I had stopped being a brother, son, friend, teacher—which was okay, sort of. But I couldn't stop being a father.

Jaimal and I sorted through the details. I had a few days' worth of frozen breast milk. I would go half breast milk, half formula, until we ran out of milk, then entirely formula. Jaimal's mother-in-law was in town to visit, and his son, Kai, was only a few months older than Jonas. I could drop Jonas at their house whenever I needed to. They would be unconditional babysitters as I adjusted. How lucky to have a friend like that.

The hospital finally called. They had found a bed for Giulia at a hospital south of the city, on the Peninsula, a full hour away from our house. Jaimal helped me pack up all of our beach stuff. I took Jonas home, collected his bottles, diapers, and onesies, and then dropped him at Jaimal's.

Then I drove to the hospital.

The drive took seventy-five minutes, not sixty. I was fuming by the time I arrived. How could they have sent her to a hospital so far away?

I forgot about the long drive once I set foot on the grounds. This was a nicer hospital, much nicer. It felt almost like a country club. There was still a locked door, and you had to call and be buzzed in to enter. Once inside the ward, there was another check-in desk, to make sure you weren't bringing in anything that wasn't permitted. Those features were never going to change. But that's where the similarities ended. You called from the main reception of the hospital, so there was no claustrophobic, glassed-in waiting room. Instead, when you got to the door, they let you in, and you were there.

The main door opened into the non-acute section of the psych ward, where patients milled about freely, reading magazines, playing board games, watching TV. Large glass-panel sliding doors led to an expansive patio, which opened onto a big grass field. Diagonally from the entrance was a long hallway with all the bedrooms. The hospital had done an impressive job of making the place feel welcoming.

Giulia was in the acute section of the psych ward.

The two sections were divided by a glass door. Giulia's side felt more like a hospital. There was a large central room surrounded by single-occupancy bedrooms for the patients. The lounge was more cluttered, there were IVs on wheels around the perimeter. But even this side had a door out to a patio garden that was open all day long. Giulia's bedroom window offered views of trees and flowers. There were no bars on the windows.

Visiting hours were set: seven to eight thirty on weeknights, with the addition of twelve to one p.m. on the weekends, just like the first hospital. But I never had to follow those rules. When I first called and explained our situation—hour-long drive, young baby at home—the staff made a note in Giulia's file that gave me the freedom to visit whenever I wanted.

When I was allowed through the second set of doors, the ones that led to the acute section, I encountered Giulia with a nurse. "Mark, they're trying to kill me again with these medications. Why do they always try to kill me when I'm in the hospital?"

"They're not trying to kill you, honey," I said. "These medicines will help you, just like they helped you before."

The nurse smiled as Giulia introduced me. "You must be Mark," she said. "And I'm sure that Jonas is at home in good hands," she added for Giulia's benefit. "Giulia has been talking about you both nonstop since she arrived."

I saw over the nurse's shoulder the familiar whiteboard where patients were assigned to nurses. Giulia's name was on the board, along with another patient's, under the name of one of the nurses. Only two patients. At her past hospital, her nurses were often responsible for ten patients at a time.

Giulia shrugged in agreement at what her nurse said but then returned to her worry about the medicine. "Mark, please, you know how this medicine makes me fat and lazy and sluggish. They are trying to kill me. Please, I don't want to take it."

We were back. It was terrifying, exasperating, and overwhelming, but it was also familiar. I was flooded with a sense of purpose that I knew well. While Giulia's year of psychosis and depression had been miserable, we had rarely fought during that period. We were so focused on survival that the only option was to make it through the crisis. And now we were back, and it felt unexpectedly meaningful to face the challenge of being her protector again.

"What happens if she doesn't take the medicine?" I asked the nurse.

"Oh, well, we'll just come back in a little bit and see if she's ready then," the nurse said back. "We understand she doesn't like the medication, but it's going to be so critical to help her get back home to you guys, and so I'll just keep checking back in until she's finally ready."

She didn't admit that since Giulia was on a 5150, she had seventy-two hours to reject all medicine. That would come up later, only if it needed to, but I was focused solely on getting her to take the medication. It had been only four days of difficult sleep for Giulia. Another three days of unmedicated sleeplessness felt like a lifetime lost to deeper psychosis.

I stayed with Giulia, and helped her settle in, and talked to her, and patiently coaxed her into taking her medicine. It took almost two hours. But she took both the Risperdal and the lithium. She was now back on the magic combination that had worked the first time.

I stayed for a few hours, much longer than I had anticipated. It was after dark by the time I got in my car to drive home and almost eleven p.m. when I arrived at Jaimal's house an hour later. I hadn't eaten anything since the night before. He and his wife were already asleep. They had left the door unlocked for me and some food on the table. I scarfed down my first meal of the day and then delicately lifted Jonas out of the pack'n play they had put him in. Gently, slowly, trying not to wake him, I took him down to the car, into his car seat, and home to his own bed.

Giulia's doctor, Dr. Franklin, was accessible and willing to spend a lot of time on the phone with me. On the first day she had a long conversation with Giulia's IOP doctor, who then called me after their consultation. The two agreed that lithium and Risperdal had good potential to stop Giulia's slide.

But the psychosis didn't fade. Instead, it deepened.

Even on a strong dose of Risperdal, Giulia somehow slipped further and further into her delusions, which became increasingly troubling. She continued to say endlessly that "heaven is a place on earth," but it was no longer reassuring to her. It left her disoriented as to who was alive and who was dead.

Her mantra littered the psych ward. The erasable whiteboard was covered with it, every available blank spot filled in with the phrase. The nurse told me it took her hours each day to fill out the whiteboard. She wrote it on all of her art projects from the group therapy art sessions.

For the first few days when I visited, Giulia took me outside to the garden patio as soon as I arrived. She lay on her back and stroked the grass with her arms, as if to reassure herself that steady ground was still beneath her. She was calm and thoughtful but profoundly confused, with questions that she rarely voiced but desperately wanted answers to. We didn't speak much. She knew that I couldn't give her the answers she needed.

She gathered leaves from the garden and scattered them throughout her room. When I walked in, they crunched underfoot. Giulia also piled leaves on the few flat surfaces in her room—her bed, her one shelf for clothes, her one small bedside chest for storage. She'd often scoop up a pile of the leaves and inhale, as if the smell might anchor her thoughts against floating away.

I brought Giulia's breast pump to the hospital under doctor's orders, and Giulia began the slow process of weaning herself off producing milk. She had to pump and dump, since her milk was no longer suitable for Jonas, but she never said a word about it to me. She also rarely asked about Jonas when I visited. He was all I wanted to talk about, but Giulia wasn't interested when I tried.

Of the many improvements of this hospital, one that left me puzzled was that the acute section of the psych ward had a computer, with Internet access. On Giulia's first night she logged in to her work e-mail and wrote an e-mail to her boss, telling her boss how much she loved her and to not worry, heaven was a place on earth. Giulia's boss promptly retrieved my e-mail address from Giulia's emergency contact card and forwarded it to me, along with a litany of her own questions.

Giulia still resented how I had quit her job for her three years earlier, so I called Giulia's social worker when her boss forwarded me the note. The social worker said she would handle all communication with Giulia's work to ensure that Giulia's privacy was protected and that she would be supported by her company. It would also take me out of the equation of dealing with work. The hospital, the doctor, and now the social worker—they all gave me a glimmer of hope that this time around would be so much different.

Suoc arrived on Giulia's third day in the hospital, and my mom arrived the day after. We spent a week in the house, all four of us—two grandmothers sharing the master bedroom, while I slept in Jonas's room on the guest bed. They watched him together as I made my daily pilgrimage to the hospital, but I insisted on sleeping in his room at night so that when he woke up crying for his nighttime feeding, I could be the one providing it to him.

After a week of all of us in the house, we finalized a schedule where the moms would rotate living at our house for a week, while the other returned back home. Suoc wouldn't fly all the way back to Italy but would instead go to New York. My mom would be commuting weekly between San Francisco and Japan. These were big requests, expensive requests, but they both were up for it.

I discovered a fantastic playground only a few blocks from the hospital in Mountain View, so I began to bring Jonas and whichever mom was in town down to the hospital. I was desperate for Giulia to see Jonas. We scheduled the drives around his nap times. If Giulia wasn't up for the visit, he could go to the park with Grandma. It became our daily outing—a long drive down to I-280 while Jonas had his midmorning nap, a few hours down in the sun at the playground with a packed lunch, and then the drive back for the early afternoon nap.

Giulia knew that Jonas was only a few blocks away at a park and that he would love to see her, but she always said no. She didn't explain why. It crushed me. Jonas needed his mom, and she needed him. That felt obvious to me. I even hoped a reunion might jump-start her ascent out of psychosis.

After a week in the hospital, her doctor intervened. She believed Giulia was suffering from postpartum psychosis, and Giulia and Jonas needed to see each other as a part of Giulia's recovery.

The plan to get Giulia and Jonas in the same room was baroque in its complexity. Children were not allowed in the acute section of the psych ward; Giulia was not allowed out of the acute section of the psych ward. There was a small office space that connected through the back of the nurses' station that was technically in both sides of the psych ward, since it had doors that opened to both. Giulia's doctor reserved that room for our visit so that no rules were broken but mother and child could still be together.

I went into the hospital first, to make sure that everything was in place and that Giulia was still okay with the idea. She paced in her room and smiled at me briefly. She had a few leaves in her left hand and in her right hand a collage of family pictures, which she had cut up from a stack that I had printed out and brought to her a few days into her stay. I texted Suoc, who was waiting in the car with Jonas.

Then, along with Giulia, two nurses, the doctor, and a burly orderly in case things somehow got out of hand, I waited. There was nowhere to sit. After a few minutes, Suoc knocked and then slowly rolled Jonas into the room in his stroller.

I stood next to Giulia and watched Jonas's face light up to see his mom. He reached out to her and smiled as she walked across the room to meet him. She dropped her leaves and collage, reached into the stroller to unlock his straps, and then lifted him into her arms. She had tears in her eyes—everyone did.

Jonas didn't know where we were. He didn't know that anything was wrong with Giulia. He simply knew that he was back with his mom, where he wanted to be, and I felt so relieved.

Giulia squatted down to pick up the collage she had made for Jonas—several of his pictures, along with a brightly colored portrait of our family that Giulia had drawn—and gave it to him.

"I love you, Jonas," she told him. "I'll be home soon. I'm being strong in here, and I'll be home soon." He cooed in response. It was the saddest happy moment of my life.

I felt an immense burden lifted to see Giulia and Jonas together, but it lasted barely a minute. Giulia looked back at me with panic in her face. She held Jonas out, offering him back to my care, but I didn't want this to end yet. It was too quick. I hesitated, to prolong the reunion. If we had to be in the psych ward, let us at least be there together. But Giulia held Jonas even farther out. Now I felt panic, too, so I scooped Jonas back into my own arms, where he comfortably settled in.

"That's enough for now," Giulia said, and she picked up her leaves and then walked out. The visit was over.

At our first family meeting, there was no uncertainty around Giulia's diagnosis. "Bipolar disorder," her doctor declared. "It's clear. That's why the lithium worked. She's probably going to have to stay on lithium for the rest of her life."

Bipolar disorder I, to be more specific, is characterized by soaring highs and crippling lows. Giulia somehow experienced both as negatives. Her highs were not the freewheeling spending and partying that many encounter in mania. Her mania fast-tracked directly into psychosis, with its paranoia and delusions.

The one advantage to Giulia's unpleasant mania was that it made the prognosis of caring for the disease more manageable. Those who experience mania as euphoric are loath to treat it. Yes, they hate the depression, but they often stop their own medication because they miss the highs of the mania. But Giulia's mania was terrifying, which made both manifestations of her bipolar undesirable. Dr. Franklin suspected it wouldn't be hard to convince Giulia that she would need to stay on her medication to avoid her highs and her lows.

The medical team suspected that Giulia's relapse into mania was amplified by Prozac. When she was on lithium, the Prozac was a godsend. Without lithium, Prozac probably sped up the onset of the mania.

This time around, the doctors resorted to a more traditional antipsychotic medication called Haldol, a drug far less gentle than Risperdal but also one that is especially effective in treating postpartum psychosis. The medical team wanted to clear up Giulia's psychosis as quickly as possible so she could get home to Jonas, so they brought out the big guns of Haldol.

Our second family meeting was on Halloween. Dr. Franklin was dressed up like a sock-hop girl from the movie *Grease*, which reminded me that I didn't have any plans for what to do that night for Jonas. Sure, he was six months old and wouldn't have any idea what was going on, but it was his first Halloween, and I wasn't going to miss taking him to his first trick or treat. I met Dr. Franklin in the same small conference room where Giulia had seen Jonas, and we waited for a nurse to retrieve Giulia.

When Giulia shuffled into the room, I was shocked. Her eyes were barely open. Her mouth hung agape, drool pouring out of the sides.

I reached out for her hand and she slowly turned to face me. "Good to see you, Giulia." I smiled, reverting back to my rehearsed mode for visiting her in the psych ward. She didn't say anything in response.

She settled slowly into the chair. This was awful. Inhumane, even. Giulia was barely aware. Dr. Franklin asked her questions; Giulia didn't respond. Her eyes didn't blink or search. She stayed in the room for five minutes and then got up to leave. I followed her as she stumbled to her room and lay down in her bed. Then I returned to the meeting, fuming.

"What the fuck is going on?" I said. "Giulia looks terrible. Is this the fucking Haldol?"

"Uh, maybe," the doctor said, squirming. She appeared shocked and even a bit embarrassed, like when you have to introduce your child to strangers and they pick that moment to throw a tantrum. She clearly hadn't seen Giulia yet today and had no idea that she would be in this condition. "I think she's on too big of a dose. We'll back off the dosage immediately. But I still think this is a good drug for the situation."

"Are you sure? She looked horrible."

"I'm sure."

I returned to Giulia's room to say good-bye. She was asleep on the bed. I sat next to her and watched her breathe. I wanted to go home but wanted to stay, too. When I was with Jonas, I worried about Giulia. When I was in the hospital, I worried about Jonas. I didn't know who I was anymore—a husband or a father? The two roles pulled me in separate directions, and I didn't know how to go in both places without being torn in half.

We repeated our policy that if Giulia wanted me to visit, she would call and invite me. On a Saturday morning, she called and said she didn't want any visitors that day.

"Are you sure?" I asked.

"Yes, I'm sure," she said.

"Positive?" I asked again. I hadn't missed a day yet.

"Yes, I'm sure, Mark. I don't want you to visit today."

I listened to her. It was a clear fall Saturday morning, and the whole day lay ahead of us, the first day in over two weeks that wouldn't revolve around visiting Giulia. I called up Cas and Leslie and asked if we could come and visit for an overnight. They dropped everything and said absolutely. My mom was in town, and it would be her first time sleeping over at their house.

We arrived at their house in Point Reyes and went first to the chickens, as always, which Jonas loved, and futzed around in their garden for a bit, and then we stuffed our feet into knee-high wader boots for a walk in the swampy marsh behind their house. I strapped Jonas to my chest in the BabyBjörn, and we waded through the high grass. For the first time since Giulia had been admitted to the hospital, I focused on what was right in front of me: Jonas, my mom, my best friends, the natural world. With each step, I felt my mind slowing and untangling.

And then my phone rang. It was Giulia.

"Mark, can you please come visit me? I really need to see you," she said.

"Uh, I thought you didn't want me to visit today?" I said nervously.

"No, I really need to see you today, Mark," she said. "Please, I need to see you."

I stopped walking, and everyone else stopped to hear my side of the conversation. "But Giulia, you said that you didn't want me to visit," I repeated. Point Reyes was ninety minutes north of the city, and the hospital was an hour south of it. I was two and a half hours away from the hospital.

"Please, Mark, please come visit," she begged. "Please visit today."

I immediately began to think of possible ways to get down there. Maybe I could leave Jonas and my mom here to spend the day with Cas and Leslie. I could drive down to see Giulia and then drive back and be in Point Reyes by dinner, sleep over as planned, and then head back in the morning.

Cas stopped next to me. He could see in my face that I was trying to come up with a plan to go and visit Giulia, even if it meant I was going to spend upward of five hours in the car.

"No," he mouthed. "No."

Leslie did the same. My mom was more forceful. "You need a break," she whispered. "She said no visitors. You listened to her." I looked back at them, ashamed. I was so embarrassed, even though it was my own mom and my closest friends, for them to see our family like this.

"Giulia, I'm sorry, but I can't come and visit today." I didn't want to tell her that we were in Point Reyes, one of our favorite places to go together, while she was locked up in the psych world. "You told me not to, so I've already made playdates for Jonas," I lied. "I can't change the schedule."

Giulia started crying on the other end of the line. "Please, Mark, please come visit me."

"I'm so sorry, Giulia, I can't do it today. You told me not to visit, and so I am not visiting."

"Fine. Thanks, Mark," she said angrily, and hung up.

Cas looked at me and took a deep breath. He put his arm around my shoulder. "It's okay, Mark."

He reached into the back pocket of his jeans, pulled out a small paperback book, and offered it to me. "There might be another way," he said gently.

The book, R. D. Laing's *The Divided Self: An Existential Study in Sanity and Madness*, was my introduction to antipsychiatry.

I didn't read the book that day. I waited until we got home the next day, and I went out to the beach with Goose as Jonas napped and my mom cleaned the house.

The book was published in 1960, when Laing was just thirty-three years old. At that point, the mental health profession had taken a strong turn away from psychotherapy toward medication as the treatment for mental illness. Laing hated the shift. He hated the premise that psychosis was a disease that needed to be cured. He wrote, "The cracked mind of the schizophrenic may *let in* light which does not enter the intact minds of many sane people whose minds are closed."

I grimaced at this thought. What light was Giulia's mind letting in? That she was the Devil? That heaven was a place on earth?

I flipped ahead a few pages, to read where Laing started arguing that the construction of mental illness is demeaning, even dehumanizing, and is all part of a power grab by the supposed normals to keep psychotics under control. After I read, "I have never known a schizophrenic who could say he was loved," I threw down the book in disgust. How could anyone say that I didn't love Giulia? I had done everything I possibly could to support her.

But Laing would not have seen me that way. In his construction, patients are good, doctors are bad, and family members botch things up by listening to physicians and becoming bumbling accomplices in the crime of psychiatry. I was therefore an accessory, a conspiring force to make Giulia take medication that made her distant, unhappy, and slow. I justified that the meds kept her alive, so everything else was secondary. I had never doubted the rightness of my motives. I'd cast myself in the role of Giulia's self-effacing caregiver—not a saint, but definitely a guy working on the side of good. Laing made me feel like I was her tormentor.

I called Cas from the dunes.

"Cas, what the hell were you thinking with this book? Do you have any idea how it feels to read this shit? The last thing I need right now is to be told that I'm fucking everything up and making it worse by putting Giulia in the hospital. Do you have any idea of how stressful this is?"

Cas was patient. He knew me well and had anticipated this reaction. "Mark, I'm only trying to show you that there might be another way," he said.

"What does that even mean, 'another way'?" I demanded.

"It means that maybe the hospital isn't the best place for Giulia," he said, choosing his words carefully. "Maybe taking all of these pills isn't the way for her to get better. Maybe it is, but maybe it isn't. At least consider that there are other options."

"If she's not in the hospital, what else am I supposed to do?" I yelled. "You think I can take care of her by myself with Jonas in the house? As she rants and raves about heaven being a place on earth and stays up all night? Are you fucking kidding me?"

Cas stopped me there and got very firm with his tone. "Mark, if you were to slip over a cliff, and all you had was one branch to hold on to, you would hold on to that branch for dear life. But you might be ignoring the other things that are there for you to grab on to, things which are out of your range of sight, things which others must show you."

"What the fuck does that even mean?" I usually loved Cas's parables, but I wasn't in the mood. "What does Laing say I should be doing, Cas? If I'm doing it all so wrong, and I'm incapable of loving Giulia, then what should I be doing?"

Cas returned to his initial gentleness. "I don't know the answer to that," he said. "I will never know. The answer is not up to me. It's up to you and Giulia."

"Well, I can't exactly talk to Giulia about that right now." I slammed down the phone.

Giulia's days in the psych ward added up. Before I knew it, we exceeded twenty-three days and were now in unchartered territory. Giulia was looking better, but she was easily irritated, and she still had occasional slips into delusional thinking. On day twenty-five, they moved her out of the acute section to the non-acute section. On the other side, she had more freedom to move around, more access to the outdoors, more activities, and substantially more patients to talk to. She made a few friends, one in particular named Violet. Giulia and Violet spent hours each day walking the halls together, arm in arm, listening to an old iPod that the hospital let them borrow, an earbud apiece, Coldplay's "Yellow" on repeat the entire time.

The question of Jonas visiting became more pressing, since he was allowed on the non-acute side of the ward. Giulia's doctor was strongly in favor of it. She even arranged for a back room to be cleaned out so the three of us could have some privacy. I asked Giulia all the time if I could bring Jonas to the hospital. "I don't want him seeing me in this place," she said day after day. "I just want to get the hell out of here and I will see him at home."

Dr. Franklin and I kept pushing, and Giulia relented. Suoc, Jonas, and I climbed into the car with a couple of bags of toys and went to visit Giulia.

In the back room we laid out a blanket, plopped Jonas on it, and scattered toys to coax him to crawl. He was so active with his rolling and sitting up, and I guessed that he was going to be crawling any day now. I so badly hoped that he would do it here, in the hospital, in front of Giulia.

The first visit went well and lacked the drama of the brief visit when Giulia was still in the acute section. Giulia agreed to another visit a few days later. The visits with Jonas were a welcome relief from my solo trips. Giulia and I had run out of things to say, just like before. Thankfully, she wasn't obsessively trying to explain her delusions to me during our visits anymore. Instead, her focus was entirely about coming home. It became the only thing she wanted to talk about, as if I had control over it. I couldn't give her concrete answers, which made her more impatient. Our visits alone were unbearably tense.

"I want to get out of here," she'd say. "When can I come home?"

"When the doctor says you're ready," I'd respond.

"Why do I have to wait for their permission? I want to go home. I should be able to say when I go home. This is ridiculous."

"I want you to come home, too. But we have to wait for the okay from the doctor."

Jonas's presence changed everything; he became the entertainment and conversation. We watched him, and played with him, and urged him to crawl for that toy that was out of his reach, and cheered him on, and marveled at the amazing little person we had made together.

I loved the visits with Jonas, but I also hated them. I hated that our son was a visitor at the psych ward on the day he turned six months old. I hated that Giulia was tentative and scared of how to behave around our son. I hated that these visits were the only way to have my family together.

Jonas did not learn to crawl in the hospital. He learned at Ocean Beach. He saw a sand dollar and crawled over to it. Suoc and I hooted and hollered together and took pictures and videos.

But I didn't tell Giulia. We were only a few days away from Thanksgiving. I thought there was nothing wrong with a little white lie, so why not pretend that Jonas didn't first crawl until he was there in the hospital with her, so she could experience the same pride that I felt?

I called the hospital to see if it was okay for us to bring food for Thanksgiving, and a lot of it, to share with patients and staff, and they said that would be fine.

Suoc and I spent Thanksgiving Day cooking jambalaya with shrimp, chicken, and sausage, focaccia bread, and cookies.

It took three round trips from the car to the psych ward to unload all the food, and each trip I had to buzz the bell to be let in and have the staff check to make sure that what I had with me was safe. We set up the food in our back room, and Giulia walked around the halls and invited everyone to come and eat.

Giulia sat with Jonas in her lap as people came and left. I tried to introduce myself to people, but no one wanted to talk. They just wanted a heaping plate of food and then to get out of there.

After we finished eating, I proposed that we go around the room and say what we were grateful for.

"I'm grateful for Giulia, Jonas, and Suoc," I said. "I know that none of us wants to spend Thanksgiving here, but at least we are together. Family is what matters most."

Suoc went next. "I'm thankful for Giulia, Jonas, and Mark," she said.

Then it was Giulia's turn.

"I can't think of anything I'm grateful for," she said.

"Nothing?" I asked.

"Nothing," she repeated.

We sat in silence, the air sucked out of the room, and then almost on cue, Jonas raced across the ground, crawling for a toy, the execution of my grand plan.

"Look at that," Giulia said blandly. "Jonas is crawling." She barely moved, none of the cheering or dancing that Suoc and I had shared.

I abandoned the ruse. She was still too far gone and too medicated to experience these milestones with Jonas. "Yup," I said. "He started a few days ago. He's getting so fast already. Our little Man in Motion."

We watched him go from toy to toy, his peals of laughter bringing us occasional smiles, but everything felt wrong. The jambalaya was too spicy, the bread burned on the bottom. We weren't supposed to be here. It was all so wrong. We all felt it, except for Jonas, who kept crawling faster and faster and squealing in delight with himself.

nine

November 2012

———

We had our final family meeting on Giulia's thirty-second day in the hospital. The full team gathered—Giulia, Dr. Franklin, two nurses, her case manager, and me. Giulia was the first to speak.

"I want to come home to my son and my life. Enough of this. Let me out of here." It was a short, forceful declaration. She sat back, crossed her arms, and waited for a response.

"We understand that, Giulia," Dr. Franklin said. "We've understood that for over a week now. It is the only thing you talk about anymore."

"Well, of course it is," Giulia responded. "You get to go home each night. I don't."

As I sat and listened, I thought of Cas's "other way." How would I feel if I had been locked away from my family for so long, unable to leave on my own terms? Maybe Giulia's irritation was a reasonable reaction to her situation and not a sign that she was "crazy."

"You're right, we do go home each night," Dr. Franklin said. "But we're concerned by how irritable you are about this. You are so impatient about going home and exhibit a lot of anger about it. That makes us worried."

"I'm not irritable," Giulia said with obvious irritation.

One of the nurses chimed in. "Giulia, you screamed at me today because I said I didn't know when you were going home. That's not a nice way to treat people."

Dr. Franklin added, "That kind of agitation has us worried about Jonas. What happens if he does something that doesn't feel right to you, like he wakes up crying in the middle of the night? Are you going to be angry with him?"

Giulia sat sullenly, refusing to respond, so I interjected, after staying silent for what felt like an eternity.

"Have we considered that maybe Giulia's agitation isn't part of psychosis or mania? She's been in here a long time. Maybe it makes sense that she's so frustrated."

I had never rebelled against the doctors before, and I was scared to do it now, but Laing had gotten under my skin.

Dr. Franklin sighed. She could see that our long-standing alliance was cracking.

"Yes, I hear what you're both saying." She sounded defeated. "Which gets to the point of this meeting. We're here to talk about discharge."

Giulia squealed with delight.

"We believe that Giulia can go home," Dr. Franklin said. There was no joy in her voice. She almost sounded as if she were regretting the words as she said them. "Tomorrow."

Giulia jumped out of her chair and into my lap for a hug.

"But we are releasing you Against Medical Advice, Giulia," Dr. Franklin said, interrupting the celebration. "It will say this in your medical file. We are letting you go home, but we don't think that you're fully ready for it. We simply recognize that the hospital is no longer doing you good, but we worry about the strains that the circumstances will put on your husband and your son."

"Against Medical Advice . . . does that mean you're worried about Jonas's safety or something?" I asked. "Because don't forget that I'm not working, so I'll be home all day with Giulia and Jonas. And we also still have help. Giulia's mom is in town, and my mom gets here tomorrow."

"Yes, I know," Dr. Franklin said. "We aren't worried about his safety. Giulia wouldn't be going home if it was a matter of safety. We've seen Giulia enough to not see her as a threat to people. But still. She is in a fragile state and it's asking a lot for her to be taking care of a young child. We think she needs more time to settle down, but we can see that she's not going to listen to that request. That's why this is an AMA discharge." She was clearly unhappy.

It was a tremendous relief to know she was coming home. I was thoroughly fatigued by driving an hour in each direction to visit Giulia, only to be bombarded for an hour about why I wasn't fighting to let her come home. But Dr. Franklin's disapproval had me uneasy, as though I were letting the doctor down, and maybe even letting Giulia down, giving in to Giulia's demands just because I was tired of hearing them, not because she was actually ready to come home. And then the nagging voice of Laing had me wondering if the doctor or I had any right to make these decisions in the first place.

"There are a few conditions of your discharge," Dr. Franklin said.

"Anything," Giulia declared.

"First, you are to begin an outpatient program with UCSF

starting the first day you are discharged. You leave tomorrow, we have arranged for you to begin their program the following day. It's five days a week, nine a.m. to three p.m., a full-day program."

"Fine," Giulia answered halfheartedly.

This softened my unease. Giulia was going to be in a program for the bulk of the day, substantially more than the three and a half hours of IOP on Monday, Wednesday, and Friday. Not that I didn't want her fully home, but it would certainly make the prospect of having Giulia and Jonas at home together feel more manageable.

"And you have to take your medicine, no matter what," Dr. Franklin said. "If you don't take your medicine, there is nothing Mark can do about it, and you will have to go back to the ER."

"Fine, whatever it takes," Giulia said.

With that, Giulia was coming home. It was with an asterisk, like a baseball record that has been tainted by steroids, but she was coming home.

I had exaggerated the claim that we had help at home. Suoc was leaving the day of Giulia's discharge, back to Italy. She had spent five weeks in the U.S., bouncing back and forth from San Francisco to New York. She was just as worn down as I was.

My mom was due to arrive the day of Giulia's discharge, but that would be her last week with us as well. My dad's job was transferring back to Delaware at Christmastime, and my mom had to go back to Japan to help with the move. We had help for the last five weeks, but now that Giulia was coming home, Team Grandma was going to be around for only another week.

I brought Jonas and Suoc to the hospital to pick up Giulia, so they could maximize the few remaining hours they had together.

Giulia had seen her mom only a half dozen times over the past five weeks.

It was pouring rain. I left Jonas and Suoc in the car. Although Suoc and I continued to disagree about how to care for Giulia, and even how to raise Jonas, I felt for her. She waited five weeks for her daughter to get better, to come home and be with her family. And now the day it was happening, Suoc was leaving.

I walked into Giulia's room. The meeting from the night before had rattled me. I couldn't ignore Dr. Franklin's words: "Against Medical Advice." It sounded so ominous, as though the doctor saw a storm on the horizon that I didn't. Giulia had already packed up her belongings and signed her paperwork, so we left.

We ran through the rain and puddles together out to the car. Before she got in, Giulia turned back and looked at the building. She needed to see what it looked like from the outside. She had lost a month of her life to the inside of that building, but she didn't even know how it looked from the outside. Suoc knocked on the window, but Giulia ignored her and stood still as a statue in the rain, taking in the sight of the building and the sensation of freedom. Then she finally jumped in the car.

On the drive home, Giulia talked to her mom and Jonas, but she also got lost looking out the window. Halfway there, she asked how much farther we had to go and marveled at how far the hospital was from our house and what a hassle it must have been to drive there every day.

My mom had landed and taken a cab to the house while we were gone and prepared lunch for all of us to eat. Suoc sadly reminded Giulia that she had to leave soon. Giulia, medicated and noticeably overwhelmed with being home, didn't have much of a reaction.

Which made Suoc even more upset to leave. She departed soon after lunch, isolating herself into her uncomfortable sadness.

We spent the rest of the day around the house. I smelled a dirty diaper and announced that I was going to change Jonas, and Giulia jumped at the chance to help. She took him to the changing pad, laid him down, and just sort of looked at him. I sat in the glider and gave them space, but after a few minutes of unproductive attempts to unsnap the buttons and find the wipes, we switched places.

Giulia rocked in the glider and watched me, as if studying to remember the habits of parenting. She stroked the chair's soft arms and asked, while looking down, "How is Jonas doing with the formula? Does he miss my milk?"

I looked up and she avoided my gaze, and my heart groaned. "He's doing fine with the formula, honey," I said, and handed the now clean Jonas to her. They sat and rocked together, slowly, the rain continuing to fall against the window.

The challenges began at dinner, after we had put Jonas to sleep.

I made lasagna, our favorite meal from that brief moment of normalcy when Giulia was at work and I was at home. Giulia nibbled at the food but put her fork down.

"Why aren't you eating?" I asked her.

"I'm nervous," Giulia said.

"What are you nervous about, Giulia?" my mom asked.

"Everything," Giulia said.

After dinner, it was time for Giulia's medication.

In the hospital, Giulia took big pills. To get her 900 mg of lithium, she took three tablets of 300 mg each. For whatever reason, the hospital discharged her with a three-day supply of small pills.

Her daily quota of 900 mg of lithium was going to take nine pills of 100 mg each. Same with the Haldol. Giulia and I popped all of the pills out of their aluminum and plastic sheets and laid them out on the table in front of her. There were at least fifteen pills.

"I don't want to take all of those," she said. "I didn't take that many in the hospital."

"I know, but it's the same total," I said. "These are just smaller doses, so you have to take more pills."

She frowned and picked up the first few. She put them in her mouth and swallowed them down with water. After a few seconds, she grabbed a few more. With the third dose, she tried to swallow them, but one got stuck in her throat. She drank more water, and more, and then before I knew what was happening, she threw everything up, all over the lasagna that sat untouched on her plate.

I could see the half-dissolved pills floating in the watery vomit. She heaved again, and more water and medicine came up. My mom and I watched in horror.

Giulia was embarrassed and without thinking reached into the mess to clean it up with her bare hands. She got vomit all over herself. I stopped her and took her over to the bathroom to get her cleaned up, as my mom tackled the mess on the table.

When I came back to the kitchen, my mom whispered to me, "Are you sure we are ready to have Giulia home?"

"Of course we are," I snapped, brushing off her concern.

What did we do now? Did I need to give Giulia more medication? What if I tried, and she threw up that, too? I called the hospital, got a familiar nurse on the phone, and explained the situation. She advised no more medicine tonight and get back on the routine the following day.

After my mom and I finished cleaning the kitchen, Giulia went into the master bathroom to brush her teeth. She flashed a brief smile as she set foot back in her bathroom, home in her space, where she could have privacy and not be told when and how to do everything.

The plan for the night was for Giulia to sleep in Jonas's room with me, while my mother took ours. I still wanted to be the first one on hand to respond to Jonas's cries in the night.

Giulia was asleep within minutes of lying down, but it took me much longer. I listened to her breathing next to me, and Jonas's breathing on the other side of the room from his crib. Giulia's breaths were slow, deep, and exhausted. Jonas's were shallow, fresh, and light.

I finally fell asleep but jolted awake a few hours later to the sensation of absence. Giulia was not in the bed. The bedroom door was wide-open. I jumped out of bed and found Giulia in the hallway, walking in the direction of the front door.

"Where are you going?" I asked her in a whisper.

"Nowhere," Giulia said, brushing me off and continuing down the hallway to the front door.

"Giulia, where are you going? Come back here, please," I hissed between clenched teeth, trying to keep my voice low. The last thing I wanted was to wake my mom up and further fuel her worries about Giulia being home. "What's going on?"

"Nothing," she said. "I just can't sleep."

The door to the master bedroom popped open, and my mom stuck her head out. "What's going on?" she asked. The hallway was dark, lit only by a night-light that we kept on for Jonas, but I could still see the alarm in my mom's face.

"Nothing," Giulia said. "I just couldn't sleep. I'll go back to bed now."

She turned around and walked back into Jonas's room, lay down in the bed, and was almost immediately asleep.

My mom and I stood in the hallway, stunned. I slouched and avoided eye contact with her. As I turned to go back into Jonas's room, she grabbed me by the wrist.

"We're not ready for this," she said.

I woke Giulia up at eight a.m. for breakfast and medicine, and then we drove to the Langley Porter Psychiatric Institute at the University of California, San Francisco. Langley Porter was affiliated with one of the most respected psychiatry departments in the nation, but you wouldn't know it from the aesthetics. The building was all rough concrete and right angles. Inside was the same frumpy furniture from every other psychiatric facility.

Giulia's outpatient program met on the fourth floor, and the director of the program, a petite graying woman, was waiting for us. She had the calmness and openness that I had grown to recognize in many other San Franciscans of her generation—retired hippies who had celebrated the Summer of Love in Golden Gate Park, not far from this very hospital.

"Welcome to Langley Porter, Giulia," she said warmly, shaking Giulia's hand and then mine.

Giulia didn't say anything in response, so I said, "Thanks."

"Giulia," the director said again, focusing squarely on Giulia, "before we start anything I want to make sure you know that this is a voluntary program. You don't have to be here. We think it can help you, but it's up to you if you want to come or not."

"Really?" Giulia asked, incredulous. I was shocked to hear this, too. This wasn't the plan.

"Really," the director said.

"Well, if that's the case, I'm out of here." Giulia pushed herself out of her chair and walked toward the door.

"Wait, wait, wait!" I called out. "Let's talk about this for a minute." Giulia stopped in the doorway to the office. "Remember what Dr. Franklin said. You have to do this program. It's the reason they let you out."

"Actually, she doesn't have to," the director corrected. "Giulia, this is up to you."

"Well, I don't want to do it," Giulia said. "I want to go back to living my life."

I couldn't believe this. The day before, a doctor had let Giulia out of the hospital AMA with a clear recovery plan, and now a director at Langley Porter was letting Giulia shatter that plan. I felt the same defensive anger that I felt reading Laing. Why was this director giving Giulia so much control? Did she not think Giulia needed to be treated? Did she realize she was dumping Giulia's illness—the vomited pills, the walking around in the middle of the night, the skeptical questions from family members—on me? My mom was going to be outraged if I came back with Giulia and no plan for an outpatient program.

"Giulia, we want you to go back to living your life, too," the director assured her. "I read your file before you got here. I think we can help you go back to living your life. It's going to take a little more time, but I think we can help."

Giulia looked at the director uneasily. "But what if I don't want your help?" she asked.

"Then you don't come," the director answered.

We all sat in silence. I couldn't stop shaking my head.

"You have a son, right, Giulia?" the director asked.

"I do," she said, smiling. "I missed him in the hospital, and I want to spend time with him."

"We want that, too," the director said. "Do you feel ready to be his mom at home?"

Giulia paused for a long time.

"I'm not sure," she admitted. "I'm still on all these pills that make me so groggy, and I just had another psychotic break, and I can't believe that this is my life." She started to cry. "I want to be back at work and be with my son and instead I just spent a month in the hospital and now I have this program and I have to take pills forever."

The director allowed Giulia to cry and waited until she had composed herself before she responded. "That's where we can help," the director assured her. "We want you to have all of those things, too."

There was another long pause before the director asked the pivotal question. "Do you want us to help?"

Giulia thought for a minute and then quietly said, "Yes, I do."

Giulia and I tiptoed around each other as she went to Langley Porter. She feared the return of Mark the Medicine Nazi, the guy who quit her job and signed her up for dumb art classes. I worried about what Giulia might do if left to her own choices—overdose, jump off the Golden Gate Bridge, spend all day in bed, throw away her medicine.

I grew to respect and trust Langley Porter. The director obviously was very skilled at empowering mental illness patients, while still getting good results. My sense of Laing softened. I felt less compelled to monitor Giulia's medicine or incessantly call her doctors.

The psychosis faded much the same way it had the first time—gradually, without fanfare, and leaving little cause for celebration, because it was immediately replaced with the deep chasm of depression. Giulia's Langley Porter doctor swapped out the Haldol with Risperdal, and the one-word answers and delayed responses returned as well.

I drew a firm line when it came to Jonas. I could give Giulia more autonomy, but I had to make sure that Jonas was okay, which set up the uncomfortable possibility that I might have to intervene between Giulia and Jonas.

They had alone time together. I'd step into the kitchen for some imagined chore and leave them in the living room together. From there, I couldn't help eavesdropping. It was excruciating. Jonas cooed at Giulia, who sat silently in response. There was no real togetherness. Jonas played alone and Giulia sat on the couch, impassive, as if the room were empty. Giulia's thoughts were elsewhere, replaying the suffering she experienced in her madness, questioning why this nightmare had happened again. Jonas didn't have answers, so Giulia mostly watched him in silence.

I forced myself to give them five minutes, but usually after only a minute or two I couldn't handle it anymore, and I crashed back into the room with the overwhelming positivity of Tigger.

The Giulia-Jonas dynamic upset everyone who came to visit. Friends always called or texted afterward, saying how much it broke their hearts to see Giulia and Jonas in the same room, not connected. I was ashamed and defensive reading these texts, at the implied judgment of our situation. We stopped having friends over, even though I desperately needed to spend time with other people. I interviewed nanny candidates to help us with life around the house. Our first choice turned down the job. She said the sadness was too much for her to bear.

One lunchtime, Giulia fed Jonas his mashed vegetables. She was mechanical, scooping and feeding as if paced by a metronome, and Jonas had a hard time keeping up with the pace.

"Honey, slow down just a bit," I said. "Wait until he has finished with the food in his mouth."

Giulia acted like she hadn't heard me and continued to scoop up the green mush and lead it into his mouth.

"Honey, please, just slow down a bit," I said again. "Give him time to catch up."

She again acted like I hadn't said anything and continued, as Jonas's cheeks started to bulge with excess food.

I laid a hand on her arm. "Giulia, just take a second to let him chew what he has." The gentleness in my voice had disappeared.

"I'm fine, leave me alone," she said, shaking my hand off as she continued to scoop and feed, scoop and feed.

"Goddamn it, Giulia, look at him!" I shouted. "Stop feeding him! He doesn't have any room left!" I grabbed the spoon out of her hand. Jonas spit the food out of his mouth. Giulia sat with her head down, embarrassed and angry by the scolding.

I eventually began to treat Giulia like a visiting guest when she was with Jonas—no expectations to change a diaper, cook, clean, grocery shop. I did my best to isolate her experience of parenting to only the fun parts and remove all the stressful, frustrating, and inane parts. I realized that the doctor's concerns about Giulia's ability to handle the unpredictable challenges of a baby were justified, so I shielded Giulia and Jonas from ever having to wade into that precarious territory. I kept telling myself that this was temporary, that this depression would go away as it had before, that Giulia wasn't a bad mom, that she was just sick. I wasn't always successful at convincing myself.

One night after Giulia and Jonas had gone to sleep, I got hit with a stomach virus and spent the whole night on the toilet with diarrhea. I had full-body shivers and was in such pain that I had to crawl on the floor to get from room to room.

Jonas began to cry at around three a.m., hungry for his nighttime bottle. Giulia didn't budge. We had returned to sleeping in our room, Jonas in his, after my mom left, and from across the hall, Giulia didn't hear Jonas's cry for food through her medicated slumber. She never did. I was the one who responded, and I had grown to love it, because it meant I could leave our bedroom and go to his. His room felt so much warmer and more hopeful than ours, which had been consumed by Giulia's depression. Middle-of-the-night feedings were pure, an unfiltered hour of tenderness. On a usual night, I rocked him during the feedings and gently sang songs, and after he finished eating, I lay with him in the guest bed as he drifted back to sleep. I tended to sleep there with him. I preferred it to going back to my wife in our bed.

But this night there was no gentle rocking and sleeping. I could barely stand up, and I panicked when I heard him cry. I was horribly dehydrated and shaking with a fever. I crawled from the toilet to the kitchen, propped myself on the kitchen counters, scrubbed my hands with soap, and mixed a bottle of formula. I limped to Jonas's room, lifted him out of the crib, and set him up on the floor to change him and feed him on blankets. I lay next to him and tried to quiet the shakes and the surging pain in my belly. I usually talked to Jonas through the feedings, but I had nothing to say because all I could think about was, How could I possibly hold up these two lives on my shoulders? What if something happened to me, then what would happen to them?

Giulia left the program at UCSF after a month and transitioned to her original IOP program, from nine to twelve on Monday, Wednesday, and Friday. This meant more time together, which took some getting used to. Jonas and I had adapted well to dropping Giulia off each morning and picking her up in the afternoon. I explained to Jonas that we were taking Mommy to work, and for the rest of the day, I returned to the fantasy of being the stay-at-home dad while Giulia was off at her job.

Now, we were home together all the time. Outbursts like the one over the feeding became more frequent, and I reached my breaking point. I had completely stopped surfing and running. I didn't see any friends. I was doing a horrible job of taking care of myself, and it showed with my shortened patience. Granted, the demands of two working parents make for a lot of stressed nerves, but this was different. I spent all day focused on Giulia's depression, Jonas's well-being, and even Goose's needs. The support I craved wasn't there because Giulia needed as much care and attention as our child. It became harder and harder to stay patient with Giulia, and I lost my temper with her more regularly.

I did finally manage to hire a nanny, and our savings continued to dwindle. We were definitely not going to be able to afford a house anymore and were probably going to be renting for life. Giulia had enrolled on disability, and her job kept us on their insurance, so there was some money to count on, but I worried more and more about money.

I eventually started to trust Giulia with more freedom. I had to. I first had to let go of driving her everywhere, even though it felt dangerous for her to drive. She couldn't even focus on something like feeding Jonas. For weeks, Jonas and I had driven Giulia everywhere she wanted to go, whether it was IOP or a meeting with a friend. Giulia hated this. It was one of our biggest sources of tension. She agitated for the freedom to drive as much as she had lobbied to come home while in the hospital. Letting her drive felt so irresponsible that I couldn't let it go. I needed to be convinced by a professional. I called her doctor, who said there was no medical reason that Giulia couldn't drive, but it still didn't feel safe to me. Finally, after a month at home, I relented.

Without me babysitting her, Giulia gravitated toward her friends, especially the ones she had made in IOP, like Marie. Marie was a brilliant artist with bipolar who had been hospitalized ten times. Over the course of Giulia's first, eight-month stint in IOP, Marie had been enrolled in IOP on three separate occasions. Marie was the type of bipolar patient who took herself off her medication regularly, because she hated how it sapped her creativity. While unmedicated, she often relapsed, hence the frequent in and out of the psych ward and IOP. She lived in the Outer Sunset, only a few blocks north of us. The two didn't talk too much after Giulia had bounced out of her first episode, but now that she had relapsed, they were inseparable. They called and texted each other constantly. As soon as Giulia kissed Jonas good night for bed and handed him off to me to finish bedtime, she took her phone into the bathroom and called Marie. The two talked in hushed tones about how they were doing and how to get through the depression they were battling. They were a part of each other's support systems. If Giulia had a bad day, Marie could help her make sense of it, and vice versa.

It was a relief for Giulia to connect with a friend who understood her so intimately. I had depleted my capacity for talking about suicide three years earlier, but Marie was always there to listen to Giulia when she felt suicidal. Marie had experienced the psych ward, and suicidal depression, and could understand Giulia's feelings and fears in a way that I couldn't, no matter how empathetic I tried to be.

But I also feared their friendship. Both were deeply frustrated with being told what to do by doctors and therapists, and they encouraged a rebellious spirit in each other. After all, Giulia and Marie had come up with the Medicine Nazi nickname together. There were times when both were stuck in the muck of their depression, and they talked each other deeper. They shared strategies for how best to kill themselves. It was Marie who told Giulia that overdoses are rarely successful.

Their friendship was exactly what Laing wanted: patient supporting patient, empowering each other to choices that make the most sense to them. And as much as I wanted to encourage it, I couldn't help having my guard up.

Five months after her discharge, Giulia walked with me and Jonas at Ocean Beach. Even though neither of us was working, and Giulia was in IOP for only a few hours every other day, we spent a surprisingly small amount of time together. In her first bout with depression, we were inseparable. This time around, with her freedom to ride her scooter, Giulia was absent a lot more, leaving me and Jonas behind. This beach walk together was one of our first in a few weeks.

I noticed her stride had more certainty and purpose. She wasn't shuffling along apathetically. Her distant, blank stare was lifting, too, replaced by a spark and vigor of healthy times. She was also more communicative with Jonas, playing peekaboo and digging shapes in the sand for him to crawl through and smash.

It was great to see her like this. "You seem like you're doing better, Giulia."

Giulia looked down at Jonas, who was crawling toward her sand castle. She had sand up to her elbows and sweat on her brow from the digging.

"I'm doing better because I stopped taking Risperdal," she said, returning to her creations.

"What?" I asked.

"I said I stopped taking Risperdal."

"Did the doctor tell you to stop?"

"No," Giulia said. "I just did it."

"*What?!?!*" I screamed. "You stopped your fucking Risperdal? Do you have any idea how dangerous that is?"

I had reassured myself that it was important to give Giulia more space, that maybe Cas and Laing and Marie and the director of Langley Porter were right: I had suffocated Giulia with how much I managed her care. But I was never really comfortable ceding control because I feared that she might make a reckless decision, and that's exactly what she had done. I didn't know how to process it.

"Dangerous?" she said mockingly. "Look at me. I'm doing better. You said so yourself."

I jumped up and began pacing wildly away from Giulia, so angry I couldn't even look at her. I punched myself in the chest over and over because I had to punch something.

"Giulia, you don't get to play your own doctor!" I screamed at her. "Last time you stopped your Risperdal, you were a complete mess, the most suicidal and weepy I've ever seen you. What if that happened again? While you were alone? Or with Jonas?"

At the mention of Jonas I came running back, picked him up, and walked away. I shook with anger.

A quarter of a mile down the beach, I finally felt more in control. I sat back down in the sand with Jonas, baby-talking him in faux cheery tones to try to quiet the anger ringing in my ears.

A few minutes later, Giulia approached. At a distance she called out, "I don't like those pills, Mark. I don't need them anymore. They help me when I'm psychotic, but I haven't been psychotic in months. They don't do anything but make me feel bad."

"I don't care," I said calmly. I didn't want to lose my temper again in front of Jonas. "Tell that to your doctor. Families lose when people treat mental illness like it only impacts one person. This is your illness, but it's actually all of ours. Yours, mine, Jonas's, even Goose's. We all live through this. You can't make decisions like this that could put so many of us in harm's way. What if you had a bad reaction while walking Jonas and you decided to step in front of moving traffic? It is so dangerous to rip yourself off your meds. You have to taper off them. You don't get to play your own doctor."

"You try to play my doctor," she said.

I didn't respond to that, even though she was right. I was so angry that I didn't have space for her to be right. I forced myself to smile at Jonas and pretend that I wasn't furious.

"Did you stop all your pills, or just the Risperdal?"

"Just the Risperdal," she said. "I'm still taking my lithium. And look at me: I'm doing better."

"You have to call your doctor and tell her you stopped your medicine," I said.

"Okay," she said. "Mark, I hate this medicine. I'm feeling better and I don't think I need it anymore. You can't take this so personally."

By now, Giulia was standing next to us. There was no way to not take it personally. I felt trapped by the impossibility of the situation. I didn't trust Giulia to make her own decisions. I wanted to make them for her, which led to her resenting me for not trusting her. I didn't want Giulia to resent me, but the only way to do that would be to allow her to make her own decisions, even if that included choices that could hurt or even kill her. It wasn't going to work if I remained in charge, and it would be too risky if she was in charge.

"Giulia," I pleaded with her, "how can I trust you with medicine ever again?"

"You just trust me."

ten

April 2013

Giulia's doctor and therapist did not worry about Giulia stopping her medicine as much as I did. Her doctor was planning to taper her off the Risperdal soon anyway, and since her reaction was so positive, it wasn't a big deal to him that she decided to stop her medicine herself. He discharged her from IOP and encouraged her to get back to living her life. At the last IOP meeting, he prescribed Giulia a full bottle of Risperdal to keep in the medicine cabinet, just in case. She shoved it behind her makeup, and we never talked about it.

There was no celebratory text at the conclusion of IOP, no date night out for pho. We instead just returned to living. Despite Giulia's abrupt return to "feeling better," I still couldn't remove myself, and my needs, from how Giulia wanted to manage her mental illness. I was adamant that we treat Giulia's illness as a shared experience for our whole family, which meant we had to be open and honest about it. When I brought this up with Giulia, she reminded me of the many times I had spoken about her to her doctor, or therapist, or parents, without being honest to her about what I was saying. The dishonesty and betrayal went both ways, and we were once again in a fragile state of distrust and even resentment.

Following the advice to get back to living life, Giulia and I both started to look for jobs. It had been three years since I had worked as a salaried teacher. I loved freelance writing and caring for Jonas, but I couldn't shake the memory of how much pressure Giulia had felt as our sole income provider before her second psychotic break.

I polished up my résumé, added some writing clips, and fired it off to some of the most progressive schools in the Bay Area. I was elated to get a job offer teaching history at a groovy school in the East Bay, but I knew that if I took the job, we would have to move. The drive across the Bay Bridge and through the Caldecott Tunnel was just too far.

Giulia and I had lived at Ocean Beach for seven years. It was more than just a neighborhood to us. It was where we first built our home as a married couple. All of our closest friends lived there. Jonas had learned to crawl on the beach. Goose's favorite activity was to dig rocks at the beach. The ocean nurtured my spirit through surfing. Our lives were defined by Ocean Beach.

But Ocean Beach was also a cold and foggy place. While the rest of the Bay Area spent summers eating dinners on the deck and running through sprinklers in shorts and T-shirts, residents of the Outer Sunset bundled up in hoodies and corduroy. One summer I went a full forty-five days without seeing the sun. Besides, in the East Bay we could afford a place with more space and a yard and wouldn't have to worry about the public school options when Jonas was ready for kindergarten.

Most of all, Ocean Beach was the place where Giulia got sick. Not once, but now twice. All of our favorite streets and restaurants felt tainted with psychosis and depression.

I accepted the job offer, and we packed up our belongings. My heart was heavy, but I felt optimistic and relieved. I kept the wax on my surfboards. We were moving only forty-five minutes away from the beach, after all.

In the rural outskirts of Martinez, California, we soaked up the sun. We hung a hammock in the backyard and immediately set up a garden with tomatoes, zucchini, peppers, and herbs. The house we rented was surrounded by fruit trees, and Jonas loved to watch as I climbed them to pick apples, apricots, and peaches.

The beach was no longer at our fingertips, but our new home was across the street from Briones Regional Park, a six-thousand-acre open-space park I had never even heard of until we moved to its front door. We translated our beach walks into hikes through the golden hills. I was struck by the unexpected beauty of the place. John Muir had set up his family home in Martinez. Good enough for John Muir, good enough for me.

Jonas took his first steps in our new front yard. When he started to wobble around, Giulia and I bounced and shrieked in celebration. The neighbors poured out of their houses, drawn by the commotion, and then returned back inside, smiling and shaking their heads in pleasure. What a joyful relief to experience a milestone together, like normal parents.

We missed our friends, but I was surprised by how little I missed surfing. Instead, I turned to trail running. I had always run for maintenance, but I'd never identified as a runner and always did my best to avoid hills. I didn't consider running the Briones trails until I met a retired firefighter while out on a hike with Jonas and Goose. He invited me to join him for a trail run. I agreed. The firefighter turned out to be the fittest fifty-year-old I'd ever met.

He ran me into the loopy, sultry glow of a runner's high. I was hooked.

Running became my meditation, a hot, sweaty replacement to the now distant surf. I ran early, before Jonas woke, or at dusk, after he fell asleep. Once the school year started, I even ran on my lunch break. The twenty thousand acres of Mount Diablo State Park were only a few hundred yards from my classroom door.

There was something beautifully primitive about stripping down to a pair of shorts and shoes and running through the grass and forest. I felt like I was doing what we humans had evolved to do, a pleasant alternative to my thoroughly modernized life. The pace of my thinking slowed to the rhythm of my footsteps. I could lesson plan on my runs, but I mostly spent the time thinking about Giulia and Jonas.

I didn't find any answers to the questions surrounding Giulia's illness or solve the riddle of my marriage. But I did find the patience and perspective to deal with them and the optimism that we would work through them.

The more I ran, the more deeply I appreciated my surroundings and running. The runner's high is so much more immediate and reliable than the elusive surfer's stoke. A surf session can be ruined by tide, wind, attitude from other surfers. A run is just you and the landscape. I occasionally ran with other people but mostly took the time to myself, to set my own pace, to choose when I wanted to soar and when I wanted to suffer. Running gives you plenty of both.

On a painfully hot Saturday afternoon, when the only available window for a run was during Jonas's afternoon nap, I trudged out into the sun and was drenched in sweat within the first few minutes.

A mile into the run, my head was spinning and I could see spots around the perimeter of my vision, but I kept going. I loved to push myself to my limits. I knew this could get dangerous—it was hot, I could pass out, no one knew precisely where I was. But courting risk, and the surge of adrenaline that accompanies it, was another reason I ran on these trails.

While I stumbled over roots and struggled against the hills, the spots somehow faded and my head felt solid on my shoulders again. Not just that: I became invincible. I charged through the tall grass at a rip-roaring pace, scaring grasshoppers to flee ahead of me, but I caught them a few steps later, and we ended up racing against each other on a single-track trail. It felt so right to be out there in the heat with those bugs, running myself into a deluded frenzy, thinking about my son and my wife, knowing that these eye floaters and our spinning heads were just a part of being a family together, and we would run through them together.

School began in August, and I felt exhilarated to be back in the classroom. I immediately remembered why I had been so drawn to teaching in the first place: the curiosity, the energy, the constant stimulation, the frantic, consuming pace.

Soon after my school year started, Giulia landed a job, her third in five years and the fifth since we moved to California. In the job interview, her new employer admitted that they loved a lot about Giulia's résumé and how she presented herself, but they were wary of her checkered past with working at companies for only a year or so. Giulia set the goal of staying there for five years. Her career trajectory had been nothing like what she had planned.

We had become a family with two working parents, which meant we needed to find a day care for Jonas. The search was heartbreaking, since he had been home with one of us, but mostly both of us, for his first fifteen months. We visited a few day care centers, curiously watching how Jonas interacted with the teachers and the other kids in the class, and knew we had come to the right place when we found one whose tagline was "A child's work is to play."

When Giulia began work in mid-September, Jonas began his new routine at school. The first day I lingered in the classroom after I put him down. He didn't want to let go, and he cried when he realized that I wasn't staying. I cried the whole drive to school. When I picked him up that afternoon, he leapt into my arms, and we had never hugged more tightly.

Within a week, we had settled into our new routines. This restart pushed us to move beyond Giulia's second episode.

We worked hard to put Giulia's sickness behind us. We didn't have a word to talk about normalcy the way we used "sick" to talk about the times of crisis. Health? Stability? Bipolar management? Whatever it was, we now knew that these good times could be punctured by another bout of the sickness. Giulia was in the 90 percent who relapse. No one knew when or if the psychosis would return.

One night Giulia stayed up late, until almost midnight, painting furniture. She usually went to bed early, only an hour or two after Jonas fell asleep. Sleep was important, and we both knew it. I suggested she go to bed.

"But I'm having fun," Giulia said.

"Good," I said. "But it's midnight. Go to bed."

"No," she said.

"You realize what this looks like, right?" I said.

"No, I don't. What are you talking about?"

"I'm not saying that you're manic, but on the surface, this looks like mania. Staying up late, painting, feeling full of energy . . ."

Giulia exploded. "How dare you tell me what to do? Stop running my life! You're not in charge."

The fight lasted days. Anything that echoed how we acted when she was sick became a sore spot for us. We played nice in front of Jonas, but for the next few days all tiny missteps triggered titanic reactions.

Then, a week later, Giulia had a tough day at work. As we got in bed to go to sleep, she said, "I'm scared about how stressed out how I feel."

I responded in high alert. "What do you mean? What's going on? Let's talk about it."

She stonewalled. "I don't want to talk about it because I need to sleep, but I'm scared."

Which in turn scared the hell out of me. She was worried about her mental health. I tried to swallow my anger and fear that she wasn't taking care of herself, but I couldn't calm down. I didn't sleep that night, I blamed it on her, and we fought for another few days.

As much as I loved running, I regularly checked a surf forecast app on my phone, in the desperate attempt to sneak in a surf session when possible. I found a Saturday morning that looked promising and cleared it in advance with Giulia. She agreed, but I could feel her tension. She and Jonas still didn't spend a ton of time alone together, and as she agreed to let me go surfing, the unspoken question hung in the air: What would Giulia do with Jonas while I wasn't there?

I woke up at four thirty a.m. so that I could be in the water for almost an hour before the sun even rose and could be back by nine a.m. I left out clothes for Jonas, fixings for his breakfast, puzzles, books, and Goose's leash, with a map of Briones. I figured they could eat breakfast and then the three of them could go for a hike. Easy enough morning.

The surf was fun, but nothing memorable, which was fine if you lived only a few blocks away, but since I left my house at four forty-five a.m. and surfed in the dark in order to get waves, I was a bit disappointed. Granted, I had gotten into the ocean and caught a few, so it was hard to call it a waste of time. But Ocean Beach will do that to you: make promises of sparkling fun waves based on the tide and swell period and wind forecast and then serve up midsized, sloppy mush.

I came home, expecting that Giulia and Jonas would either be out or doing a puzzle. Instead, they were cuddling on the couch, watching a movie. Goose greeted me at the door, his tail a frenzy with the impatient wagging of a dog who had not got his morning walk.

"What's going on in here?" I asked, trying but failing to not make my question sound like an accusation.

"We're watching *Cars*," Giulia said. Jonas cheered in agreement.

"What about the books?" I asked.

"We didn't read them."

"Did you guys go hiking?" I didn't need to ask. They were all still in pajamas.

"No," Giulia said, shuffling out from under Jonas. "You can take them hiking. I'm going to go out and run a few errands now that you're home."

"Okay . . . ," I said, my tone once again accusing, even though I said only a single word. I didn't know that Giulia had plans to go out for the morning.

"You got to go surfing for four hours while I took care of Jonas, so now I get to go out for four hours." She sailed through our house into our bedroom to change. I trailed behind her.

"Yeah, but you guys just watched a movie. You didn't take Goose out. You didn't even change Jonas out of his pajamas, or the diaper he has been in all night. So when you say you 'took care of him'—" I hadn't even finished my thought before Giulia erupted.

"How dare you tell me how to spend time with my son?" Giulia yelled. "I don't tell you how to spend your time. Let me make my own choices. I'm sick of you telling me how to run my goddamn life!"

She was changed and out the door within a few minutes. She came home almost precisely four hours later, just as she had promised.

Our old patterns had found us, after all.

The further Giulia's episode faded into the past, the more I thought about Laing. I no longer had the knee-jerk reaction of wounded pride. I stewed on some of his concepts, especially the skewed power dynamic that certainly existed in our family. Laing boiled down the treatment of psychosis to power. Who gets to decide what behavior is tolerated? Who chooses how and when to enforce the rules? Even with Giulia's psychosis faded, we battled over those questions.

Cas and I had long ago patched up the tension created when he gave me Laing's book. I began to delicately ask him what exactly his "other way" might entail. He was a self-described "psychic adventurer" who had wrestled personally with and researched intensely issues of identity, fragmentation of the psyche, and power in relationships while in a PhD program, so I figured he had plenty of ideas. We now visited Cas and Leslie more regularly, and Cas and I carved out Sunday mornings for just the two of us. He hopped on his mountain bike, I put on my running shoes, and we rode/ran out to Arch Rock on Point Reyes together and talked the whole way. Our trail was mostly flat, and Cas patiently pedaled his bike at my running pace, which meant that he did most of the talking and I grunted in agreement as I tried to keep up. Our conversations were more like philosophy lectures, sprinkled with advice from a close friend.

"I had a torrid love affair with Nietzsche," he said on one of our outings. "I fell deeply for Nietzsche in every possible way, but then he crushed me like an empty Coke can, and left me in ruins," Cas continued. "You need to read *Thus Spoke Zarathustra*, because I think you'll see a lot of yourself, and what you've tried to do in caring for Giulia, in his concept of the Superman. But first you should read Jung's *Man and His Symbols*. That's going to speak to you a lot. It'll really give you a new perspective on Giulia's delusions, and what they might be hinting at."

While Cas gave me dozens of book recommendations and theories to consider, he always left it up to me to decide how to proceed. "It's not up to anyone else to dictate the terms of your relationship with Giulia, except for you and Giulia."

Even with this prodding, I was intimidated to address questions of Giulia's health, and the way we dealt with it, directly with her. So I did some reading and research on my own, picking at the uncomfortable questions I had about Giulia's time in the hospital and some of the medication she took. I had already exhausted the Internet's capacity to explain to me what side effects might look like. I needed to hear from people who felt the same degree of frustration with their recovery treatment that Giulia felt. I was so emotionally absorbed in her recovery that I had a hard time hearing her without taking things personally. But if I could read about strangers, I could listen without feeling judged or be relieved from trying to control the outcome.

On the pretext of doing research for a magazine article, I e-mailed and called various people who were outspoken critics of psychiatry. I talked to Robert Whitaker, author of *Mad in America* and *Anatomy of an Epidemic*, who kindly schooled me on the history of antipsychiatry in its many manifestations. Laing was one of the first, and many followed in his footsteps to create the Mad Pride movement, which modeled itself on gay pride, reclaiming the word *mad* as a positive identifier instead of a slur. Mad Pride came out of the psychiatric survivor movement, with its goal of taking mental health treatment decisions out of the hands of doctors and well-intentioned caregivers and putting those decisions into the hands of patients.

Even though I had my frustrations with Giulia's two hospitalizations and outpatient programs, I didn't hold any of the medical professionals at fault. No one had acted with malice toward Giulia, even the nurses from the first hospital, who were clearly overworked. There was only one psychiatrist to manage a ward with a revolving patient group of thirty people. No wonder he didn't return my calls. They were all doing the best they could, often in overworked and overcrowded circumstances, in a field of medicine that the mainstream expected to be objective and scientific but the insiders knew was far from it.

I also spoke with Sascha Altman DuBrul, one of the founders of the Icarus Project, an alternative medical health organization that calls mental illness "the space between brilliance and madness." I was nervous when I spoke to Sascha. I wanted to hear his stories, but I was also there to ask for advice, and I feared what he might say. Was I doing everything wrong? Was I part of the problem?

Sascha instantly put me at ease. He started by arguing that each person's experience with mental health is unique. This may sound obvious, but psychiatry, to some extent, has been built on generalizations. Sascha didn't like how psychiatry stuffed patients' singular experiences into one of a handful of available boxes.

"I have a diagnosis of bipolar disorder," Sascha told me. "While that term can be really useful for explaining some things, it's lacking in a whole lot of nuances." He said he found the label "kind of alienating." All that resonated with me. For Giulia, too, none of the diagnoses seemed quite right. In her first psychotic break, psychiatrists ruled out bipolar disorder; in her second, they were certain she was bipolar. Besides, as Sascha put it, no matter the diagnosis, psychiatry "gives you terrible language for defining yourself."

As for medication, a constant source of tension between Giulia and me, the Medicine Nazi, Sascha believed that the question of whether or not to use pharmaceuticals was more nuanced than just yes or no. The best response might be *maybe, sometimes,* or *only certain medications*. For example, Sascha himself took lithium every night, because after four hospitalizations and more than a decade with the label *bipolar*, he was confident that the medication was a positive part of his care. Not the whole solution, but a piece.

All of this was very comforting, and far from the guilt and judgment that I feared Sascha might heap on me, but I really perked up and started paying careful attention when he introduced me to the concept of mad maps. Like advanced directives for the dying, mad maps allow psychiatric patients to outline what they'd like their care to look like in future mental health crises. The logic is if a person can define health while healthy, and differentiate health from crisis, that person can shape his or her own care. The maps are not intended to be rejections of psychiatry, though they might be that. Instead, they are designed to encourage patients to plan ahead—to treat a relapse as possible or even likely—in order to give them more control and avoid, or at least minimize, future mistakes.

I loved the concept, but I pushed back on Sascha. "These maps sound incredibly useful, and pardon me for asking this, but do you have any children? Are you married? Did you make your map with your family?"

"No," he admitted. "I made mine with my best friend."

"That's my big issue," I told him. "Giulia might have a vision for how she wants to care for her illness, but it's clearly different from mine. And we live together. We share bank accounts. We have a son. That makes things much, much harder."

Sascha paused for a minute. "We've never met before, Mark, we don't know each other, but I really feel for you, man. You're trying to do the right thing. That's the best we can all do."

In December, Marie killed herself.

She had texted Giulia the day before, saying that she was having a terrible day. Giulia had texted back that Marie was the strongest woman she knew and that everything would be okay. Then Giulia didn't hear back. Marie's employer knew of her mental health struggles and that if they couldn't locate her, they were to call the police. When she didn't come back after lunch, they called. The cops busted through Marie's door and found her in her bed.

We heard the news in such a cold, bizarre way. Giulia had written a blog post on our round-the-world travel blog about Marie's artwork years before, and the night after her suicide, her brother left a comment saying, "What a nice tribute to Marie, we miss her." As cohosts of the blog, Giulia and I both got an e-mail alert that someone had commented. Giulia was at a party with friends in our old neighborhood, only a block away from Marie's house, when she got the e-mail. She called me, and all I heard was Giulia weeping. She could barely speak. I drove out to Ocean Beach to pick her up, and I hugged her, but there wasn't anything to say. Giulia had lost her most genuine companion in her recovery, the one who could immediately understand her based on their shared experiences.

I had long ago given up on the notion that suicide is a cowardly cop-out. I think that anyone who feels suicidal is presented with one of two types of courage. Giulia had one type, which was to face the feelings each day and still choose life. No matter how much life hurt, this courage helped her wake up each day.

Marie had the other type of courage, one I wish no one had. She believed in her feelings. So deep was her sense that things would never get better, and that there was no way out, that she ended her whole world.

Giulia had the first type of courage. But the more she thought about Marie, the more she feared that she might find the second type, and what it would mean for me, and Jonas, and the rest of the people she loved.

"Marie always told me that the second hospitalization is the hardest," Giulia said the night after she got the news. "It's the one where you realize that this isn't going away. I've had my second hospitalization. There might be a third, or a fourth, or a fifth. I don't want what happened to Marie to happen to me."

"I don't want that either, Giulia," I said.

"So how do I avoid it?"

"I don't know," I said. "You've avoided it so far."

"I think we need some type of plan."

I waited for Giulia's grief to ease before we tried to create a plan. She told a lot of stories about Marie; she cried; she listened to old voice mails and read old texts; but thankfully she avoided a relapse, something I feared might be possible. But Giulia's grief was clearly not just for Marie. The way she talked about Marie's death, it was as if Giulia were grieving for herself as well. She knew that it could have been her.

Finally, one evening when we were in bed, after Jonas had fallen asleep, as Giulia was getting ready to watch *Friday Night Lights* on the iPad, I cautiously brought up the idea of a mad map.

"So, about that plan," I said. "I think it's time we talk about it."

Giulia didn't say anything.

"I think we should talk about the Risperdal in your medicine cabinet, first."

"What's there to talk about? We have Risperdal in the house. Big deal. Are you afraid I'm going to take it all?" Already, she was getting defensive.

"No, that's not it," I said. "I'm talking about taking Risperdal as prescribed, in the event that the psychosis returns. I think we need to figure out what it would have to look like in order for you to take it. Last time it was only four nights of no sleeping before you were in the hospital."

Giulia cut me off. "I don't want to talk about this, Mark. I'm not going to go psychotic again. I don't want it to happen, so it's not going to. Just have some faith in me."

"I don't want it to happen, either," I said. "But it might. You said so yourself. We should make a plan for it now, while you're feeling good, rather than wait until a crisis hits and I end up making all the decisions for you."

"You mean like quitting my job for me," Giulia said, taunting.

"Yes, I mean like that," I said.

"And refusing to listen to me when I say that I'm ready to come home," she added with increased hostility.

"Well, I guess that's how you see it," I said. "I was just trying to listen to what the doctors said."

"Or forcing me to take medication I don't want to take." She was fired up now.

"Or keeping you alive so you don't jump off the fucking Golden Gate Bridge!"

"Well, this is a great idea, Mark," Giulia said, standing up out of bed. "Thanks so much for having faith in me that I'm going to have another psychotic break!" She stormed into the bathroom and slammed the door.

"This has nothing to do with faith, Giulia," I called out. Giulia locked the door in response. "This is because I realize that we both made huge mistakes in how we handled your hospitalizations.

Those mistakes hurt us. Of course I don't want you to go psychotic again. But I'm not sure how much we're in control of that. And if it does happen, I definitely don't want to make the same mistakes again."

The door stayed locked. Giulia muttered, "Whatever," so I backed away from the door and returned to bed.

I tried again a week later, after Jonas's bedtime, when we both were fried, the only chance for two working parents to talk among themselves.

"We really need to talk about what it would have to look like for you to take Risperdal," I said.

"I'll take the Risperdal when I'm psychotic," she said, barely glancing up from the iPad.

"When do you know that you've gone psychotic? It's never been clear to me, it just kind of gets worse with each day that you're not sleeping. I wonder if you could take it before you get to feeling psychotic?" I said.

She groaned and put down the iPad. "Do you want me to start taking it right now?" she said. "Then I'll never go psychotic! And I'll never feel anything, either."

"Honey, I don't want to fight," I said.

My lack of a rebuttal calmed her down.

"I don't want to fight either," she answered. "But I don't want to have to take Risperdal unless I have to."

"Well, I think that if you can't sleep, then it's a 'have to' situation. I think that if you can't sleep one night, you should take Risperdal."

"That's ridiculous, Mark," Giulia said. "One night is not going to do anything. How about after two nights of sleep, I take one milligram of Risperdal."

"That's ridiculous, too!" I said. "Last time it only took four nights. And one milligram of Risperdal won't do anything. Three milligrams, first night, that's my suggestion."

"Well, my suggestion is one milligram after two nights."

The battle lines were drawn. But at least we were negotiating.

We decided to take the conversation to her psychiatrist.

Giulia had seen at least a dozen doctors in the past three years. There were the hospital doctors, the outpatient program doctors, her doctor in the city, and now her doctor in the East Bay. Her new psychiatrist, Dr. Stefania, was very sharp and very convincing. She had a no-bullshit air about her, just as Giulia did. In fact, I think I liked her because of how much she reminded me of Giulia—stubborn, ambitious, focused on a goal.

"So, we need a plan for when to take Risperdal in the event of a relapse," Dr. Stefania said from behind her desk. "I think if you can't sleep, you need to take your medicine. Period."

"Exactly," I said. I leaned back into my chair in triumph. "Sleep is so important for you."

"I know it is," Giulia said. "But just because I can't sleep doesn't mean I should take antipsychotics."

"Well, then how about this," Dr. Stefania offered. "If you can't sleep, you take one milligram by midnight. If that does the job, then you're fine. You sleep, you go to work. If you can't sleep, then by two a.m., take two more milligrams, for a total of three. You shouldn't go to work on three milligrams of Risperdal, so call in sick that day. And call me, so I know you had to take the medicine. And then we will play it day by day."

"Okay, I can do that," Giulia said.

"This sounds good to me, too," I said.

"That it? You guys are easy," Dr. Stefania joked.

We were both shocked. After only a few minutes with Dr. Stefania, it was done. We had a plan for the Risperdal.

"Now get out of here and go live."

There was much more to discuss than just the Risperdal, but at least now we had the confidence that we could figure things out. We knew that we disagreed on almost every aspect of our road map, but it didn't have to be so impossible to find a plan that worked.

We made a point of addressing a different detail each month. In February, we agreed that Giulia would never take Zyprexa or Haldol again. If a doctor recommended it while Giulia was in the hospital, I would refuse on her behalf. In March, we confirmed that if she was hospitalized again, I would not speak to her work and would instead leave all communication up to her assigned social worker. In April, we agreed that since Giulia had medicine and was willing to take it, we would try to wait out the psychosis at home for a little while before racing off to the emergency room. Hypothetically, Giulia would already be on Risperdal and in communication with her psychiatrist, so why not see how things went at home a bit first. In May, the month of Jonas's birthday, we agreed that he would not come and visit in the hospital.

Each agreement was a small victory, a genuine step in the right direction in a world where such steps are rare. The conversations typically got tense, but we powered through. We resolved many unknowns, but there were still other questions to address. We had to figure out what type of help to accept from our parents. There was still the question of having more children. We both wanted more, but the idea evoked any number of disastrous scenarios.

But we stuck to our commitment to come up with a plan, even though setting aside time to work on that plan felt like we were scheduling time to fight. The subtext underlying these tense conversations was that we were making progress. When we sat down to discuss medication doses, or a timeline for getting pregnant, or the risks of taking lithium during pregnancy, we were essentially saying "I love you." My exact words might have been "I think you're rushing things," but the subtext was "I want you to be healthy and fulfilled, and I want to spend my life with you. I want to hear how much you disagree with me, about something that is as personal as it gets, so that we can be together." And Giulia might have said "Give me my space," but in her heart, it was "I value what you've done for me, and appreciate how hard you're trying to be open and flexible in your support, and let's make this work."

eleven

October 2014

———

In the midst of all of this was Jonas, growing steadily and proudly and always the anchor that made us stick to searching for a way to make the best of what we had. After his first steps in our front yard, Jonas was off and running through life. He hit his first Wiffle ball off the tee a month later and was hitting underhand pitches at eighteen months old. Football, soccer, anything that allowed him to throw, kick, or catch, and he was hooked, especially if he could wrestle someone in the process. He loved nothing more than to run the bases and slide into home plate. I loved to watch how much he explored his world through his body, much as I did through my running and surfing.

I marveled at his physicality, but beyond his size was the sheer power of his positivity. He laughed and smiled all the time, even when things were most challenging with Giulia. He loved to crawl in our laps and cuddle through story time, and after moving into his big-boy bed, he still found his way into our room at some point almost every night so we could all wake up a tangled mess together in the morning. Our Man in Motion earned a new nickname from us: Sweet Sauce.

The truth is I needed Jonas as much as he needed me. I turned to Jonas more than anyone else for joy and comfort, even though I knew I was placing an unfair burden on the shoulders of a toddler. He was my escape while Giulia was lost to her depression.

His pediatrician assured me that young children can adapt to challenges facing their parents as long as one of the parents can continue to show reliable love and affection, and I took that charge seriously. I adored him and wanted him to adore me back, for both our sakes.

As Jonas learned to talk, he mostly asked for "Daddy." I noticed, and I know that Giulia noticed, too. We didn't speak about it with each other, but it lingered uncomfortably between us. Neither of us knew how to handle it. Giulia wished she were more in Jonas's spotlight, and I didn't blame her for it. I cherished my special relationship with Jonas, but I didn't want to flaunt it. So we didn't talk about it and instead held our breath whenever Jonas said "Daddy" and not "Mommy" and hoped for the best.

One day—he must have been around two and a half—we asked him to describe our bulldog, Goose. "What's Goose like, Jonas?"

Jonas looked quizzically at Goose and then proudly answered, "Handsome!"

We all laughed.

"What's Mommy like, Jonas?" Giulia followed up.

He turned his attention to her, studying her closely. I was nervous as he took a while. No one had never asked him so directly to describe Giulia.

"Gorgeous!" He beamed, elated. Phew. We laughed again.

"What about me, Jonas? What's Daddy like?"

"Happy!" Jonas answered immediately. We laughed a third time.

"All right, Jonas, last question." He looked at me eagerly. "What is Jonas like?"

He chewed on his finger as he thought about his answer. Then his face lit up.

"I'm happy, too. Just like Daddy."

It was a wonderful fall. We picked pumpkins and brainstormed Halloween costumes. Jonas wanted to be either a baseball player or an elephant. The Giants were in the playoffs, fighting for a thoroughly unexpected third World Series win in five years. School was going great. Giulia's job was going great. Nobody could really believe it.

And then on a Monday night, Giulia couldn't sleep. She couldn't explain why—she didn't have anything in particular keeping her awake. But on 900 mg of lithium, which had worked solidly for two years, she couldn't sleep.

I lay awake with her through the long, quiet hours of the night, fighting my heavy eyelids. I frequently faded off and awoke with a startle. I listened to her breathing and for the sounds of rustling that would give clues to whether she was awake or not.

We had our plan, which had felt so solid in the abstract, but now that it was time to enact it, I was afraid—afraid to say something that might anger Giulia or, even worse, wake her up if she had fallen asleep. I waited until three a.m. to suggest maybe it was time to take 1 mg of Risperdal. Giulia resisted. She wanted to go to work the next day, and if she took the pill now, at three a.m., she would have a hard time waking up when the alarm went off at seven thirty.

So she stayed awake, and in the eerie quiet she e-mailed her doctor and her therapist to see what they thought she should do. The e-mailing put her at ease, and she fell asleep soon after putting down her phone. I woke up to my work alarm at five forty-five and rushed through my morning of getting Jonas and myself ready. Giulia slept through it all. I decided to let her sleep and to take Jonas to day care myself, even though that was usually Giulia's favorite part of the day. Before we left, we tiptoed in to kiss her good-bye. I asked her how she was feeling. She mumbled a non-response from under the covers and was back asleep before we left the room.

She woke up to her seven thirty alarm and had e-mail responses from her therapist and doctor, who both said that tonight we should stick with the plan: 1 mg Risperdal at midnight, 2 mg more by two a.m. She set up an appointment for the next day with her psychiatrist, who encouraged her to stay in daily contact. Then she otherwise pulled herself together and went to work.

I checked my phone throughout the day for updates from Giulia, but none arrived. I texted her a few times and got bland responses: "I'm ok." "I'm tired." Midafternoon, I picked up Jonas as usual and took him and Goose to our nearby park, checking the time every few minutes, eager for Giulia to get home.

We gently embraced when she walked through the door. She looked fine, just tired. I was on high alert for signs of psychosis—pacing; weight shifting from one foot to the other; nervous, twitchy eyes—but I couldn't let her see that I was watching her.

With nothing else to do, we turned on the baseball playoffs. It was an odd combination—Giulia's sleepless night and the Giants against the Cardinals in the National League Championship Series, the winner going to the World Series—and I felt torn in two directions. On the one hand, I wanted to care for Giulia and go through all the meditations, massages, and relaxation techniques we had acquired over the years. Whatever it took. On the other hand, I was a Giants fan, and so was my son. There were certain rituals of fatherhood that I was committed to—the tousling of hair, the serious talks, the camping trips—and watching your home team in the playoffs was one of them. I wanted it for my sake as well as his, so someday Jonas could say that he and his dad had watched the games together in 2014, when the Giants surprised everyone and made it deep into the postseason.

Besides, Giulia and I had our plan. The main reason to have a plan was to allow us to continue with our lives and to keep psychosis from destroying everything like a wrecking ball. Watching baseball was continuing with our lives. The plan gave Giulia space to be in charge of her experience, without me breathing down her neck.

Jonas cheered when we finished dinner and I told him we were going to watch the Giants game. I flipped on the TV and kicked my feet up on the couch. Jonas loved the rare times we watched baseball together. He settled into my lap but bubbled with questions, asking for the names of every player and explanations for what was happening with each play. He quickly became impatient with being only a spectator. It took only a few outs for him to scramble off to find his own glove somewhere in the mess of the garage. A few minutes later he came back with his glove and a Wiffle ball, and he spent the next hour throwing the ball around the room and diving on it, passionately narrating a game that he was playing out in his mind, full of home runs, and megahits, and really fast pitches.

Giulia sat next to me, and I massaged her neck, and scratched her head, and rubbed her earlobes. She seemed settled at first, but as the game progressed and the sky darkened, I could feel her body tense up next to mine.

With only two innings left, she abruptly stood up. "I'm gonna go walk outside," she said. Her body was tense. She couldn't keep her feet settled beneath her or her eyes focused on one thing.

"Where are you gonna go?" I didn't like the idea of her walking around by herself. "Why don't we come with you?" I said, an obviously halfhearted offer.

"No, it's okay," said. "You and Jonas watch the game. I won't go anywhere if it makes you nervous. I'll just walk around in the backyard. I won't go anywhere."

Giulia walked out and began to pace in the backyard, back and forth across our modest patch of grass. I went out with her, but she assured me that she was fine and just needed some space for herself. So I returned to the living room, with Jonas and the game and the fun of the postseason. Between innings, I went back outside to check on her. She was taking big, deliberate breaths as she walked, her shoulders rising and falling with her inhales and exhales. Her hands were all over the place—behind her back, holding each other against her chest, pressed up against her face.

My throat tightened each time I walked out to check on her. Inside, in the living room, Jonas and I were continuing with life as normal. The Giants were losing, but it was a great night of baseball. Outside, barefoot in our backyard, Giulia was trying, and failing, to stay calm as she approached her bedtime.

"Giulia, it's getting dark, and cold," I said gently. "Why don't you go and take a bath? Jonas already had his, that might feel nice."

"That's a good idea," she said, nodding. "I'll start my bath, and maybe you can handle bedtime until I'm done. I'll come in after I'm done."

"Sounds good."

I went back to the game, which was wrapping up. Jonas smiled at me at the indulgence of watching TV on a school night. He whined when the game ended with a Giants loss, and I carried him off to his bed.

Bedtimes with Jonas lasted forever. He loved books and fought against his exhaustion to stay awake through the endless stories that I read. I stole glances as I flipped the pages to see if his eyelids sagged and fluttered. But if I stopped reading for more than a few seconds, he roused himself to insist, "Keep reading, Daddy."

I was deliberately slow to switch from one book to the next, so I could listen to the sound of jostling water from down the hallway, to assure myself that Giulia was still in the bath. I kept reading, and Giulia stayed in the bath. When Jonas fell asleep, Giulia was still in the tub.

I stuck my head through the door. "He's asleep. Sorry you didn't get to come in and say good night."

"Oh, I'm sorry, too," she answered. She was submerged as much as she could be in the tub without the water going into her eyes, the waterline drawing a tight circle around her face. She seemed to be finally calming down. "Thanks, honey. This bath feels good. I think I'm not going to wait until midnight tonight. I think I'm just going to take Risperdal. I want to get some sleep. I'm tired from not sleeping last night."

"That sounds like a great plan, Giulia. I'm proud of how you're being so responsive to this."

I stepped over the pile of towels on the floor and sat on the edge of the tub. I searched through the warm, bubbly water and found her hand and held it.

"Thanks, honey," she said quietly. We were being so tender with each other. We knew we were walking on a narrow tightrope. Any slip could be consequential.

I lay in bed, at a distance, as Giulia took the Risperdal in the bathroom. She flashed me a quick look of fake optimism and kissed a quick good night before we turned on her favorite playlist and flicked off the lights. We lay in bed together, quietly waiting for sleep. So much of my life had become about the threshold between sleep and awake and the fragile waltz back and forth across the two.

Giulia didn't sleep. She took more Risperdal.

She still couldn't sleep.

The next morning, we cleared our work schedules and were at Dr. Stefania's office for her first appointment of the day.

"We need to get you a blood test, first and foremost," the doctor said. Giulia had been on an uninterrupted regimen of 900 mg of lithium for almost two years, but it had been at least a year since her lithium levels were measured. "There's the chance that Giulia's body has started to metabolize the medication differently, and she might not be on the therapeutic levels that she needs." She typed an order into the computer, requesting the blood work.

"Now, let's talk about what's going on," she said.

"Well, it's now been two days and I'm having trouble sleeping," Giulia explained.

"Are you getting any sleep at all?"

"Yes, a little bit," Giulia said. "I guess I fall asleep around four or five in the morning. But then I have to get up and go to work a few hours later."

"Are you having any delusions? Any of the religious fixations that you have had in the past when you couldn't sleep?"

"No, none of that," Giulia said.

"Has anything big happened at work?"

"No." Giulia had recently celebrated completing her first year at her job, something she hadn't done in three years. One down, four more to go to hit her goal.

"Are you sure you're taking your medicine? You haven't stopped it in secret or anything, have you?"

"No," Giulia said, offended by the question.

"I have to ask," Dr. Stefania said, backpedaling. "I'm not accusing, I just have to make sure. Because this is coming out of nowhere."

"I agree," I chimed in. I had finally stopped mansplaining during Giulia's appointments, but it didn't mean I sat in silence. "She's taking her nine hundred milligrams of lithium. She's doing everything right. What's going on?"

"I don't know," the doctor responded. "But I'm going to prescribe a sleep medication on top of the Risperdal. Giulia, stay on one pill of Risperdal, and take one sleep pill tonight. Take both at bedtime. If you're still not asleep four hours later, take a second sleep pill."

"What if I'm still not asleep after that?" Giulia asked.

"Then you should take a second Risperdal." Giulia's eyes widened in response. "But I doubt you'll still be awake," Dr. Stefania added hastily. "That's a lot of medication to take."

"What about work? I really don't want to lose my job. Mark and I have a plan in place, and we have a lot of goals we've agreed upon. The two biggest ones are that I don't want to go to the hospital, and I don't want to lose my job. This is the first job I've been able to hold down for a while, and I really like it." Giulia was getting herself worked up. I leaned across from my chair and held her hand.

"Those are my goals, too," the doctor affirmed. "But if you're taking all these drugs, you probably shouldn't go to work. Can you take some time off?"

"Yeah, I guess. I mean, I took the morning to be here today, and I haven't ever taken a sick day, so I definitely have some of those saved up." Giulia shrugged.

"Why not take tomorrow off, too? When you do fall asleep, this will allow you to sleep in, and you won't have to worry about your alarm. Then, after a good night's sleep, you should already be feeling better. If you can get two good nights in, then we can pull back off the meds. It's Tuesday now, we can hopefully have this wrapped up by the weekend."

"I was going to go to New York City this weekend. My brother just got engaged, I want to celebrate with him," Giulia said. "Mark and Jonas are going camping. They already have a campsite reserved."

"Well, let's see how you feel. Going to New York might not be a good idea. Let's check in about that on Thursday."

We left her shiny office, hand in hand. We had been to so many appointments before, but this felt much different. We were in charge. No, Giulia was in charge. I was supporting her decisions because we had already talked through the contingencies before. This was going to be different. It was going to be fine. We went back to work, ate dinner, put Jonas to sleep. All felt encouraging.

Except that Giulia didn't sleep that night.

The Giants continued their march through the playoffs, and Giulia continued to not sleep. I watched the next game on TV as Jonas played around in the room with me, Giulia paced barefoot in the backyard, and I tried to wrap my head around why this was happening.

Her two prior psychotic episodes had such similar origins. I figured that work was the main culprit in both cases, a new job with unexpected demands. But nothing was tumultuous at work right now; in fact, it was the exact opposite. Work was going great. And she was on lithium, which she hadn't been taking for the previous two episodes. She should not be sleepless. None of this should be happening. It disrupted the pattern. It made no sense.

The only constant was the time of year. In 2009, she was hospitalized in September; in 2012, it was in November; now, in 2014, we were smack in the middle of October.

Her blood work confirmed that her lithium levels were in fact low, and her doctor e-mailed that Giulia should increase her dose to 1500 mg, which Giulia did immediately and without complaint. "If Dr. Stefania thinks more lithium should help, I want to take more lithium," she said.

We called our parents and explained what was going on. Both sets offered to come out and help, but we told them not to. Beyond Giulia's sleeplessness, everything else was as it should be. I was still working, Giulia was still working, and Jonas was still going to day care. We had daily contact with a doctor and access to all the right pills.

On Thursday, October 16, the Giants were up three games to one against the Cardinals. Game five was in San Francisco at AT&T Park, an immaculate stadium perched on the San Francisco Bay. They needed only one more win to go to the World Series, and here was the chance to do it at home, in front of forty-two thousand rabid fans.

Our routines were now set: Jonas and I watched the game, Giulia paced in the backyard. She walked in the cool green grass barefoot. A few early-season rains had already fallen, and our dead brown grass was growing back. The hard-packed dirt had been softened to a gentle mud. Giulia was often on the phone with friends, like Sachi and Leslie, but she paced in silence just as often. I always came out to check with her in between innings and offered to stay with her and talk, but we both knew that I should return inside to Jonas, who was waiting for me.

Game five of the 2014 NLCS between the Giants and the Cardinals was a game of historic drama. The Cardinals took a 3–2 lead in the fourth inning and looked in control. In the eighth inning, the Giants sent in pinch hitter Michael Morse, a charming goofball with forearms the size of tree trunks. Morse hit a majestic, earth-shattering home run down the left field line to tie up the game. He rounded the bases with his arms held aloft, as if he were a child running through a park, pretending to be an airplane. Jonas and I jumped up and down in celebration and ran around the house like airplanes as well. Giulia came in at the sound of the commotion and stayed with us to watch the ensuing final inning.

In the top of the ninth, our hearts were racing as the Cardinals loaded up the bases, but they failed to score. On to the bottom of the ninth, with the game tied and a trip to the World Series on the line. The Giants quickly got two men on, through a hit and then a four-pitch walk. The relief pitcher for the Cardinals was clearly struggling with his confidence. As he prepared to throw the next pitch, I said to Jonas, "Watch, Jonas. He's going to throw a meatball right down the middle, to remind himself that he can throw strikes."

That's exactly what the pitcher did. He lasered a strike right over the plate to the Giants hitter, Travis Ishikawa, who connected with the pitch and a hit a line drive that beelined toward right field. The second he made contact, everyone knew that the Giants had won. The ball rose up out of the infield, over the outfielder's head, and kept soaring. It bounced on top of the right field wall, and the Giants won the pennant with a home run in the bottom of the ninth inning. It was a mythic baseball game.

We erupted in our living room, and so did our whole neighborhood. Car horns were honking, people were running through the streets. Jonas was jumping up and down on the couch, screaming, "Meatball! Meatball! Right down the middle!"

In the celebration, I fell for one of the biggest illusions in professional sports: I felt like this win somehow belonged to me. I found narratives from the baseball diamond and applied them to my life. I knew it was silly to do so, but I did it anyway. The guys in orange and white celebrating on the infield didn't know that my wife wasn't sleeping and was steadily taking more and more pharmaceuticals to stave off psychosis. Their walk-off home run had nothing to do with us. Yet I felt elated and interpreted it as a sign that everything was going to work out.

And of course, Giulia didn't sleep that night.

———

Giulia canceled her trip to New York. Jonas and I didn't go camping. We didn't get refunds on the plane tickets or the campsite. Giulia took every pill she was directed to take. But she still couldn't sleep.

After a week of sleeplessness, we agreed to take a week off together, a medical leave of absence from our jobs, so we could be at home and not worry about the pressures of work. We hoped that a week would be all the time off that we needed. We turned off our morning alarm so we could wake when our bodies were ready for it, especially so Giulia could sleep in, if she slept at all. Although Giulia usually dropped off Jonas around eight, we now went together, something we never did but he loved, and we arrived after nine a.m. His teacher looked at us quizzically when we showed up together, and an hour later than normal, but she didn't say anything.

Then we had the whole day at home together, to try to do meaningful, calming activities—my newest iteration of art classes. We went on long walks in Briones with Goose. We grocery shopped and cooked together. We cleaned. We spent a lot of time in the garden. Giulia loved the sensation of the dirt in her hands, and while I weeded, she slowly rubbed the soil between the palms of her hands. We lived days as we had done five years before, but instead of creating a schedule in response to her time in the hospital, we were living this way to keep her out of the hospital in the first place.

With the week away from the office, Giulia spent a lot of time on the phone calling friends. Ellie, a friend from our days of living at Ocean Beach, invited Giulia to spend the day out in the old neighborhood with her daughter, who had just celebrated her first birthday.

"It'll be great, Mark," Giulia said, formulating a plan for the visit from the passenger seat as we drove together to drop off Jonas. "I can't wait to see Ellie and the baby. You can surf while I'm there. You deserve to surf! Let's not bring Goose, though. Just you and me, so you can surf and I'll be at the house with Ellie and the baby, and it will be great. It will be so fun to see Ellie and the baby. I can't wait. And you should totally surf. It's a good idea. It will be great." Fidgety and energetic, she repeated herself over and over on the way home from day care.

"Maybe we should tell Ellie how you're doing," I said. "I know you're not delusional, but you're pretty clearly anxious and on edge. Ellie is home alone with a one-year-old. I think it's only fair for her to know that this isn't exactly a typical visit."

"Jeez, Mark, give me some credit, would you?" Giulia said. "Don't you have any faith in me? I'm fine. We don't have to tell her anything."

I packed the car with my board and wetsuit but had low expectations about actually getting in the water. None of our friends had seen Giulia in her escalating psychosis. Plenty had seen her suicidal, but this degree of anxiety and restless energy was something entirely different. I fully expected to be asked to stay around and not disappear into the ocean for a few hours. So I wanted to bring Goose, but Giulia was adamant that everything was going to be fine, leave Goose at home, otherwise he would be stuck in the car while I surfed.

As we drove to the city, Giulia chattered the whole time and jumped erratically between topics: work, seeing Ellie, the friends she was calling, gardening, the ocean. None of it was delusional, but it was entirely out of character. On a normal day in the car,

Giulia was quiet and content to listen to music. Not so today. She spoke with a desperate intensity, as though the rapid stream of words would prevent the silence from swallowing us up.

At Ellie's house, Giulia bounded up the stairs. I followed slowly, anticipating defeat. Within a few minutes, Giulia was shooing me away. "Go surf, Mark! That's why I'm here! This is time for you to have fun. Let us girls have some mama time!"

Ellie walked me to the door. As I stepped outside, she whispered to me, "I don't know how to say this, so I'll just say it: Please don't get in the ocean. I need you to have your phone handy in case she becomes overwhelming." She was obviously embarrassed to say this and had a hard time making eye contact with me.

"I tried to get Giulia to tell you," I said in response. "I wanted her to say how she was doing, but she didn't want to." I hung my head in shame. After all these years, I was still embarrassed when people saw Giulia in her time of sickness. It was so far from the Giulia that we all knew. Which was why I had wanted to call ahead, and sometimes did anyway, violating Giulia's sense of privacy, so our friends could brace themselves to see her act so unlike herself. "She's not delusional," I continued. "She's definitely not dangerous. She's just . . . anxious. And wired from not sleeping."

Ellie nodded, accepting what I said, but she repeated her request. "Please keep your cell phone with you."

"Of course, of course," I said. "Good luck."

I trudged down the stairs. I didn't know what to do. Surfing was out. I had no dog, no book to read, and no interest in calling any of my old friends.

I drove to the beach, plopped myself in the sand, and watched as guys in black wetsuits hooted and hollered their way through head-high waves. I stared at my phone, waiting for either Ellie or Giulia to call. Two hours later, Giulia called. I picked her up, we drove home, and Giulia rambled the whole time about how great it was to see Ellie and the baby, and asked why didn't I surf, and said how we should have brought Goose, and I couldn't say anything back because I was too embarrassed and defeated and angry to make a sound.

One of the best strategies to help Giulia stay calm was to exercise. I couldn't convince her to go to the gym on Monday or Tuesday, but she conceded on Wednesday. I hate gyms as much as I love trail running. I considered sending her off by herself, so that I could use the time for a much-needed run in the hills, but I changed my mind and went with her.

Giulia slogged away on the elliptical as I cranked a few fast miles on the treadmill. It was bland and monotonous, but running was running, and it felt good to lose myself in exercise. Giulia was only a few machines away. She didn't read anything, or listen to music, or even really look anywhere. She plodded along steadily, with no expression on her face.

I went downstairs to lift a few weights, and we agreed to meet in the lobby at one forty-five p.m. Giulia has been impeccably prompt for as long as I have known her, so I made sure I was in the lobby by one forty-three. My shirt and shorts were soaked in sweat. Even my feet squished in my soggy socks and shoes.

I stood in the lobby, self-conscious about the sweat puddle I was making on the floor. We were at one of those fancy new gyms: spotless tile, crystalline glass doors, perky smiles on the faces of the uniformed employees. A huge flat-screen TV played a tennis match on mute.

No sign of Giulia. I shuffled my sweaty feet as the clock ticked along—1:46; 1:49; 1:52.

Had she fallen asleep in the locker room? I knew that she had wanted to go sit in the sauna a bit. Maybe she had dozed off. I was just about to ask someone at the front desk to check on her in the locker room when an employee came sprinting down the hallway.

"Someone call 911! There's a woman in the locker room saying that we are all dead, she's dead, her husband is dead, her son is dead. She needs help. We need to call 911!"

I knew she was talking about Giulia.

The employees who had been lounging behind the front desk sprang into action, the red uniform shirts a blur as they formed an impromptu huddle in the lobby. I jumped right in the middle of them.

"It's my wife," I said. "I'm sure it's her. Don't call the ambulance." They looked at me, their eyes wide with fear, and chose to trust me.

Everyone spoke at once as we padded down the carpeted hall. The employee who had seen Giulia kept repeating the same thing: "She wouldn't stop saying that we were all dead and something about us not being in this life anymore." I kept trying to calm down any potential overreactions and avoid a 911 call. "It's okay, it's probably my wife, I can handle this, don't call an ambulance."

We reached the door of the women's locker room, and the female employee who alerted us all to the situation went in first. Immediately inside the door was Giulia, sobbing and huddled over. She looked frail and in pain.

"Oh, Mark. We're all dead now," she said to me through her tears. "All of us. Even Jonas. We're all dead."

I wrapped my sweaty arm around her. "It's okay, Giulia, we're fine, let's go home." I propped her up and ushered her out of the locker room. She felt lifeless under my arm. "It's okay," I said to the small army of stunned employees around us. "It's okay. I know what's going on. It's okay, I've got her."

We walked down the hallway together, Giulia slumped against my body, and I was overwhelmed with a memory from many years before, long before Giulia had her first psychotic break. On a rare sunny weekend at Ocean Beach, the two of us sat in beach chairs and soaked up some rays. A carefree, naive life—pre-dog, pre-child, pre-psychosis.

We watched a family crossing the dunes when the mother, a woman in her sixties, suddenly collapsed onto the sand, screaming that she was burning alive. I nervously walked over to offer some water—she refused. Her children, all adults, tried to calm her down, but it wasn't working. I ran back and grabbed our beach umbrella and ended up standing over the woman to shade her. That helped a little, but she was still hysterical.

It felt like an eternity before the husband arrived after parking his car. He broke into a sprint when he saw the scene—a small crowded gathering, his wife squirming in the sand, a stranger holding a beach umbrella over her. "It's okay," he said to us when he arrived, panting. "Thanks for the help, but I can handle this now."

I remember how scared I was by the woman, who shrieked that she was burning alive from the sun; how sad I felt for the husband, who looked worn down as he slumped over his wife and whispered to her that everything was okay; how unconvinced I was as he kept saying to strangers like me that it was okay and he knew what was going on.

I was now that husband. The gym employees were the ones shaking their heads in fear and confusion.

I practically carried Giulia out of the gym, all the while offering the empty reassurance that I had things in control.

Giulia cried to herself most of the drive home. I wanted to ask if she was okay, but she was still spinning in the delusions, sorting them out in her head, and I knew the best thing to do was sit in silence. The psychosis would hopefully fade on its own.

Alone with my thoughts, I panicked. Giulia was delusional. We were going on ten days of almost no sleep, she was taking all the medication, and she was delusional. Our plan, so carefully and thoughtfully constructed, suddenly felt absurd. I had considered sending Giulia to the gym on her own. How could I have left her alone? Why wasn't she in the hospital? What if she had a delusion in front of Jonas?

As Giulia wept and my mind raced, I gave up on our plan.

Giulia called her psychiatrist when we got home. By then, the delusions had faded. I shamefully hoped that the psychiatrist would say enough is enough, time for the psych ward. That would be my out. Then I wouldn't be the one quitting on the plan.

But she didn't. Giulia was calm and in control on the phone. Her doctor told her to keep staying the course. The medicine would kick in and Giulia would feel better. I shook my head in disbelief. Maybe her doctor wasn't quite tuned in, fatigued by Giulia's constant calls and e-mail. She had other patients, too. Maybe she was regretting her involvement in our doomed plan.

We picked up Jonas at school and went back to our routine. That night, the Giants lost to the Royals in game two of the World Series. It was now tied at one game apiece. Jonas and I continued to chug along with our nightly routine. After the game, Jonas jumped on our bed, cheering, "Let's go, Giants!" in his Buster Posey jersey as I videoed on my phone. Giulia lay on the bed, motionless, not listening or looking at anything.

The reality settled in: Giulia was sick again. Laing saw it as a gift, but there were no gifts here. I had promised to let her have autonomy, and I gave it to her. Ten days into an autonomous approach to psychosis, I feared what that meant for me, and her, and most of all Jonas. Psychosis is terrifying when you see it for the first time. How much scarier it must be when it's your mom and you're not even three years old.

Giulia didn't sleep that night, either.

"Where's Mommy?" Jonas asked me the next evening. We were eating dinner. Giulia had not joined us to sit down and was instead walking around in the backyard.

"She's in the backyard, Jonas," I said casually, trying to play off his question.

"Why?" he asked.

"Because she likes it," I said, the best answer I could think of.

He sat for a second and chewed on his food.

"There are monsters in the house, Daddy," Jonas said. I wasn't sure if he was changing the subject or somehow continuing on his previous line of questioning. "I can see them. Monsters everywhere."

"Monsters?" I asked.

"Yes. Big monsters. Scary monsters. But I'm not scared." Jonas always tried to be bigger than he was. He was breaking my heart.

"Well, good thing we have a special monster broom," I improvised.

"Monster broom?"

"You know the broom we have? You didn't know that it's not only for cleaning up dirt? It's also for sweeping out monsters." Jonas was wide-eyed in disbelief. "I'll go get the broom, you open the door, and we'll sweep them out."

Jonas jumped out of his chair and ran over to the front door. I rushed off to get the broom from the hallway closet, and when I returned to the kitchen, Giulia was at the back patio doorway.

"What's going on, guys?" she asked quietly as she stepped inside.

Giulia's entrance put the two of us almost standing side by side, with Jonas at the end of the hallway at the front door. When she stepped inside, Jonas immediately walked toward me without saying anything.

Giulia approached us, and Jonas held on to my leg. "Can you give Mommy a kiss, Jonas?" she asked.

Jonas tucked closer into my legs as Giulia leaned in. He kissed her, but I could feel the tension in his body.

"I'm going back outside, you guys, I just wanted to say hi."

"Thanks for saying hi," I said. "We're just cleaning out the monsters from the house." With Giulia back out in the yard, Jonas rushed over to the front door to prop it open, and I swept the monsters out, one at a time, making a big show of it, and then we closed the door and breathed sighs of relief and hope that the monsters were gone.

————

Over the weekend, Giulia told her doctor she wanted to return to work. Remarkably, her doctor agreed. She hadn't slept in two weeks.

Our routine became unbearable. Giulia worked, I worked, Jonas went to day care. I was a nervous wreck the entire day. I couldn't concentrate on my classes. I improvised my lessons as they were happening and didn't grade any of the homework that I kept collecting. I picked up Jonas and took him on hikes with Goose. When Giulia came home, she disappeared into the backyard to be on her phone. Jonas and I watched the World Series, but it felt more like a chore than a treat. The two of us lived as if Giulia were out of town.

After spending an hour getting Jonas to sleep, I went into our room, to now try to achieve the same goal with Giulia. This took even longer and was never successful. Inevitably, I fell asleep first. In a desperate effort to stay on top of my schoolwork, I set an alarm for three a.m. so I could do some of the overdue grading and lesson planning. I slept so nervously and lightly that I was often awake before the alarm went off. Whether Giulia was awake or not, she didn't acknowledge my departure as I tiptoed off to my office to work. I sat at my computer, blinking hard against the glare of the screen, until I woke up Jonas at six to get him ready for school. Then we launched into another day.

It was an unsustainable schedule. I couldn't spend four hours each night trying to get my family to sleep and then wake up a few hours later to grade papers. Even my students noticed it. One day, after I e-mailed a round of graded essays back to my students in the middle of the night, one of them said to me after class, "I got your e-mail. You sent it at four a.m. Why are you grading papers at four in the morning? Is everything okay?"

Our plan had swung me from one end of the spectrum to the other. In Giulia's previous episodes, I had been the forceful advocate, my hands in every decision, no matter how minute. In this new plan, I felt like a passive bystander, completely uninvolved, watching a psychotic episode explode around me.

Under the ruse that I was doing it for Giulia, that Jonas's habit of coming to bed with us in the middle of the night was disruptive, I started to sleep in Jonas's room. But I was really doing it for me. I liked his room, with all the life-affirming children's books on the floor and the alphabet stickers on the wall, so much better than ours.

His bed was too small for me to lie comfortably in for too long, so I rolled out our family-sized sleeping bag on the floor. When Jonas woke up in the middle of the night, I pulled him close, and we snuggled on the floor until I woke up to do more grading. Those moments on the floor with Jonas were the only times I felt at ease.

Our plan collapsed the night before Halloween. The World Series was over by now. The Giants won game seven in what many commentators considered to be the best series of the past decade, but Jonas and I had mostly given up on watching. I couldn't pretend to enjoy baseball while Giulia paced herself into a steadier stream of psychosis.

The Giants' season over, we tried to go back to usual dinners, usual bedtimes, but Giulia still spent most of the evening by herself in the yard. Giulia and Jonas didn't spend more than a few minutes in the same room together. She was very unsure of herself and nervous when she was in the room with Jonas, so she excused herself. I bathed Jonas and put him to sleep by myself, then lay with Giulia for a long while. When I couldn't keep my eyes open any longer, I moved to my sleeping bag on Jonas's floor.

A few minutes after I settled down on the floor, his bedroom door slowly opened.

"Get out of there, Mark. You can't hurt Jonas," Giulia hissed. "I won't let you hurt him. Get out of his room right now."

"I'm not going to hurt Jonas, Giulia," I whispered. "I'm just here to make sure that he doesn't wake you up if he comes to our bed. You remember, we've been doing this for a week."

"Mark, I mean it, get out of there now." She wasn't whispering anymore, and I didn't want her to wake him up. I crawled out of my sleeping bag and left his room. We stood in the hallway. "You can sleep with me, but not with Jonas," she said.

At a loss, I did something that hadn't occurred to me before: I called the hospital emergency room, which was staffed with an advice nurse. Giulia waited with me for a few minutes but then returned to our room after losing interest.

I was on hold for a long time. When I finally had a nurse on the phone, I explained the whole situation as quickly as I could—the two previous hospitalizations, the two and a half weeks of no sleep, the escalating psychosis. Giulia heard me on the phone, came into my office, and snatched the phone out of my hands. She told the nurse her own version of what was going on, but her explanation was slurred and full of delusions and exaggerations.

After Giulia's ramblings, the nurse asked to speak with me again and told me to give Giulia another sleeping pill. Yes, even though she had already taken two, and two Risperdals, she should take one more. If she wasn't asleep in two hours, call back.

I hung up, and Giulia reversed course. She now insisted that I *had* to sleep in Jonas's bed and couldn't stay in our room. She no longer feared what I might do to Jonas; she was scared of what she might do to me. I rolled my eyes and trudged back into Jonas's room. I wasn't concerned with her empty threats of danger. I knew she wouldn't hurt me. I lay in my sleeping bag and zipped it up all the way to my chin and waited out the two hours.

When I woke up around three a.m., Giulia was standing in the hallway. "It's time to call again," she said, almost with glee. "To figure out what is happening."

I spent another long wait on hold and spoke with a different nurse, reexplaining the situation, with Giulia constantly interrupting to chime in with her own delusional insights. As before, she lost interest after a while and left. With Giulia gone, the nurse immediately became very decisive.

"You have to hang up and call 911 and have the police bring your wife to the hospital," he said to me.

"I'm not going to call the police on her," I said. "We've been down this road before. She's not going to hurt anyone."

"Okay, so don't call the police, but you need to bring her to the hospital."

That phrase—"bring her to the hospital"—uttered from the lips of a medical professional, completed the final phase of our plan. I had done everything I could, *we* had done everything we could, to respect Giulia's autonomy. We had kept her out of the hospital as long as we could. But now, someone finally gave us permission to not have to wage this war alone. It wasn't because we weren't strong enough. It wasn't a defeat. We hadn't given up on the plan. But this was where the plan brought us. Psychosis was too big to manage on our own.

Giulia returned for the tail end of the conversation and heard the last few details about going to the hospital in the morning. When we hung up, she thanked me for not calling the police and then went back into our room again. She fell asleep almost immediately, as if the knowledge of her impending hospitalization was somehow a relief for her, too.

It was now three thirty in the morning. My mind was fuzzy with the exhaustion from the past two weeks, but I knew it was lunchtime in Italy. I gritted my teeth and called my mother-in-law. Through tears, I explained that I had to take Giulia to the hospital, again. Suoc surprised me with her response. "I'm so sad for Giulia, but I'm more sad for you, Mark. I don't know how you manage all of this by yourself, with Giulia and Jonas, too. We love you so much."

Suoc offered yet again to come out and help, but by that point she and I both knew that wouldn't do much. We agreed that it would be best for Jonas to stay in school, around his friends and in the upbeat environment. And without a grandson at home to watch, Suoc would have nothing to do all day. We were finally seeing eye to eye.

At four a.m. I got back into my sleeping bag, my alarm on my phone set for six a.m. so I could get Jonas ready for school. I fired off a quick e-mail to the parents of my students, time-stamped *4:17 am*, yet more digital evidence of the chaos from my life. Parent-teacher conferences had been scheduled for the next day. I canceled the meetings, promising to hold them sometime later, no specifics provided.

It was odd, and strangely reassuring, to be awake in my sleeping bag at four a.m. and to know that Giulia would be in the psych ward the very next day. I had a vague sense of what the day would look like. I knew we would mostly be waiting—at the ER to see the psychiatrist and then to find out where she would be admitted. If I took her there after I dropped off Jonas, he would be fine at school all day, and if the wait wasn't long, I might even be able to go with her to the admitting hospital before I had to pick him up. I thought ahead to the weekend: I would need a babysitter for a few hours on Saturday and Sunday so I could visit her, but then I could probably return to work on Monday, go straight from work to the hospital, and then get Jonas on the way home before his day care closed. The planning restored a semblance of control.

I mostly thought of how the day was going to feel. The ER would be an emotional tsunami. But this time, I knew it was coming. I could brace for the sadness and fear.

Or so I thought.

Jonas decided to be an elephant for Halloween. His favorite book was *The Jungle Book*, and he especially loved the scene when Mowgli tries to march with the elephants. We found an adorable elephant outfit online the week before and left it hanging in his room for the week leading up to Halloween, for Jonas to see and get excited about. He woke up with an eager smile on October 31 and squealed, "Daddy, I get to be an elephant today!"

We ate breakfast together as usual, his oatmeal and yogurt, my granola, and he stole a few spoonfuls of my granola, as always. It was all so beautifully ordinary, a whisper of joy on a day that was scheduled to be heart-wrenching. I didn't say much as he talked on and on about his elephant costume. I mumbled in agreement through my mouthfuls of breakfast and couldn't resist pulling him into my chest to kiss his head and tell him how much I loved him over and over again.

Giulia woke up as I fumbled through putting on his costume, the soft gray bodysuit, the hat with the big ears and trunk, unsure of the buttons to snap and knots to tie. He saw her come toward his room, and no one said anything. Giulia kept her distance in the doorway.

All week, Giulia and I had been promising Jonas that we would be coming to school for the schoolwide Halloween parade. I had even planned my parent conferences around seeing his parade. I knotted the laces on his elephant-feet shoes, and I was sluggish with the dread of telling him that we would miss the parade and that when he got home, Mommy wouldn't be there.

Fully costumed, backpack in hand, Jonas was ready to go to school. Giulia still hadn't said anything to him. I knelt down to be at his level and looked him in his full, brown eyes. "Jonas, Mommy is going on a business trip today. She will be gone for a little while."

Jonas tilted his head quizzically. The few other times Giulia had to travel for work, we had talked about the trip weeks in advance, not the morning of. "Business trip?"

"Yeah, she's going on a business trip, and I have to take her to the airport, so we can't come to the parade today. We're really sorry to miss it. But I promise I will still take you trick-or-treating tonight."

Jonas was quiet as he processed this, but he nodded in relief at the mention of trick-or-treating.

Giulia followed my cue. "That's right, Jonas, I'll be on a business trip. I'll miss you so much while I'm gone. Can you give me a kiss?"

Jonas approached her cautiously. He was so adorable in his elephant costume. He gave her a quick nervous kiss and backed away, grabbing my hand for comfort. I had to look away. I had expected a slower rising tide of emotion, but the sight of them kissing in his elephant suit was too much. A deep sadness overwhelmed me. My eyes welled with tears and my mouth quivered in an attempt to choke back a sob. I thought my head would explode with the effort as I stuffed it all back inside so I could get my boy off to school.

Jonas turned and rushed off to the door. I whispered to Giulia to please start packing for her business trip while I was dropping him off. I wondered if she might try to leave while we were gone.

I played the Colonel Hathi march song from *The Jungle Book* on repeat on the drive to his school, but I couldn't sing along or tell the story like usual. I knew that if I made a single sound, all of my sorrow would pour out into the enclosed space of our car. I had prepared for the feelings of sending Giulia into the hospital, but I hadn't anticipated breaking a promise to Jonas. I thought of him walking out into the crowd of parents, beaming with pride in his costume, looking for us, only to remember that we weren't there. I wanted to scream and run and rip the guts out of these monsters that tormented us.

I wore my sunglasses into his classroom even though it was a drizzly morning and rushed my good-bye. I told Jonas again, in hushed tones, holding him close to my chest, that I would be taking Mommy to the airport and I would miss the parade. But don't worry, buddy, we will go trick-or-treating tonight, you and me and Goose. He turned into the dizzying excitement of a class full of Halloween costumes and was quickly swept up in the frenzy. I waved good-bye to the flash of a gray elephant stomping around the classroom.

On my way to the parking lot, I flagged down the director of the preschool, who was racing around to relocate all the outdoor Halloween decorations that were about to get soaked in the rain. I could only croak out a whisper to ask if we could talk in her office. She looked at me—a dad who usually skipped and whistled when I was at school, now a dad slouched over, wearing sunglasses in the rain—and understood something was wrong.

The second that the office door closed, all of the sadness, regret, and uncertainty that I had been trying to hold together burst and flooded her overstuffed office. My body groaned through sobs that strained every muscle.

The stunned school director watched. I heaved for I don't know how long. Then I finally pulled myself together enough to explain that Giulia had bipolar, she was in an episode of psychosis, I had to take her to the hospital, and she would probably be there a few weeks. I was telling her this because school was Jonas's sanctuary. He spent most of his days with his teachers and classmates, and they needed to know about how vulnerable he was right now so they could carry him if I couldn't. She nodded and hugged me, which felt so warm, and then I left to head home.

I shot my mom a quick phone call to explain what was going on but hung up as soon as I pulled in the driveway, leaving most of her questions unanswered. I promised updates throughout the day.

Giulia was pacing around our bedroom when I got home. She hadn't packed a thing. Together we gathered a bag with the wisdom of experiences we wished we didn't have: toiletries, comfortable clothes without drawstrings, one of Jonas's blankets to sleep with. We drove to the ER, checked in, and went through the mechanics that had by now become familiar. Check-in at the front desk. Quick interview with a triage nurse. Placement in a room for vitals. They were waiting for us because of the phone call the night before.

Giuila's psychiatrist came from her office to see us in the emergency room. She was the head of the department, so she had authority. "I'm going to try and get her into the best facility that I can," she promised me. "One that's close, too."

I sat with Giulia in her assigned ER room, but she couldn't settle down and asked me to leave. The security guard stationed outside her room looked at us with suspicion after hearing her ask me to leave. In the past, I would have been so offended for Giulia to give someone the impression that I wasn't supporting her, but I just didn't care anymore. There were such bigger things to worry about than what a hospital security guard thought about us. I left to get food and make calls.

I spent a few hours on the phone out in front of the hospital— Giulia's parents; my parents; Cas and Leslie, who cleared their weekend to come and stay with Jonas and me and provide the babysitting I would need so I could visit Giulia over the weekend; even the dad of one of Jonas's day care friends, who invited me to piggyback on their Halloween plans that night. I didn't know what to say, so I opened with, "I call you at a time of need." I knew I wouldn't be able to take Jonas trick-or-treating by myself.

I checked in on Giulia one more time, and she told me to leave her alone. The security guard said that she had been calm while I was gone and that she said several times that she didn't want me to come back. So when she asked me to leave, I gave her a quick kiss on the forehead and left. We didn't yet know what hospital she was going to, but it felt pointless to stay there with her.

I drove home and sank into the couch. I closed my eyes, and three hours vanished into a deep, unmoving sleep. At five thirty p.m. I was awake in an instant to pick up Jonas at day care. I brought Goose and we headed straight to the house of the dad I had called. He knew better than to ask anything. A few other families were there. I meekly introduced myself to the crowd and continued the farce that my wife was away on a business trip—"A business trip on Halloween? That is brutal!"—and mostly walked by myself, relying on the slow-moving Goose as an excuse to distance myself from the group.

Jonas was ecstatic. He skipped along with the rest of the kids, and at each house he sprinted from the sidewalk to the front door, undeterred by the bigger kids who elbowed him out of the way. Each time he returned to me smiling and out of breath, candy clenched in his fist to show me before he dropped it into his orange pumpkin pail.

We got home around eight p.m. and returned to the couch. I picked a random kids' show on Netflix and was asleep within seconds. I woke up several hours later with Jonas, still in his elephant costume, asleep across my chest, Goose strewn across my legs, all of us smeared with sweat from the heat of the costume and one another's bodies. Netflix was spinning out episode after episode of *Rescue Bots*, which Jonas had stayed up watching until who knows what time.

I carried him into our bedroom, which already felt foreign without Giulia, and cracked the window to let in the cool breeze. The air was still wet and fresh from the rain of the morning.

I changed Jonas out of his costume, lay down with him in our bed, and wrapped him in my arms. As I drifted off to sleep, my last thought was a wish that we could freeze this moment and never have to face tomorrow.

twelve

November 2014

I woke with the sunrise and couldn't find a reason to get out of bed until I remembered the Switch Witch. Distant cousin of Santa Claus and the Easter Bunny, the Switch Witch comes to children's houses on the night of Halloween and turns their candy into toys. We told Jonas he could keep his five favorite pieces of candy but should put the rest by the fireplace so that the Switch Witch could perform her magic as he slept.

Jonas was curled into a tight ball against me, as he tended to do, the two of us over on the edge of Giulia's side of the mattress, most of the bed empty and unused. I felt dazed: from my first full night of sleep in almost three weeks; from going straight from the ER to trick-or-treating; from missing Giulia. I wondered how I was going to pull off the duties of the Switch Witch without waking Jonas. Everything felt fuzzy and out of reach.

As I tiptoed out of the room to retrieve the two toy cars I had hidden in the guest room closet, I heard Jonas rustle in the sheets, but he didn't wake up. I smiled with pride when I reached the living room and saw that he had remembered to put his bucket of candy at the base of the fireplace, with his five chosen pieces on the coffee table nearby. For that brief moment, all I felt was a love for my son that eclipsed the worry and dread.

With Jonas still sleeping, I had time to be alone in the silence of the morning. I sat on the couch and tried not to think, but how could I not think? There were too many logistics to figure out. Cas and Leslie should be at our house by noon. I would visit Giulia during Jonas's nap. I would visit again on Sunday morning before they left. Then I'd need to figure out Monday, with work and day care and another hospital visit. Then Tuesday. Wednesday. And then how much longer was this one going to last? We had gone from twenty-three days to thirty-three days. And what was going to happen with Giulia's job?

When Jonas woke up, he found me dozing on the couch. I jumped up and made a big production out of the toy cars from the Switch Witch, and he set out to play with them, inventing stories of the cars as they did huge jumps and crashed and zipped all around the room.

We lazed through the morning as I watched the clock, waiting for Cas and Leslie to arrive. I held it together till they got there and I could put my guard down. I knew what lay ahead of me with Giulia. But for now I was with friends, and my son, and I wanted nothing more than to be vulnerable and feel loved and connected and unafraid.

Cas and Leslie brought a DVD of the dreamy Japanese anime movie *My Neighbor Totoro*, their favorite pick for sad, rainy days. The movie doesn't have much of a plot, just two sisters befriending a gentle monster in the forest, who takes care of them and helps them as their mother is in the hospital. Not much happened, but *Totoro* felt so comforting, with its stunning colors, charming soundtrack, and gentle dialogue. I had never seen the movie before, even though I grew up in Japan in the era of *Totoro*'s peak popularity, but I was captivated, and so was Jonas. The characters became friends with Totoro and a bus shaped like a cat, and that was kind of it as far as the story was concerned.

Acorns are an important part of *Totoro*. The sisters and the monster give each other acorns as gifts, sometimes wrapped in leaves. Sunday morning, we all went for a hike in Briones, and in early November the mighty oaks were flush with acorns. Jonas was ecstatic as he collected acorns, and we left piles of them along the trails as gifts for Totoro. I pocketed a few dozen acorns so that later I could wrap them in leaves and hide them along our favorite trails for Jonas to find. He needed to feel protected by a kind forest monster like Totoro.

I loved to make believe with Jonas. As a dad, I wanted to build a world for him where logic, gravity, time, and other restrictions didn't matter. All that mattered was that Jonas was loved and cared for. Everything else was fluid. So we made up stories of Totoro in Briones, friendly coyotes who came to our back door at night and brooms that could sweep monsters out of the house. I wanted to build for Jonas a cocoon against the harshness of the world, a safe, beautiful retreat. I needed that, too.

All the while, Giulia was lost in her own world of make-believe. So lost that she was once again in the hospital, heavily medicated, unable to live in the rational world.

The hospital was in Oakland, about thirty minutes away from our house. The weekend disappeared, and it was Monday. I was alone with Jonas. I dropped him off in the morning, only a few minutes after his school opened. I taught all day. I raced out of school and drove to the hospital. I stayed an hour and then ground through bumper-to-bumper traffic to pick up Jonas, only a few minutes before his day care closed. One of the kids first dropped off and one of the last picked up. Then it was a matter of figuring out what was in the fridge, what I could cook, and the inevitable acceptance that it was going to be another night of takeout. I bathed Jonas and bundled him in his pajamas, and we retreated to the master bedroom to sleep together. I didn't even try to put him to sleep in his own bed. I drifted off after the first book, even as he was still awake beside me. Then my body woke up around midnight, no alarm necessary, painfully aware of how much schoolwork I was failing to do. I sometimes fell right back to sleep, but most of the time I worked for a few hours, until three or so, then slept again until the six a.m. alarm rang and started it all over again.

The psych ward was much smaller than the other two Giulia had been in. We held our visits in a cramped, closet-sized space called a "quiet room," which was offset from the TV lounge. I never visited during traditional visiting hours, so I didn't know where visitors typically went.

Giulia was calm and settled in the hospital. She didn't seem scared. Her fixation now wasn't on the Devil or heaven, but on helping the other patients in the hospital. She adopted a mothering role with all of them. Each time I visited, people came up and introduced themselves to me, to say what a helpful presence Giulia was for them. They also made fun of me behind my back after I left and called me Mr. Buttoned-Down Shirt.

I missed a few visits. One afternoon I was hung up at a work meeting and couldn't make it in. Another day I simply didn't have the energy to drive to Oakland for another visit that I knew would be mostly the same thing it had been for twenty-three days, then thirty-three days, and then now. Most of all, I couldn't stomach the guilt of leaving Jonas in day care for eleven hours. When Giulia was first hospitalized five years earlier, I was appalled to leaf through the guest book and see so much white space, so many empty slots from families who didn't visit. If they did visit, they didn't stay long. I was becoming those families.

"Can Jonas come and visit?" Giulia asked on the phone.

"No, honey, he can't," I said. "Remember, we made that a big part of our plan. No Jonas visits."

"But I really miss him," she said.

"I know you do. He misses you, too. But he can't visit. We agreed."

Jonas was now two and a half. He had questions. He had memories. Impressions would linger. I didn't dare bring him into the psych ward. I didn't even ask the hospital if Jonas could visit, but Giulia did. Their rules prohibited children under the age of fourteen. She asked them each day anyway, unwilling to take no for an answer, but they didn't budge. Thank God.

I called Jonas's pediatrician for insight on how this might impact him—the time away from Giulia, her strange behavior in the days before the hospitalization, his signs of being scared of her.

The doctor was unflinching. "You have to protect your son, above all else."

"Jonas is fine now. Giulia's in the hospital, I don't have to protect him," I said.

"Yes, but she will be coming home. She probably wants to come home soon. You might have to refuse it. If she's not ready to be around Jonas, you can't allow it." I felt nauseated hearing this advice. "He's so little. He doesn't have the capacity to process what he might be feeling, nor the words to explain himself. I know this is hard to hear, but your wife is an adult. She's in the care of professionals. If things need to be uncomfortable for anyone, it's her, not Jonas. He is a little boy. He needs to be protected."

I knew she was right, but I couldn't say "yes" or "okay" or in any way verbalize that I agreed with her. Not because I disagreed, but because agreeing was acknowledging that I might have to make such an awful choice.

"If it comes down to a choice between Giulia and Jonas, you have to choose Jonas. You have to."

One afternoon I arrived to find Giulia and a few other patients in music therapy class, out in the garden. The social worker was playing "Let It Be" on the guitar. The group had written their own song lyrics to express how they felt. The chorus: "Let me free . . ." Even Giulia, who wasn't much of a singer, sang along.

I had a hard time being fully present with Giulia during our visits. From my seat in the quiet room, I faced a giant clock on the wall behind her, and I glanced up at it constantly. I knew that the longer I stayed, the worse traffic would be, which meant a later pickup for Jonas, no walk for Goose, more takeout for dinner.

Our script was overplayed. We had exhausted our psych ward conversations on the first hospital stay and were no better now. I told stories about Jonas, and she told me about the other patients, and group therapy, but those ended within ten minutes. I wanted to make sure that Giulia was safe and in good care, which she was, but I knew by now that I couldn't unlock the mystery to her psychosis. We were just in a waiting game for the medicine to kick in.

One day our typical chat was interrupted by the loud thud of someone smashing into the wall. The door to our room had a glass window on it, but we couldn't see anything. We just heard it. Loud, profane screams—"Fuck you, motherfuckers! I hope you all fucking die!"—amid a swarm of firm, professional voices.

Giulia and I sat in chairs across from each other, but at the startling noise of the confrontation, she got up and sat in my lap.

She recognized the voice as belonging to a woman who had been admitted that morning. The new patient railed over and over again at the staff: "Get the fuck off me! I'm going to fucking kill you! Fuck you and die!" The nurses, doctors, and orderlies worked together to keep the woman pinned to the floor. We could hear the sound of her arms and legs flapping against the tile as she resisted.

"Are you okay?" Giulia asked me over the noise. She looked worried, not for herself but for me, as though she wanted to protect me.

"Yeah, sure, I'm okay," I said. I was surprised that she was checking in on me. "Are you okay?"

"Yes, I'm okay," she said. "I just want to make sure you're okay. You don't spend a lot of time in here, and don't see what happens here."

"Yeah, I'm fine, honey, thanks for asking."

We waited and listened to the whole thing. It was disturbing to hear someone driven to such hatred and violence by the thoughts in her head and the violation of orderlies restraining a person for her own safety and the safety of others. It was even more unsettling because we couldn't see anything but heard it all in vivid detail. Disturbing, unsettling, but I wasn't scared. I'd shed my fear of the psych ward years ago.

But the longer it dragged on, the harder it became for me to avoid my fear. The woman wouldn't stop screaming, and Giulia and I looked at each other with each outburst. In her mothering psychosis, she was clearly worried about me.

But the thing was, I wasn't going to stay here. Once we got the "all clear," I could walk out of the quiet room and through the locked doors, gather my phone and keys, and drive home.

But Giulia wasn't leaving. This was her home, at least for now. She was going to sleep here and walk these halls, with this woman. The same nurses and orderlies could pin Giulia down if she ever exploded like that. Giulia had real reasons to be afraid: for her own safety and of her own mind. I had somehow forgotten how terrifying this place must be for her.

I knew I had to protect Jonas from a world like this. I didn't need the pediatrician to tell me that. But in the charge to protect Jonas at all costs, I couldn't forget that I had to protect Giulia from a world like this, too.

We stayed in the quiet room for an excruciating thirty minutes that felt like hours, until the staff subdued the woman and took her to a different part of the hospital. A nurse checked in to make sure we were okay. She explained that the patient's family had visited, which had agitated her.

The nurse led us out of the quiet room through a hallway I didn't know existed. "Are you okay?" Giulia asked me again.

"Yes, I'm fine," I said. "Thanks for checking, but I'm okay."

"I don't want you to be scared," she said.

"I'm fine, I promise."

Standing in the hallway, she leaned into my body and rested her head on my shoulder and gently slipped her arms around my waist.

"Good, I'm glad," she said, releasing a big sigh. "I don't want you to be scared," she repeated.

I gave her a kiss on the forehead, but it was time to go, so I left. I walked to the locked doors, gathered my phone and keys, and got in the car to drive home.

On hospital day six, a Thursday, I called my parents on my drive from the hospital to Jonas's day care. I called so I had someone who would talk with me and keep me awake on the drive.

"Come to Delaware this weekend, Mark," my parents suggested. "You need to be with family."

I balked. I couldn't imagine flying across the country right now.

"Why would I fly to Delaware? That's so far."

"We've already talked to your siblings," my mom said. "They are ready to come for the weekend if you are. You need a pick-me-up."

"Wow," I said. They were spread around the East Coast, but they were ready to drop everything and go to Delaware for me. "That actually does sound really nice."

"We have another suggestion," my mom said gently. "Maybe, just think about it, but maybe you should leave Jonas here with us."

"What?" I asked in alarm. "That makes no sense. Jonas lives here. He has school. I'm going to pick him up there right now. This is his home. I'm taking care of him."

"Just think about it, Mark," my mom urged. "You won't have to work in the middle of the night. You won't have to scramble in the morning to get him ready and then rush to pick him up and get him to bed. You can have some time to take care of you."

"I don't know, Mom. I kind of need Jonas right now."

"Sure you do," my dad said. "But you also kind of need to take care of yourself."

"Just think about it," my mom said again. "Let's talk tomorrow on your drive to work, and see what you think then."

I drove the rest of the way home sullen, smothered by guilt. Guilt at not being at the hospital long enough, not picking up Jonas sooner, not caring for Goose well enough, not having the attention and patience for my students. No music, no phone calls, just guilt beating the shit out of me as I gripped the wheel tighter and crawled through jam-packed traffic.

I didn't even make it to Jonas's school before I called my parents back. They were right. I couldn't do this anymore. I selfishly wanted to keep Jonas with me, but our life right now wasn't what was best for him. He could be with his grandparents, whom he adored, instead of being dragged around as a companion to my worry. "Okay," I said. "Let's do it."

That night I bought a round-trip ticket for me and a one-way ticket for Jonas. We would take a red-eye on Friday, the next night. I would fly back Sunday morning. Jonas would stay. I didn't know for how long.

I visited Giulia Friday afternoon and explained the plan to her. She was on edge and asked a lot of questions about discharge, so it took me almost an hour of diplomatic dodging before I brought it up.

"I don't like it," she said. "I want Jonas to be at home."

"I do too, Giulia," I said. "But it's so hard for me. I'm so tired. Besides, he loves Grandma and Grandpa."

"I want him home when I get home," she said.

"I do too," I said. "I'll do my best."

We flew out of San Francisco International Airport at ten thirty p.m. and were eating breakfast through heavy eyelids at my parents' house by seven thirty a.m. My flight home was twenty-four hours later. At nine a.m. my sister, Cat, arrived with her husband, Alex, and son Memphis. Jonas and I stood in the driveway with my parents, waiting for them. Jonas jumped into their arms and was immediately off and playing games with the toys Memphis brought, and Cat and Alex turned to me and bear-hugged me tightly. An hour later, my brother Carl and his husband, Jeff, arrived, and we returned to the driveway for more hugs and hellos. I was so tired, but it felt so vital to be with my family.

After lunch, the children napped and we adult kids went for a run along the Brandywine River. We started with a slow jog together and chatted around the question of Giulia and Jonas and our twisted lives. At the turnaround point I separated from the group and ran through the cold so fast that I could feel my heartbeat pounding in my ears, and I gasped for breath as I waited for them to catch up.

Sunday morning I was awake an hour before my six a.m. alarm, puncturing through the thin sleep of my nervousness. Jonas was in the bed next to me, and I was the most tired I've ever felt, but I knew I couldn't sleep. I lay with him and gently held his hand and spent the hour reminding myself that this was what was best for him, and that was what mattered most. I was ready to protect Jonas from Giulia's illness. I never thought I'd have to protect him from my own inability to navigate the impossibility of our circumstances. It was terrible. I was dropping him off in his elephant costume all over again.

I said good-bye to Jonas as he was still waking up. My mom was in the room with us and she took over, playing with him as I fumbled through my sloppy tears to kiss him good-bye. I trudged down the two flights of stairs to my dad's car.

My mom opened Jonas's bedroom window, and I heard him innocently ask, "Where's Daddy going?"

"He has to go back to work, but you will see him soon," my mom said.

Then Jonas started to panic. "I want to go with Daddy," he said. He shouted out the window, "Daddy! Daddy! I want to come with you! Let me come with you!"

I couldn't look up, I was crying so hard from where I sat in the passenger seat. I yelled out, "I'll see you soon, Jonas, have so much fun with Grandma and Grandpa," and my dad started the car.

Jonas kept yelling, "Daddy! Daddy! I want to come with Daddy! I want to come with Daddy!" My mom tried to reassure him, but he wouldn't stop yelling, and I was dying to stop the car and bring him with me, but we drove away through the lifelessness of winter and I hated myself for not having enough courage to bring him home with me.

Monday, I taught a full load of classes and then had four hours of parent conferences, and it felt like the easiest day of the month. With that schedule, at school from eight a.m. until eight p.m., I once again couldn't visit Giulia, which meant I hadn't seen her in three days, the longest I had ever gone without visiting her in the psych ward. I called her as I drove home from school.

"Mark, they think I'm almost ready to come home," she told me.

"That's great," I said, not believing it. Giulia was clearly doing better. This was her best hospitalization by far. Her psychotic ramblings were in check within a week of arriving. The two weeks of taking antipsychotic medication may not have kept her out of the hospital, but they set the stage for a shorter stay. "You remember that Jonas isn't here right now, right?" I asked. "He's with my parents."

"I know," she said. "When is he coming back?"

"I don't know," I admitted. "It depends upon when you're coming home."

"Well, I think I'm coming home soon, in the next day or so. And I want Jonas home when I get home."

"We'll see," I said.

"No, we won't see," she snapped back. "We have a family phone conference tomorrow, and I want to come home and I want Jonas to come home. Are you going to fight for me, Mark? I want to come home. Get me out of here. It's been long enough."

"Yes," was all I could say.

"Mark, are you going to fight for your wife?" she said. "Are you going to fight for your wife?"

"Of course I am, Giulia," I tried to interject, but she kept repeating herself.

"Are you going to fight for your wife?" she asked me over and over, each time emphasizing different words. Are *you* going to fight for your wife? Are you going to *fight* for your wife? Are you going to fight for your *wife*? She was furious. It wasn't a psychotic anger; it was her first release of the pent-up agitation of being locked away for the third time. Half of me didn't take the outburst personally, because I could only imagine how frustrated she must have felt. But the other half was crushed at her accusations. I had followed our plan down to its finest, most unreasonable detail, and she was still mad. Each query took a piece away from my crumbling sense of myself as a husband and father.

She must have asked me twenty times, so quickly that I couldn't say anything in response. It was the one moment she granted to herself to be the bad patient, the one who spoke her mind against the injustices of being locked away from her family. She had learned that following orders with a smile got you out of there quicker, and she had been on her best behavior as soon as the psychosis faded enough to give her that sense of control. But on the phone, it was just the two of us, and she let all of her simmering agitation with the hospital explode, if only for a few minutes.

She finally calmed down and then quietly, one last time, she asked again: "Are you going to fight for your wife?"

"Yes, Giulia, I'm going to fight for you," I said. "I've been fighting for you for five years."

She sweetened up at that answer. "Well, that's good," she said. "It's going to be so good to be home. I can't wait to see you and come back home to help out with Jonas, you must have been so busy at home without me there . . ." And on she rambled for five more minutes with as much kindness as she could.

But I was still going to fight for Jonas, too. I was going to *fight*. For *Jonas*. Even if it meant that I might have to fight against Giulia and her psychiatrist. Jonas's pediatrician never specified what I had to protect Jonas from, so I had to trust my instincts. If Giulia's good behavior was just an act, and there was still sleeplessness and paranoia and delusional thinking, then I was going to have to put my foot down, no matter what her psychiatrist said.

I was going to fight for Jonas.

———

The family conference call on Tuesday was during my lunch break, and it was quick and decisive. The doctor felt that Giulia would be ready to come home the next day. He was confident that she would be fine with Jonas home as well.

The night before, she was aggressive. Now, she was remarkably self-aware.

"I'm so glad I get to come home, but you need to remember how fragile these hospitalizations leave me," she said. "I've been thinking that maybe it's a good thing that Jonas stays with your parents for a few more days. I miss him so much, but I know that it's already overwhelming to be home, and that it will be even more so if Jonas is there."

I breathed a huge sigh of relief. There was going to be no fight. Giulia would come home to just me, and I could see how that went for a few days before we brought Jonas back into the mix. I had been worried about a showdown—Giulia home, demanding that Jonas be there, me skeptically checking to see if it was the right environment for him—for over a week, but we would avoid a confrontation for the first few days.

Giulia was pleasant and steady when I picked her up Wednesday morning. We took Goose for a hike, which was now becoming a post-hospital tradition. We Skyped with Jonas and my parents in Delaware. He was ecstatic to see Giulia for the first time in two weeks. We drove to her favorite sushi restaurant to celebrate. It was a smooth night. No vomiting up of medicine. No waking up at two a.m. to try to sneak out of the house. Just a quiet, comfortable sleep together, husband and wife, back in our bed, our bulldog snoring between us.

It all went remarkably fast. I worked on Tuesday, picked up

Giulia on Wednesday, and was back at work on Thursday. Giulia enrolled again in her IOP and set to filling the rest of her time with horseback riding and volunteering. It was clear that the hospital doctor had been right: Giulia was ready to be home, with all of us. There wasn't going to be any showdown.

My parents flew with Jonas back to California on Saturday morning. He had been gone for a week. Giulia had built up noticeable confidence over the three days she'd been home. We drove to the airport together and were waiting curbside. Jonas's smile lit up when he saw us, and he ran to me and I grabbed Giulia into my side so when he jumped he was jumping into both our laps, right there on the curb at the airport, a tightly wound hug of smiles. Jonas chattered nonstop on the drive home about the different outings he'd had with Grandma and Grandpa. My parents stayed overnight but politely kept in the background as we found our new footing.

I resumed waking up with Jonas and dropping him off at school before I went to work. Giulia busied herself throughout the day with IOP, dog walks, and grocery shopping. There were no signs of the post-psychosis depression that had hit her so hard in the past. In the afternoon, I picked up Jonas from day care, and we all spent the evening together. Within a few weeks, Giulia tapered off the antipsychotic medication. I didn't have to watch her take her pills, because I knew that she had conceded how important they were for her recovery.

The single biggest difference of Giulia's third hospitalization was that she didn't leave her job. She took a full month off, but after that she returned to a twenty-hour week and then, when that went well, a thirty-hour week. She found her greatest sense of value by returning to the job she loved to do.

We had mostly followed our plan. It was far from perfect, and I had already identified tweaks we needed to make, but those could wait. What mattered most was that we had used the plan we created. Now here we were, a month after her shortest hospitalization, feeling in control and optimistic that this time would truly be different.

Giulia's impressive rate of recovery—discharged from the hospital after thirteen days, back to work on a limited schedule only two weeks later—lasted through December. But in January, the depression returned with unforgiving intensity. Giulia insisted that she keep working, and she trudged through her day and sat at her computer and somehow got her work done, but she heard the nagging voice of suicidal depression all day long.

By February, Giulia was coming home from work defeated by the effort it took to focus on her job, without much energy left over for us. She almost never talked about her feelings. She didn't go to any support groups and saw her therapist only every other weekend.

While at first it felt like we had discovered how to prevent her bipolar from ruining our lives, now I worried that we had resumed normal life too quickly, pretending that if we ignored Giulia's depression, it would go away on its own. But it wasn't going away, and the old routine of her depression left me standing alone as the sole parent. Just as when Jonas was six months old, Giulia was too withdrawn into her depression to engage with us. She wasn't on antipsychotics, so at least she wasn't sluggish and muted, but she was distant all the same. At night she just wanted to sit in the bathtub while I played with Jonas, then lie in bed alone as I put him to sleep. She didn't wake up with us in the morning, so I handled solo the mad dash of dressing Jonas, wiping yogurt out of his hair, and shepherding him into her room to kiss her good-bye before we left.

The one exception to Giulia's disengagement was our nightly dance parties. We resumed the ritual borrowed from Cas and Leslie and their boys, and every night after dinner we cranked up the music and danced around the house.

I was the DJ. We had our favorites—"Bright Whites" by Kishi Bashi and "Inside Out" by Spoon—but the number one hit was "True Believers" by the Bouncing Souls, a punk band I first saw in concert when I was fourteen years old. I've never forgotten the intensity of that show, how the crowd of individuals morphed into a single living entity that was fueled by the strumming of the guitar and the banging of the drums.

Jonas loved to look at his reflection in the glass door as he pretended to be a rock star. I taught him the difference between playing air guitar to regular songs and playing air guitar to punk songs: regular guitar is about the wrist, but for punk songs you have to drive the strumming through your elbow. Jonas had already perfected his glam face of puckered lips and intense eyes, and as the Bouncing Souls blasted through the speakers, he danced and strummed his imaginary guitar, his eyes always on himself.

Our dance parties were a collective moment of escape, just like our aerobics class in the red-carpeted gym years before. We danced to shake free of our worries, if only momentarily. We danced together in the same room, but we mostly danced alone, working up a sweat so that we could feel our hearts race with endorphins and freedom.

In the bath one night after an especially energetic dance party,

Jonas asked me what a true believer is. He'd been paying attention to the song lyrics: *The kind of faith that doesn't fade away. We are the true believers.* I thought about how to answer without too many big words. It was an important question.

But I never got to the answer. Before I organized my thoughts, Jonas smiled and said, "Oh, I know, Daddy. A true believer is me. I'm a true believer."

"That's right, Jonas, you are a true believer," I said.

"And Daddy, you're a true believer, too."

"And Goose?" I asked. Goose always sat in the bathroom with us during bath time.

Jonas looked at him and smiled and said, "Yes, Goose is a true believer." Then:

"Is Mommy a true believer?" Jonas asked. Giulia was in bed, as she always was after our dance parties, not to go to sleep, but to sort through her thoughts and reconcile the fitful joy of our dance parties with the heavy suffering of the rest of her day.

I wanted to tell him yes, but I needed him to say it instead. He had identified himself, Goose, and me as true believers, and I wanted him to be the one to include Giulia in that circle.

"Do you think she's a true believer?" I asked Jonas.

"Yes." He nodded seriously. "Mommy is a true believer."

It was decided. We were all true believers.

From then on, Jonas had a new question to ask strangers, as a part of his interrogation of getting to know them better: "Do you like the Giants?" "What's your favorite color?" "Are you a true believer?"

I signed up for corrective laser eye surgery so that I wouldn't have to wear contacts ever again. Giulia and I both started wearing glasses in the fifth grade, another one of those small coincidences we learned we had in common. I tried to get her to sign up for Lasik as well.

"No more glasses, no more contacts. Wake up each morning and be able to see. What freedom!" I said, trying to convince her one morning as we lay in bed together. "Besides, the surgery pays for itself in fifteen years. Tally up all the costs of wearing contacts, with the new contacts, and solution, and eye appointments. Each year after that, you're actually saving money."

"Yeah, but I don't know if I'll be alive in fifteen years," she said.

"None of us knows that, Giulia. But I plan to be alive in fifteen years, so I think it's worth it."

"I don't know if I'm planning to be alive in fifteen years," she said quietly. "I still don't know if I'm going to make it or not. I've made it through three episodes, Mark, but that doesn't mean I'll make it through four, or five, or six."

"Oh," I said, disoriented by the quick change from a conversation about Lasik to one about suicide. I waited to see what else she had to say. I stayed quiet and listened to the hum of the humidifier from across the hall in Jonas's room. I could sense that she wanted to pick up her phone and forget about this moment. This was a rare moment when she opened up about her feelings.

"I will say this," Giulia said, breaking the silence. "If I get sick again, I'm not as scared of it."

I said nothing.

"I mean, of course I don't want to go psychotic again," she said. "But if I do, I know it's okay. I've been in the hospital before, I know what to expect, it's not as scary as it was the first time. I know that you and Jonas will be okay while I need my time to get back under control. . . ." Her words got lost in the marbly sound of her tears, and she trailed off.

"I've got this thing for life, Mark." She looked up at me, gracious and dignified under the weight of her diagnosis. "Call it 'bipolar,' call it a 'disease,' call it whatever you want, but the main thing is that it's not going away. It will always be with me. But at least I'm not as scared of it anymore."

Her rise out of her third depression was muddled and lethargic. There was no flick of the switch as with the first two. But by March it was mostly gone.

"You seem like you're doing well lately," I said to her one evening as we picked weeds around the tomato plants that we had just planted. Even though the plants were barely saplings, they filled the garden with promising smells, and we liked to come out there and just breathe.

"I guess so," she said, her eyes still on the soil.

"I mean, it's been a few weeks since you've talked about suicide."

"Yeah, I guess you're right," she said.

"Do you still feel suicidal?"

"No, not really," she said. "I haven't for a while."

"So would you say that this episode is behind us now?"

She sat back on her heels and looked up at the sky for a moment and then at me. "Yeah, I think I would. I don't feel sick anymore. I think the third episode is over."

We were hit with a soaking rainstorm in early April, and all of California rejoiced. We were in our fourth year of drought, and the snowpack and reservoirs were at historic lows. The California drought was an international news story.

We always rushed out into Briones for a celebratory mud hike whenever it got wet. We loaded up the back of the car with towels and changes of clothes and trekked out.

The clay of the East Bay hills turns exceptionally sticky in the rain, and it takes only a few steps for the mud to cling to your shoes. The mud attracts more mud, and soon enough you are walking with mud Frisbees on your shoes as you slip and slide along the trails. Which for a toddler is about as fun as it gets. Jonas adored our mud hikes. We all knew he was going to get soaked and dirty, so Giulia and I just let it happen. He was always grinning from ear to ear.

On this day, I wanted to explore a trail that I had been eyeing for a little while but had never followed. Our family map had grown, with the addition of places such as Mommy's Favorite Hike, the Ridge Hike, the Totoro Tree. Still, I sought new places to call our own.

The trail wound near a picnic area and then disappeared into thick trees. We followed it through the forest into a gorgeous opening, a flat valley between two steep hills. The basin was full of old trees, gnarled and leafless in the winter, half of their branches dead. They were arranged symmetrically like an abandoned orchard, except they gave no fruit.

I had run so many miles in this park and thought that I knew the geography pretty fluently, but this was new.

We plodded through the puddles and the mud, running our fingers along the wet, mossy bark. The grass between the trees was a green so vibrant that it pulsed. Clouds hung low over the hills.

There wasn't a sound besides the pitter-patter of rain and those that we made.

We walked farther and I said to Giulia, "Let's make one of these trees our tree. We have so many places in this park, let's make another one."

"Sounds good," she said. I could see from her face that she was in pain, that my interruption had pulled her away from a deep sadness.

We explored deeper into the field. Ten minutes later, Giulia said, "This is the one."

The tree wasn't any different from any of the others, but I agreed. "This is it. This is our tree.

"Did you hear that, Jonas?" I called to him. "This is our tree." He was already exploring the perimeter, looking for California newts that might have wandered away from the nearby creek.

"We need to make it ours somehow," I said to Giulia. "Let's get some sticks and make a sculpture."

"Sounds good," she said again.

We gathered a few dozen sticks of all sizes, but I was hit with the sudden urge to climb. If this was going to be our tree, I had to see the view. I left it to Giulia to build something out of the sticks while I set off to climb the tree.

I heaved up on a sturdy branch and scrambled up a few feet before slowing down to pick my route more delicately. I didn't get too high, about twenty feet. I found a perch and settled in.

Giulia had started to arrange the sticks into the outline of a heart. She dragged big logs for the base and reinforced them with the smaller branches we had gathered, and when those ran out, she gathered more.

Jonas ran through the grass and mud and was playing a game that only he understood. He leapt from one spot to another, to a third, then retraced his steps and did it again.

Goose watched them both and decided that he liked one of the logs that Giulia had laid down inside the growing heart. He started to gnaw.

I watched my family from a distance. I spent so much of my life in their midst, with a tendency to dominate the group. For the moment, I took myself out of the equation so I could see them for themselves, independent of me.

I watched Giulia, and I knew how much she had suffered. Even though she declared the third episode to be over, I knew it still weighed on her. She would never again be as carefree as before she was sick. I thought about how many times she had considered killing herself and how many times I had pondered her death. I had already grieved a life's worth of mourning for her. I wanted her to survive her bipolar, but I knew that something, someday, was going to take her away. But that didn't unhinge me anymore.

Up there in our tree, as the April rain breathed life into the thirsty grasses and trees, and my son stood tall, and my bulldog meandered through middle age, and my wife created the shape of a heart, all I could think about was death.

Giulia shooed Goose away from the middle of her heart so she could keep building. Our dog had been with us through all three hospitalizations. He was six now. I remembered when Giulia was pregnant, and when I thought about having a child, for some reason my mind always skipped ahead to the moment when Goose would die. I'm not sure why, but the impending arrival of a new life made me think of the lives we would lose. I could see us burying

Goose and imagined that would be the first time that our child saw us cry.

Out beyond Giulia's heart, still wrapped up in his game, was Jonas, my beginning and my ending. I had thought about his death, too. As a parent, your mind goes into dark places when feeling protective of your child—a car crash, leukemia, a bad accident at the playground. I hated imagining these possibilities, but they also felt important to consider, because they made each day, even in its most frustrating moments, feel like a treasure.

The only death I avoided thinking about was my own. I wasn't afraid to die for my own sake. I knew that I lived a charmed life. My fear of death wasn't for me. My life has been good. It will be nice if it is long, but it doesn't have to be. I've already been given more than I deserve.

I didn't think about my own death because it brought with it the fear of what would happen to the creatures below me, the ones playing with sticks in the mud. Who would take care of them? Could they take care of themselves, and each other, without me? It was a narcissistic fear, but a realistic one, given the past five years.

And so I sat in my perch and watched them be alone, if only for a few minutes. Jonas eventually saw me up in the tree and pointed and laughed, and I climbed back down, and I stood inside the heart with Giulia. Jonas wedged himself between our legs and looked up at us.

"This is the Love Tree," Giulia declared.

"That's a perfect name," I said.

"Let's come here when times are bad and we need to focus on us."

"That's a perfect idea, too."

Jonas kept tugging on our legs, so we squatted down to his level and wrapped our muddy selves around each other. "The Love Tree," Giulia said again.

"The Love Tree," Jonas parroted, delighted with himself.

We stood up, walked outside of our heart of sticks, and trod back through the tall, wet grass to our car, our hearts warmed by the hope of our new sacred place.

As we walked away, Giulia promised our tree, "We'll be back."

Acknowledgments

This book has been in the works almost since Giulia was first hospitalized, when I wrote long e-mails at night to our parents to try to make sense of what was going on. There have been so many people who have touched and protected our lives and this book since those e-mails from seven years ago.

Along the way, three guardian angels have stood out: Bonnie Solow, Liz Weil, and Karen Rinaldi.

Bonnie, as I've said time and again, you are so much more than an agent to me, and I knew that was going to be the case when you agreed to meet for a hike and make-your-own-pizza at our house. You have given me the protection, advice, confidence, and friendship to believe that this was a book worth writing.

Liz, we never quite pinned down what exactly your role was in this—editor, book doctor, mentor—but I'm okay with that because no title would do justice to how critically you shaped this book. You turned a wordy, overly detailed mess into something that I am so proud of. I can't imagine writing without you by my side.

Karen, I'm so grateful you took a chance on me, a high school teacher with a magazine article, and coached me through writing this book. You pushed me in ways that I've never been pushed, and I grew as a person and a writer through your guidance. I'm so grateful that you believed in this story enough to want to share it with the world.

Besides my guardian angels, I have been lucky enough through the sheer coincidence of being a surfer in San Francisco to meet some amazing writers who fed me opportunities to grow and expand as a writer, especially Brian Lam, Jaimal Yogis, Tom Prete, Matt Warshaw, Mat Honan, and Zach Slobig. Beyond my beach friends, I'm so grateful for the professionals who accepted my pitches, especially Dan Jones, Meg Bowles, Amanda Hess, and Maria Streshinsky.

The team at Harper Wave has been so amazing to work with. Hannah, you are a godsend to me, and have been so patient through my cluelessness. Thanks to everyone for making this such an exhilarating experience.

I want to acknowledge the many people who have spent their lives caring for the mentally ill. Whether as a professional, family member, or friend, your patience and courage helps to inspire us all. I've been fortunate enough to get to meet some of you, but there are a lot more of us out there than we realize.

I had so many friends reach out and help me through these years of caregiving. I have been given wisdom, companionship, milkshakes, and hugs from so many people, especially Jean, Allison, Brian, Austin, Nicholai, Jaimal, Jamie, Chris, Paul, Eric, Drew, Adam, Hovey, Molly, Fr. Martin, Scott, and Willy, just to name the tip of the iceberg. And then to the many people who offered their love to Giulia: Briana, Jan, Sachi, Nan, Abby, Megahn, Vanessa, Joya, Heidi, Leah, Hanna, Carel, Annie, Nancy, Fio, Sarah, Danielle, Sophie, and Cathy.

Cas, Leslie, Bron, and Blaize: you changed my life when you invited me to dinner at your house. You expanded that generosity to Giulia, then Goose, and then Jonas, and have shown us what friendship really is. And what homemade vegan food really is. Point Reyes is our sanctuary because you are our sanctuary.

Thanks so much to our siblings, our best friends. Carl, Jeff, Cat, Alex, Matt, Grace Ann, Pietro, and Charlie—I can't believe how lucky we are that we all have so much fun together. And our parents—Mary, CJ, Mariarita, and Romeo—we wouldn't have made it without you guys. You stopped your lives to take care of us, and we will spend the rest of our lives trying to earn all the love and support you have given us. We're all in this together.

Our dog Goose has been at my side through all of this. And while it might be ridiculous to thank a dog, I wrote most of this with Goose sleeping at my feet. You're our rudder, Goose. Seriously, people, if you're going through a tough time, get a bulldog. They are the best.

Jonas, you give me more joy than I thought possible. I can't believe all that you are already capable of. I'm excited for you to read this one day when you're old enough.

And most important, my lovely wife Giulia. This is a big deal. None of this has been easy—the illness, the writing about it, the book publishing. This is our story but there is no story without you opening yourself up to the world like you have. Thank you for trusting me to tell this in a way that honors your bravery. You always say that we both got stronger because of your illness. I agree, and I think this book has done the same.

About the Author

Mark Lukach is a teacher and freelance writer. His work has been published in the *New York Times*, the *Atlantic*, *Pacific Standard*, *Wired*, and other publications. He is currently the ninth-grade dean at the Athenian School, where he also teaches history. He lives with his wife, Giulia, and their son in the San Francisco Bay Area.